Thinking with the Poem

RECENCIES SERIES:
Research and Recovery in Twentieth-Century American Poetics
MATTHEW HOFER, Series Editor

This series stands at the intersection of critical investigation, historical documentation, and the preservation of cultural heritage. The series exists to illuminate the innovative poetics achievements of the recent past that remain relevant to the present. In addition to publishing monographs and edited volumes, it is also a venue for previously unpublished manuscripts, expanded reprints, and collections of major essays, letters, and interviews.

ALSO AVAILABLE IN THE RECENCIES SERIES:

Rethinking the North American Long Poem: Form, Matter, Experiment edited by Ridvan Askin and Julius Greve
"A Serpentine Gesture": John Ashbery's Poetry and Phenomenology by Elisabeth W. Joyce
Amiri Baraka and Edward Dorn: The Collected Letters edited by Claudia Moreno Pisano
Yours Presently: The Selected Letters of John Wieners edited by Michael Seth Stewart
All This Thinking: The Correspondence of Bernadette Mayer and Clark Coolidge edited by Stephanie Anderson and Kristen Tapson
Geopoetry: Geology, Materiality, Ecopoetics by Dale Enggass
Ingenious Pleasures: An Anthology of Punk, Trash, and Camp in Twentieth-Century Poetry edited by Drew Gardner
A Description of Acquaintance: The Letters of Laura Riding and Gertrude Stein, 1927–1930 edited by Jane Malcolm and Logan Esdale
Evaluations of US Poetry since 1950, Volume 1: Language, Form, and Music edited by Robert von Hallberg and Robert Faggen
Evaluations of US Poetry since 1950, Volume 2: Mind, Nation, and Power edited by Robert von Hallberg and Robert Faggen

For additional titles in the Recencies Series, please visit unmpress.com.

Thinking WITH THE Poem

Essays on the
Poetry and Poetics of
Rachel Blau DuPlessis

EDITED BY Andrew R. Mossin

UNIVERSITY OF NEW MEXICO PRESS   ALBUQUERQUE

© 2024 by the University of New Mexico Press
All rights reserved. Published 2024
© 2024 by Rachel Blau DuPlessis for quotations from poetry and prose. All rights reserved to author. All citations from *Drafts* © 2025 by Coffee House Press.
Printed in the United States of America

ISBN 978-0-8263-6720-4 (cloth)
ISBN 978-0-8263-6721-1 (paper)
ISBN 978-0-8263-6722-8 (ePub)
ISBN 978-0-8263-6723-5 (pdf)

Library of Congress Control Number: 2024943524

Founded in 1889, the University of New Mexico sits on the traditional homelands of the Pueblo of Sandia. The original peoples of New Mexico—Pueblo, Navajo, and Apache—since time immemorial have deep connections to the land and have made significant contributions to the broader community statewide. We honor the land itself and those who remain stewards of this land throughout the generations and also acknowledge our committed relationship to Indigenous peoples. We gratefully recognize our history.

Cover image courtesy of Rachel Blau DuPlessis
Designed by Isaac Morris
Composed in Alfabet, Garamond Premier, and Swear

This book is dedicated to Miriam Nichols
for her support and friendship across the years.

CONTENTS

Acknowledgments ix
List of Abbreviations of Works Cited xi

Introduction 1
ANDREW R. MOSSIN

Part I. Feminist Practice and the Poetics of Crisis

CHAPTER ONE. Inner Speech in Rachel Blau DuPlessis's Poetry 19
PETER MIDDLETON
CHAPTER TWO. "First Feminism" in Rachel Blau DuPlessis's *Drafts*: "Draft 49" as Counter-Archive 41
MEGAN JEWELL
CHAPTER THREE. Infinite History and the Mortal Body: Rereading the Unending *Surge* 59
AMBER MANNING

Part II. Materialities of Making: Collage, Detritus, and Waste in *Drafts*

CHAPTER FOUR. Intertexuality as Collage, Text/Textile Interstices, Layering: Art Practice as Embodied Feminist Philosophy 81
MARIA DAMON
CHAPTER FIVE. "daily politics, weird shit": Feminist Weak Resistance and Waste in Rachel Blau DuPlessis's Later Work 99
ERIC KEENAGHAN
CHAPTER SIX. En Dehors Garde Collage Homage 121
SUZANNE W. CHURCHILL, LINDA A. KINNAHAN, AND SUSAN ROSENBAUM
CHAPTER SEVEN. An Extra Horizon Can Be Spun: On Publishing Rachel Blau DuPlessis's *Numbers* and *Life in Handkerchiefs* 139
ARIEL RESNIKOFF

Part III. Across Traditions: Romanticism, Objectivist and Projectivist Poetics, Secular Judaism, and the Witness of History

CHAPTER EIGHT. Between Objectivist and Projectivist Poetics: Rachel Blau DuPlessis and the "Force Moving"   153
JEANNE HEUVING

CHAPTER NINE. "Immerginated Raptures": Rachel Blau DuPlessis's *Drafts 1–38, Toll*   173
JOSEPH DONAHUE

CHAPTER TEN. Spark Me Up, or The Light of Shattered Language: The Holy Un[]hole in Rachel Blau DuPlessis's "Psalm 151"   197
ADEENA KARASICK

CHAPTER ELEVEN. "Moth: Ode to Psyche" and the Active Romanticism of *Drafts*   205
JEFFREY C. ROBINSON

Contributors   229
Index   233

ACKNOWLEDGMENTS

I am grateful to many individuals who contributed their time, effort, and work to this project. First, I must thank all the contributors to this volume, without whom the book that readers can now hold in their hands wouldn't exist. A project of this kind relies on the faith and persistence of all its contributors to become a reality. I am grateful beyond words to all those who wrote essays for this book and continued to work on them through the revision process, as they did so staking belief in this project's vitality and significance.

To Elise McHugh and Matthew Hofer and the entire team at the University of New Mexico Press, I extend deep and profound thanks. I am especially grateful to Elise's shepherding of this book through all the stages of its production and her patience with my many queries along the way. James Ayers and his design team were particularly generous in working with me through multiple iterations of the cover design to produce the stunning version that now adorns this book. Thanks to Anna Pohlod and Patricia Kot for their work in finalizing the manuscript and producing the copyedited text of this book. Special thanks to Lys Weiss, whose extensive knowledge of the areas covered in these essays was invaluable in her creation of the index for this book.

Heartfelt thanks to Bradley Fest and an anonymous reader whose comments and suggestions for revision were decisive in making this book both more coherent and clearer in the articulation of its central arguments.

Finally, I owe a major debt of gratitude to the subject of this book, Rachel Blau DuPlessis. Her thinking and stance toward poetry and poetics have been decisive across my own career as a poet, scholar, and essayist since I came to know Rachel in the first year of my graduate study at Temple University in 1989. As the subject of this book, Rachel always understood that her role could be advisory at most, but her own long experience in scholarly writing and academic publishing was an indispensable aid to my work on this collection. The result is a gathering of essays that speaks to the long-standing and dynamic influence Rachel has had on so many of us, across generations, geographies, and poetic affiliations. If my effort to make Rachel's unique brand of thinking poetics visible in new and complex ways has been successful, it is in no small measure thanks to Rachel's instructive example and generous spirit as this project unfolded.

ABBREVIATIONS OF WORKS CITED

Poetry

ATW: *Around the Day in 80 Worlds*
DW: *Days & Works*
GN: *Graphic Novella*
LW: *Late Work*
N: *Numbers*
P: *Drafts 39–57, Pledge*
PI: *Pitch: Drafts 77–95*
PR: *Poetic Realism*
S: *Surge: Drafts 96–114*
SP: *Selected Poems*
T: *Drafts 1–38, Toll*
TF: *Drafts 15–XXX, The Fold*
TR: *Tabula Rosa*
W: *Wells*

Criticism

BS: *Blue Studios*
GRRC: *Genders, Races and Religious Cultures in Modern American Poetry*
PG: *The Pink Guitar*

Collections Edited by Rachel Blau DuPlessis

ON: *The Objectivist Nexus: Essays in Cultural Poetics* (coedited with Peter Quartermain)
SIG: *Signets: Reading H.D.* (coedited with Susan Stanford Friedman)

Introduction

ANDREW R. MOSSIN

> In poetry, one wants to make statements in language in all the social-sensuous means and hyper-saturated nuances that can be mustered toward pleasure and a reverberating impact from formal, tonal and syntactic understandings. Real rhetorical pulse of sheer poesis, not "rhetoric" in the limited sense of straining or poseur manipulations, not in one "position" only. I think that has led me away from "period style." The only "position" I might hold in poetry is the tertium quid—a perpetual sense of the between, often between fixed doctrines. I sometimes think I want more from poetry than most poetry has been designed to give.
>
> —Rachel Blau DuPlessis, "'Thinking the Poem; Thinking the Poem Writing': An Interview with Rachel Blau DuPlessis," conducted by Andrew R. Mossin

> To vow to write *so that*
> *if*, in some aftermath, a few shard words,
> chancily rendered, the potchked scrap of the human
> speck
> washed up out of the torn debris, to write
> so that
> *if* your shard emerged from the shard pile
>
> people would cry, *and* cry aloud "look! look!"
>
> —Rachel Blau DuPlessis, "Draft 14: Conjunctions"

IN THE FALL OF 1989, as a graduate student in the creative writing program at Temple University, I attended a reading by Bruce Andrews and Rachel Blau DuPlessis sponsored by Temple's Poets and Writers Series. Not much of that evening has remained with me, except this: when Rachel took the podium to introduce the work she'd be reading—most likely "Writing"—she offered that the work might appear confusing at first to some in its use of laminate sheets projected onto a screen behind her so that the pages appeared as palimpsests, overlays, moving in multiple directions at once.[1] But DuPlessis hoped that the work would also provide something else: pleasure. The word is a decisive one for DuPlessis, and, as the contributors to this volume all attest in various and important ways, this concept is a valuable one in our consideration of a poet notable both for the pleasures of the texts she has produced across her career and for her cultural acuity and interrogation of the relationship between poetic production and other genres and formats, including hybrid essays, scholarship, and the visual artwork she has done in collage. The motif of pleasure has been particularly important to DuPlessis's work within the framework of the long poem, beginning with her multivolume serial work, *Drafts* (1986–2012), and the poetry that has followed since. In each instance, the entwined strands of writerly and readerly pleasure have been central to the work's evolution and hold on our attentions as readers.

Extending on questions DuPlessis herself raises, the contributors to this volume point their interrogations in a number of important directions: What are the connections between subjective experience, the body, and historical trauma? How does the poetic subject recognize herself as both divided and unitary, speaking and silent? How are feminist theory and practice galvanized in root works of the contemporary long poem—while at the same time rethinking key precepts of modernist and postmodernist thinking about the ethical and political responsiveness of this culture work? In what ways are other art practices such as collage integral to the projects undertaken by DuPlessis, affording her work a material and textile praxis that in turn complicates questions of refuse, waste, debris, the disused and under-seen? What are the cosmological and theological bases of this work? What claims does DuPlessis make in poetry that is both deeply secular in its orientation and impulses and, at the same time, provisionally engaged in Hebraic lore and mysticism and an approach to poetic production that engages in its own enactment of midrash?

Beyond these questions, this volume also quite rightly asks: what constitutes an adequate response to the expansiveness of DuPlessis's career, one that by its sheer productivity amounts to a massive accumulation of work? The array of publications is daunting, beginning with her multibook serial poem, *Drafts* (1986–2012); followed by a series of new books included under the title of *Traces, With Days* (2017–); a hybrid of critical essay and socio-intellectual biography, *A Long Essay on the Long Poem* (2023); her *Selected Poems* (2022); to be followed by the whole of *Drafts*, a presentation of the complete long poem by DuPlessis that will be published by Coffee House Press, and still more books of poetry awaiting publication. Through all this work, DuPlessis has established herself as one of the central contributors to post–World War II postmodern poetry written in English. In addition to the poetry, DuPlessis has remained a central theorist and explicator of contemporary poetry, poetics, and feminist discourse in her critical and scholarly writing, including foundational books such as *Writing Beyond the Ending: Narrative Strategies of Twentieth-Century Women Writers* (1985), *The Pink Guitar: Writing as Feminist Practice* (1990), *Blue Studios: Poetry and Its Cultural Work* (2006), and *Purple Passages: Pound, Eliot, Zukofsky, Olson, Creeley, and the Ends of Patriarchal Poetry* (2012). DuPlessis has produced a formidable array of materials that have established formative new modes of thinking in relation to poetry, the sociopolitical construction of gendered subjectivity, and the critical nexus between poetry as a field literary expression and poetry as cultural critique. In responding to the range and multifocal aspects of DuPlessis's work in poetry, the essays gathered in this volume provide vital case studies in how to approach work that is marked by multiple intellectual and cultural entry points. As such, each writer here establishes a different vantage line of inquiry—both in terms of career timeline and sites of investigation—from which to assess DuPlessis's contributions.

All this work comes in the wake of earlier scholarship and writing on the poet. During the past decade, there have been several serious articles on DuPlessis's poetry, though concentrated critical attention has not been the focus of a single anthology until this book. With the exception of an appreciative and important feature on DuPlessis's work curated by Patrick Pritchett that appeared in *Jacket2* in 2011, contemporary readers of DuPlessis lack a benchmark anthology of essays that responds to the scope and ambition of her multifoliate poetry and poetics. For readers following this poet, there have been to be sure important recent contributions by a number of scholars, including Hélène Aji, Marina Camboni, Bradley Fest, Elisabeth Frost, Alan Golding, Walter Kalaidjian, and Paul Jaussen, to name just a few. Notably, there have been several recent featured interviews with DuPlessis in *Contemporary Literature, Golden Handcuffs Review, Asymptote, Tupelo Quarterly, Oxonian Review,* and *boundary2*, indicating a growing interest in the literary contributions of this poet/critic. By establishing the long view, this volume contributes an important set of documents that both reassesses the trajectory of a poet whose work has been in the public eye for more than forty years and provides critical ballast to the next stage of inquiry. In this sense, *Thinking with the Poem* importantly traces both early pre-*Drafts* work in which DuPlessis was establishing the textual, linguistic, and formal lines she would pursue and her later, post-*Drafts* material (post-2012) that navigates the materiality of language, cultural and subjective memory, and the provisionality and precarity of public life. Doing so, this book provides a vital record of intricately related moments of poetic history across key decades in the development of post–World War II Anglophone innovative poetries as these are represented by DuPlessis's own activities. At the same time *Thinking with the Poem* eschews any effort at a career overview or honorific appreciation. The clear through line of this collection is its inquiry into the hows and whys of a body of work with which we are just beginning to reckon.

In certain key aspects, then, this is a book that casts a long view backward and forward, across many decades of DuPlessis's poetic production, and attends anew to its singularity and surging, empowering waves of language and cultural study that course through the work. Who will write the book of any of us, might be one of the questions proposed by DuPlessis's poetry; and this too: once we get there, what next? Both fiercely cognizant of poetry's long history and the poet's own presence—complicated, fitful, diffident, and austere—within that history/herstory, DuPlessis forces into the open the questions of necessity and drive that are also acknowledged vectors of the scholarship this volume presents:

> It was all necessary,
> the desire, the loss, the itch, the anger,
> the impossible push,
> the separated cartilage.
> And what now?
> Acknowledge
> that it was necessary?
> Or just refuse to concede?
> ("Useful Knots and How to Tie Them," *Late Work*)

This book is, then, part query, part critical intervention in a career that continues to produce works of importance—discretionary, provisional, critical in their gaze on *now*. As DuPlessis's work continually reminds us, no language is ever done once committed to the page. It moves, resettles, finds new locales, habitations, spaces to wander/wonder: "No poem is totally the poem you meant to write, but every poem you've written is the one you did or could write, brought to the poise or level of interest to which you could then bring it. That is, the poem escapes the poem. Or the poem escapes the poet. Or is it, the poem escapes the poetics? With the simultaneity of making and a sense of loss, something escapes inside the work. This 'escape' authenticates the work" ("Preface," *Surge: Drafts 96–114* 15).

The essays gathered here are about these escapes, these spaces of time and location and language that drift across our awareness, pull us in, reveal our deepest subjectivities to us, incorporating latent gestures of polyvocality and pluralized identity en route to utopic presence, phenomenological awareness, lingering social hopefulness. "But time is only forward in the world we know," DuPlessis writes toward the end of *Around the Day in 80 Worlds*. In that event these are essays devoted to the forward movement of time, its principled and intricate progression, "orphic and eurydic communiques" ("Per Se"), while positioned like Benjamin's *Angelus Novus* between an incommensurate past and an incommunicable future.

As the first full-length collection of essays devoted to the poetry and poetics of DuPlessis, *Thinking with the Poem* gathers contributions from several well-known scholars of DuPlessis's poetry to provide a nuanced and wide-ranging exploration of her poetry and poetics across more than four decades of writing. While DuPlessis is best known for her decades-spanning long poem *Drafts*, which "closed up" in her terms with the publication of *Surge: Drafts 96–114* in 2013, she has continued her exploratory work in serial composition. In poetry that extends on the investigative ambition and feminist orientation of *Drafts*, DuPlessis has further expanded on the material and conceptual power of poetry as a medium of analytic thought and cultural intervention in recent books, including *Graphic Novella* (2015), *Days and Works* (2017), *Around the Day in 80 Worlds* (2018), *Late Work* (2020), *Poetic Realism* (2021), and *Daykeeping* (2023). Asking of her readers a willingness to interrogate their own assumptions about the manifest realisms of everyday life and the connections between our subjective experience of these realities and the language we deploy to represent our political, historical, and identitied selves, DuPlessis nourishes a complex poetics of nomadic inquiry through poetry that continues to exert pressure on normative understandings of and assumptions about poetry as a genre and field of study. As I suggested in the introduction to my 2021 interview with DuPlessis, her work since *Drafts* "further explore[s] the connections between the visual page, the poem as documentation of thought, and collage as a visual medium in dialogue with and in movement alongside the poems" (37).

A collection that probes different contexts of DuPlessis's cultural and poetic production across her lengthy career, *Thinking with the Poem* integrates several overlapping layers of engagements that move across DuPlessis's career as both a poet and scholar. Hence, this anthology necessarily responds to both, as each of these essays integrates formal analysis of the poetry with a congruent emphasis on DuPlessis as a central voice of feminist criticism and scholarship. In groundbreaking books such as *The Pink Guitar* (1990), *Blue Studios: Poetry and Its Cultural Work* (2006), and *Purple Passages: Pound, Eliot, Zukofsky, Olson, Creeley, and the Ends of Patriarchal Poetry* (2012), DuPlessis established ways of reading and responding to modernist and postmodernist poetry that are syncretic, adaptive, non-hegemonic and variously informed by cultural theory (notably Theodor Adorno and Walter Benjamin, to cite just two influences on her thinking). Thus, while the writers of this anthology are responding to DuPlessis as a poet, their thinking is inevitably informed by this influctual and foundational set of texts that have laid the basis for several generations of poet scholars taking up the challenges with which DuPlessis's writing presents us. DuPlessis's description of her work in *Drafts* from *Blue Studios* provides an appropriate example of her own approach—as both poet and theoretician of the poem: "*Drafts* could be described as heterogeneric, making allusive loops around and through concepts of genre that the poems both appropriate and disturb, genres such as midrash, elegy, ode, autobiography, and meditation. In texture they are heteroglossic—open to a range of voices, tones, verbal textures, social codes and rhetorics" (215). The practice is emphatically open, principled, and ethically driven by the demands placed on the writer by poetry as a cultural test of—and testimony of—written form. DuPlessis's reading practices—carried through and between the variant forms of writing that compose her oeuvre—are signal verifiers for many of us about what to look for in a poem, and how to read what's in front of us with care, diligence, and ethical discernment.

In an important recent essay on DuPlessis, "Emergent Midrash: Rachel Blau DuPlessis Glosses Modernism," included in his book on the long poem, *Writing in Real Time: Emergent Poetics from Whitman to the Digital* (2017), Paul Jaussen has observed the stakes couldn't be higher in DuPlessis's effort to develop "a poetic form that acknowledges historical displacement while attempting to ethically comprehend it. . . . A poetic ambition made all the more poignant in light of the historical erasures of subject and cultures that preoccupy DuPlessis" across her career (137). In these and other ways, *Thinking with the Poem* responds to the critical need for a book that thinks through the enormity of the questions DuPlessis has set before her readers—questions that come from many directions at once and that situate DuPlessis's materials in a network of cultural, political, and historical associations.

As she has posed the task in "Draft 18: Traduction":

> I'm after everything and after nothing.
> A belatedness so strong
> I come,
> even after what is
> not there,
>
> after eradication
> Who inhabits one's own time
> who can be witness
> after the eclipse of witness
>
> cannot not speak. O poetry
> —again and again no more poetry.
> (*Toll* 120)

DuPlessis's account here foregrounds the struggle her poetry and poetics enact: to write "after eradication" without the consolatory narratives of witness or the provenance of Poetry as a canonical and canonized form of written response to social life. Each of the writers in this collection asks us, from different perspectives, to chart our responses to the eclipse of witness and the condition imposed on us in real time of being both unable to speak and needing to speak in poetry.

Given the range of the contributors, their positions and interests, *Thinking with the Poem* integrates different modes of cultural investigation and literary scholarship to explore potential answers to these and other concerns raised by DuPlessis's poetic and scholarly output. As Jeanne Heuving suggests in her introduction to *Inciting Poetics: Thinking and Writing Poetry*, "Poetics now finds itself in a far more diversified and uncertain terrain. Radical social and cultural change with respect to identity movements and their evolution continue as well as an accelerated technological and media revolution" (xi). DuPlessis has contributed importantly and demonstrably to many of these cultural and literary shifts, as her own "Statement on Poetics" from this same collection exemplifies. The essays collected in *Thinking with the Poem* likewise promise to complicate both our understandings of and desire for poetry that is "radical" in its cultural inquiry and adaptive to the changing social, political, and historical worlds in which we locate ourselves and are located in turn by forces outside our control.

Indeed, as each of the writers here documents, DuPlessis's multifocal investigations of the connections between poem-making and social change demand our attention precisely because of her formidable belief documented in book after book, poem after poem, in the value of poetry as a culturally significant and ethically responsive art form—one with specific responsibilities, commitments, and availabilities for political intervention.

Thinking with the Poem is separated into three sections: Part I: Feminist Practice and the Poetics of Crisis; Part II: Materialities of Making: Collage, Detritus, and Waste in *Drafts*; and Part III: Across Traditions: Romanticism, Objectivist and Projectivist Poetics, Secular Judaism, and the Witness of History. Organized into these discrete yet intersecting units of analysis, each of these sections and the individual contributors within them provide meaningful extensions on already extant scholarship, while establishing overlapping and convergent concerns across the volume. Thus, in its attention to the long poem and formal concerns related thereto, this volume acknowledges the continued relevance of such decisive earlier studies as Lynn Keller's *Forms of Expansion: Recent Long Poems by Women* (1997) and Joseph Conte's *Unending Design: The Forms of Postmodern Poetry* (1991), while it promises to extend on the work of more recent volumes, including Linda Kinnahan's *Lyric Interventions: Feminism, Experimental Poetry, and Contemporary Discourse* (2004), Matthew Carberry's *Phenomenology and the Late Twentieth Century American Long Poem* (2019), and Paul Jaussen's already mentioned *Writing in Real Time*.

The writers included in Part I of *Thinking with the Poem* offer a particularly suggestive set of readings of feminist practice in relation to the long poem, the intersection of public histories, poetic formation, and the ongoing cultural work of texts that enact subversive and alternative versions of poetic making. This section gathers important new thinking on the development of feminist thought in DuPlessis's work and shows the depth of this inquiry that moves across multiple disciplinary and theoretical levels. The section opens with Peter Middleton's "Inner Speech in Rachel Blau DuPlessis's Poetry," which focuses readers' attention on DuPlessis's later poetry, *Surge: Drafts 96–114*, *Poetic Realism*, *Numbers*, and *Late Work*, and argues that this work reveals an acute ear curious to listen in on her own inner speech, treating it with respect, caution, challenge, and irreverence, alert for the revealing *clinamen*. In "Angelus Novus" from *Late Work* she asks questions of Walter Benjamin's gnomic description of Paul Klee's angel, appearing at moments to be dialectical, writing an essay in verse, while repeatedly falling away from such formality into asides, snark, frustration, even silence: "If you can't represent this, // you just can't." Stalling with: "I am not I." Accordingly, Middleton queries the tendency to divide contemporary poetry too sharply into voiced and unvoiced poems, personal lyrics, and open field poems on the one hand and various modes of "languagey," nonexpressive writing on the other and asks instead that readers see the deeply resonant inner voicing evident in DuPlessis's late work.

Following on Middleton's critique of vocality and contemporary poetics, Megan Jewell, in "'First Feminism' in Rachel Blau DuPlessis's *Drafts*," identifies the ways in which *Drafts*, in its conception and execution, is influenced by DuPlessis's specific engagement with post–World War II feminism in the United States and her long-standing commitment to twentieth- and early twenty-first-century feminist thought. In an expansive rethinking of the cultural trajectory of feminism and its impact on DuPlessis's poetry, Jewell argues that such a clear delineation of the major feminist ideas and relevant biographical information contributing to *Drafts*'s composition and form is essential for scholars and students hoping to understand the ways in which DuPlessis's fluid yet longstanding feminist commitments to women's expression are specifically documented in what is her own "poem about history."

In the final contribution to Part I, Amber Manning's "Infinite History and the Mortal Body: Rereading the Unending *Surge*" argues that in "Draft 97: Rubrics," "Draft 99: Intransitive," "Draft 111: Arte Povera," "Draft 113: Index," and "Draft 114: Exergue and Volta" (among others), DuPlessis deploys images of flowing, floating, surging, and drowning in poems whose forms mimic the swell of the sea to reconcile the mortal body and the crests of history. This imagery, when coupled with the poet's contradictory claims about ending, creates a text that uniquely answers H.D.'s query about whether the third wave would be the last: "it is / finished but it is / not complete." Finally, Manning proposes that it is in this reading of unfinished histories that DuPlessis's *Drafts* makes its signal contribution to serial form and the postmodern long poem.

Part II represents forward-looking responses to the materiality of poetic production. Here, each of the writers (and group of writers in the case of Chapter Six) is invested in establishing new ground for reception of DuPlessis's more recent books that often incorporate or are based in collage procedures and other multimedia elements. Thus, Maria Damon's essay probes the confluence of feminist philosophy and collage to reposition DuPlessis in an art tradition that includes such practitioners as Cecilia Vicuña and Jen Bervin. In "Intertexuality as Collage, Text/Textile Interstices, Layering," Damon places her argument firmly in the connection between feminist philosophy and artmaking; this essay proposes that DuPlessis participates in the growing artistic and scholarly attention to "craft" as art (i.e., a reevaluation of "women's work"). Thereby, DuPlessis joins the crossover text-textile poetry movement whose most prominent practitioners primarily identify as visual artists. Focusing on DuPlessis's preoccupation with salvage, materiality, and repurposing as a form of eco-minded conservation, Damon argues that DuPlessis's consistent aesthetics continue to expand in their forms of expression and contribute to timely and urgent conversations and praxes with specific ethical consequences.

Eric Keenaghan, in "'daily politics, weird shit': Feminist Weak Resistance and Waste in Rachel Blau DuPlessis's Later Work," argues that as DuPlessis struggles to produce new meanings out of the detritus of the everyday in her more recent work, she contributes in vital ways to an alternative modernism and postmodernism, an alternative rooted in gendered alterity. Positing that waste is the stuff of the margins—it's the stuff of daily life for those who are women (cis or trans) and those who are queer—Keenaghan situates DuPlessis's recent work (post-*Drafts*) in a cultural conversation that asks: Is this work political? Or is it ethical? If so, in what ways? What kind of future is this work going to produce if all that's seen is the social *refuse*, rather than the poet's *refusal*? In so doing, Keenaghan reconsiders DuPlessis's recent poetry as a varied and multimodal assemblage of texts that continually takes into account the excluded, the world of waste, all that is otherwise marginalized in the name of the ideal. In this way, Keenaghan moves his critique to a central locale within DuPlessis's expansive cultural critique, providing readers with new tools with which to examine the plethora of referential and sociopolitical detritus these projects both point to (deixis as the prominent figure of cultural critique) and weigh as intricately interconnected fields of public knowledge and accountability.

In their collaboratively produced essay "En Dehors Garde Collage Homage," Suzanne W. Churchill, Linda Kinnahan, and Susan Rosenbaum draw on the feminist strategies DuPlessis has modeled in her own writing to weave together, collage-style, personal reflections on how her work has influenced and energized multiple generations of feminist scholars and teachers. Thus, these authors consider the groundbreaking influence of DuPlessis's scholarly work in early venues like *HOW(ever)*, experimental scholarly essays in *The Pink Guitar*, and compositions foregrounding collage and visual dimensions that cross genres of poetry, theory, scholarship, and visual composition/poetics. Both interpersonal autobiography and social critique, this essay illuminates in particularly resonant ways the sites of contact and confluence that have animated each of these writers' relation to DuPlessis's work across several decades of writing, talking, and thinking. In so doing, they enact key principles of ethical engagement central to DuPlessis's project as it has developed across multiple venues, formats, and audiences with different stakes in different parts of the conversation.

As DuPlessis's publisher via Materialist Press, Ariel Resnikoff in "An Extra Horizon Can Be Spun: On Publishing Rachel Blau DuPlessis's *Numbers* and *Life in Handkerchiefs*" attends to DuPlessis's recent book-length collage poem, *Numbers*, from the perspective of editing and publishing this work (Materialist Press in 2018). Commenting and reflecting on the already long biography of this poem, Resnikoff tells the story of how the book came into the world, while at the same time he moves through the hybrid poem as a curator might in a gallery, addressing the text and collages together, thereby foregrounding the materiality of this work. Though the essay focuses specifically on *Numbers*, Resnikoff also examines other pertinent examples of DuPlessis's collage-poetic praxis, making a larger argument and observation about the flux and coalescence of various factors in her prolific oeuvre that have found a dwelling place in her late practice of collage poetry and poetics. Poignant in its imagining of a conversation that might take place with the poets Charles Reznikoff and George Oppen in the room "sitting together over this wild numerological-poetic work [DuPlessis] had created," Resnikoff's essay charts his reading of the text first as admirer of DuPlessis's previous work, then as scholiast examining the complex Jewish histories inscribed through the book's collagist wandering. Taken together, the essays in Part II both provide much-needed history of the intersectional and collaborative aspects of second-wave feminist production in the 1980s and '90s and a useful way of understanding DuPlessis's developing position during the last twenty years as a major voice in independent publishing and innovative poetries.

Part III explores the interrelationship of multiple strands of cultural, poetic, religious, and literary traditions in DuPlessis's poetry. The opening essay of this section, Jeanne Heuving's "Between Objectivist and Projectivist Poetics: Rachel Blau DuPlessis and the 'Force Moving,'" circles back to some of the initial concerns raised in Part I related to the feminist orientation and praxis of DuPlessis's work, while extending on this conversation to pursue a fundamental rethinking of DuPlessis's well-established linkages to George Oppen and objectivist poetics. In her piece, Heuving offers a remapping of DuPlessis's early career during which she sought ways to integrate the objectivist practices of Oppen and the projectivist practices of Charles Olson and Robert Creeley into her poetry. In her reading of the relationship between DuPlessis's essays and poetry, Heuving demonstrates the impact of the strictures and constraints of both Oppen's brand of objectivist poetics (bounded by the constraint of "sincerity") and Olson and Creeley's projectivist poetics (famously organized around the principle "form is never more than an extension of content") on DuPlessis's ability to move out in her own decidedly feminist direction. Heuving proposes that it was through DuPlessis's bridging of the seemingly conflictual gender and poetic issues of her time emblematized by these two contrary positions within contemporary poetry and poetics that the poet was able to create her epic *Drafts*. It is in this extended serial work that DuPlessis was able to achieve a poetry that combines critique *and* presence to mark a decidedly new turn in innovative poetry and poetics.

In "'Immerginated Raptures': Rachel Blau DuPlessis's *Drafts 1–38, Toll*," Joseph Donahue provides a detailed examination of the relationship of Oppen's poetics to DuPlessis's development of her own formation of the political and ethical sublime, one that would revise elements of Oppen's materialist praxis to engage the spiritual and numinous, the sacred and Hebraic as foundational conductors of poetic making/meaning. Throughout this meditative narrative of a poet's growth, Donahue pursues the significance of a single word elided from the Keats epigraph from which *Toll* takes its title; the word is "forlorn." In his pursuit, Donahue reconsiders DuPlessis's place within the tradition of H.D., Robert Duncan, and Robin Blaser, as well as Oppen and Louis Zukofsky, as he examines one of the boldest and most distinctive of DuPlessis's contributions to the postmodern concern with myth and its relation to poetics: the transformation of deixsis—the fundamental capacity of language to point out—into a cosmological gesture. Meditating on the connections between Oppen's objectivist poetics and the work of DuPlessis's early *Wells*, Donahue establishes a recurring and formative motif in DuPlessis's later work, the figure of the well, and proposes a way of reading DuPlessis that anchors her textuality in and through the intergenerational haunting instantiated through her revisiting of Oppen's thinking across decades of writing. As Donahue importantly points out, in his linking of DuPlessis to other predecessor figures, such as Emily Dickinson, long part of the lyrical canon, "the great strength of *Drafts* is its refusal to concede the sublime, to forsake the grandeur of poetry's past however much it must be tested on the pulse of the post-Vietnam world."

In ways that extend on Donahue's discussion, Adeena Karasick traces the connections between the Kabbalah's concept of breaking of the vessels (Shevirat ha Kelim) as a central topos for consideration of DuPlessis's as yet uncollected poem "Psalm 151" (2021). In so doing, Karasick provides a corollary reading to Donahue's of the intersection of Jewish mysticism and postmodernist poetic form as she "highlights how language is not only a creative force that engenders a multiplicity of communicative possibilities, but a means to continually re-activate the world." Situating DuPlessis's more recent work in this nexus of midrash and spiritual scholia, Karasick anticipates the next phase of scholarship in relation to DuPlessis and others who follow the syncretic pathways of Hebraic teaching and thought through the lens of contemporary poetics.

Finally, Jeffrey C. Robinson rereads an early work of DuPlessis's in his "'Moth: Ode to Psyche' and the Active Romanticism of *Drafts*" (1984) to link DuPlessis to a key text of Romanticism, John Keats's "Ode to Psyche." Reading DuPlessis in relation to the Keatsian predecessor text to *Tabula Rosa*, Robinson demonstrates how words and phrases from "Ode to Psyche" are frequently quoted backward from poem's end to beginning as a sign of the inescapability of the poetry of the masculinist tradition but also its availability for (feminist) transformation. In focusing on the connection between the Keatsian sublime and DuPlessis's reworking of this trope in her early poetry, Robinson argues that "Moth: Ode to Psyche" is paradoxically at once a pivotal moment in DuPlessis's poetics, a singular moment of feminist postmodern refashioning of Romanticism, and a demonstration of the radicalism of British and American Romanticism's precepts for postmodernist poetic practice.

As open-ended inquiries into the relationship among multiple traditions and intellectual trajectories, Part III closes out *Thinking with the Poem* with rigorous and exacting readings of DuPlessis's multizonal thinking and the ways in which, as one of the central practitioners of feminist and postmodernist poetics across the last half century, she bridges critical gaps along the way from modernist to postmodernist poetry. Insofar as DuPlessis can be firmly located in the tradition of poets mentioned above—John Keats, Robert Duncan, H.D., George Oppen, Robin Blaser—she is most recognizable to us for the heterogeneity with which she has responded to the conditions of our time through serial compositions that reject any singular locale or methodology through which to confront the phenomenological and political realities of the current age. These conditions, as explicated in each essay included in this volume, are not static nor set on perpetual rewind. DuPlessis's most recent work confirms both the importance of poetic thought in our era of digital media, ChatGPT, Instagram, TikTok, and the like, and the susceptibility of any work to become too quickly categorized as one thing. As DuPlessis's work so clearly delineates and as each of the contributors to this volume recognizes, the questions raised by DuPlessis's inquiry rely on a nimble form of parataxis; no one answer is sufficient. In the concurrences of "and and," this book registers the formal, po-ethical, and cross-historical movements that DuPlessis's work manifests.

Near the end of *A Long Essay on the Long Poem*, DuPlessis addresses her readers with the following questions:

> But what precisely is the meaning of those very long poems in the twentieth and twenty-first centuries? Not, what do they mean? But why did people feel the urgency to write them? What is the meaning of (translation: what do *we* think was going on with) those overwhelming acts of writing chosen by a number of poets? What was the longing they evinced, and how did each work this out? (225–26)

She then goes on to answer some of these questions:

> It is the longing to name a collective socio-cosmological and sometimes political shape—the shape of "everything" affecting our lives and driving our histories, filled with contradictions and cross pressures . . . long poems as a praxis—a real practice within culture but beyond the literary . . . different poets' drives to write poems of great and very great length, what it feels like in relation to language and one's time, what motivates the poet within the mechanisms of poetry, in the traditions of poetry, in the world issues—secular and spiritual, historical and ontological—that each poet chooses to confront. (226)

Arguably, as DuPlessis has moved from *Drafts* to segmented books that coexist in relation to one another, carrying forward elements of long-poem thinking while producing work that is in scope of a different scale and differentially related to poetry's praxis as assemblage and the format of the book, some of her discussion here has differential application to the poetry she's produced across the last decade since she brought *Drafts* to a stopping point. Yet in ways that are significant to her ongoing meditations on and interventions in poetic practice as intra- and interpersonal realms of transitive thought, DuPlessis's comments above provide another lens through which to consider the contributions of the writers gathered in this book.

In their varied approaches to DuPlessis's body of work, each writer here represents responses to the material as varied as the work itself. In responding as they do to the multifoliate compositional arc of DuPlessis's career, the contributors to *Thinking with the Poem* explore, explicate, and provide important conjectural models for further discussions of poetry and poetics in the already long twenty-first century and stage a set of concerns that will continue to animate discussions of innovative poetry and poetics and require new modes of thinking—with and through and across poetries. The richness of this conversation suggests a variable and potentially inexhaustible set of new directions for a new cohort of scholars to explore. As Bradley Fest has pointed out, "This is not easy work. To participate in textual enormity without perpetuating the sense of totality concomitant with patriarchal late capitalist modernity ... requires of DuPlessis a vigilant ethics of debris, a poetics of documentation and an unwavering lifelong commitment to theorizing her own poetry" (159). The writers in this volume meet DuPlessis in these commitments, joining in her own hermeneutic and midrashic engagements and further complicating and extending on work that has already been done on the long poem and DuPlessis's central place in the history of this conceptual framework of modernist and postmodernist poetics.

What are the stakes of all this work? As DuPlessis observes with the last word of her book on the long poem, nothing less than "poesis" itself is at stake. Which is to say: the entire scope of traditions, positionalities, and cultural conditions signified by this word. "The poem finally chooses you," DuPlessis tells us at the end of *A Long Essay on the Long Poem*. "You must essay to be worthy of its trust and of the insights you fabricate with it" (229). That condition, as the writers in this volume have suggested, is a weave of differing obligations, assignations, commitments, intellectual engagements, subjectivities, and identity positions. The result is a book without end, one that ends over there, or nowhere, or is always en route, never finished. A long poem of books, each written into the world as each of us may experience such: contingent, precarious, nomadic, all of a piece. Recognition of the endeavor remains dialectical, shaped by vision and revision, response and critique, ethicality and intervention, through which the poem chooses us, and we choose the poem.

Note

1. While not entirely certain, DuPlessis has confirmed for me that "Writing" (which appeared in her collection *Tabula Rosa* in 1987) was likely the text she read in 1989 at Temple: "'Writing' as a poem was written in 1985. The handwriting in *Selected Poems* has been done as pretend handwriting in a typeface. The 'technology' then was laminate sheets (transparencies) slid over a transparency projector, changed by hand. It was a fine effect. Light streamed through. For a while in that early period, I thought people at readings would like to see the poem's complexities, not the poet. So I did many readings that way" (personal email with the author, March 23, 2023).

Works Cited

Altieri, Charles. *Modernist Poetry and the Limitations of Materialist Theory*. Albuquerque: University of New Mexico Press, 2021.
Carberry, Matthew. *Phenomenology and the Late Twentieth Century American Long Poem*. New York: Palgrave Macmillan, 2019.
Conte, Joseph. *Unending Design: The Forms of Postmodern Poetry*. Ithaca: Cornell University Press, 1991.
DuPlessis, Rachel Blau. *A Long Essay on the Long Poem*. Tuscaloosa: University of Alabama Press, 2023.
———. *Selected Poems*. Tucson: Chax Press, 2022.
———. *Poetic Realism*. Buffalo: BlazeVOX Books, 2021.
———. *Late Work*. New York: Black Square Editions, 2020.
———. *Numbers*. Cincinnati: Materialist Press, 2018.
———. *Around the Day in 80 Worlds*. Buffalo: BlazeVOX Books, 2018.
———. *Days and Works*. Boise: Ahsahta Press, 2017.
———. *Graphic Novella*. West Lima, WI: Xexoxial Editions, 2015.
———. *Surge: Drafts 96–114*. Cromer Norfolk, UK: Salt Publishing, 2013.
———. *Purple Passages: Pound, Eliot, Zukofsky, Olson, Creeley, and the Ends of Patriarchal Poetry*. Iowa City: University of Iowa Pres, 2012.
———. *Blue Studios: Poetry and Its Cultural Work*. Tuscaloosa: University of Alabama Press, 2006.
———. *Drafts 1–38, Toll*. Middletown, CT: Wesleyan University Press, 2001.
———. *The Pink Guitar: Writing as Feminist Practice*. New York: Routledge, 1990.
———. "Psyche, or Wholeness." *Massachusetts Review*, vol. 20, no. 1, 1979, 77–96.
Fest, Bradley J. "'Is an Archive Enough?': Megatextual Debris in the Work of Rachel Blau DuPlessis." *Genre*, vol. 54, no. 1, 2021, 139–65.
Finch, Annie. *The Body of Poetry: Essays on Women, Form and the Poetic Self*. Ann Arbor: University of Michigan Press, 2005.
Heuving, Jeanne, and Tyrone Williams, editors. *Inciting Poetics: Thinking and Writing Poetry*. Albuquerque: University of New Mexico Press, 2019.
Hofer, Matthew, and Michael Golston, editors. *The Language Letters: Selected 1970s Correspondence of Bruce Andrews, Charles Bernstein, and Ron Silliman*. Albuquerque: University of New Mexico Press, 2019.
Jaussen, Paul. *Writing in Real Time: Emergent Poetics from Whitman to the Digital*. Cambridge: Cambridge University Press, 2017.
Keller, Lynn. *Forms of Expansion: Recent Long Poems by Women*. Chicago: University of Chicago Press, 1997.
Kinnahan, Linda. *Lyric Interventions: Feminism, Experimental Poetry, and Contemporary Discourse*. Iowa City: University of Iowa Press, 2004.
Middleton, Peter. *Expanding Authorship: Transformations in American Poetry Since 1950*. Albuquerque: University of New Mexico Press, 2021.

Morris, Adelaide, and Thomas Swiss. *New Media Poetics: Contexts, Technotexts and Theories*. Cambridge, MA: MIT Press, 2006.
Mossin, Andrew R. "'Thinking the Poem; Thinking the Poem Writing': An Interview with Rachel Blau DuPlessis." Conducted by Andrew R. Mossin. *Golden Handcuffs Review*, no. 30, 2021, 37–60.
Pritchett, Patrick. "Drafting Beyond the Ending: On Rachel Blau DuPlessis." *Jacket2*, 14 Dec. 2011, https://jacket2.org/feature/drafting-beyond-ending.
Sadoff, Ira. *History Matters: Contemporary Poetry on the Margins of American Culture*. Iowa City: University of Iowa Press, 2009.

PART I

Feminist Practice and the Poetics of Crisis

CHAPTER ONE

Inner Speech in Rachel Blau DuPlessis's Poetry

Peter Middleton

WHEN RACHEL BLAU DUPLESSIS began work on the long poem sequence *Drafts*, she hoped for "a voiced text," to create "a stance capacious, ready, open-throated, alert and altered, serious" (*BS* 229), and she knew that this seemingly simple aspiration was anything but. Voice in poetry, lyric or long form, confessional or abstract, was a subject of controversy among poets and literary critics. As a scholar she was already immersed in contemporary debates about language, and she wanted to extend this interest into a poetry sequence, while going beyond academic argument.[1] She wished, in words that Lisa Robertson uses to describe Simone Weil's writing (words that would fit Robertson's own poetry), to throw "open her subjectivity in order to be fundamentally changed by language" (24).

DuPlessis had signaled hopes for her poetry in her early haunting essay "For the Etruscans," which was also my first introduction to her work. Reading it with hindsight, two principles stand out. The first is commitment to a facture that can encompass large-scale knowledge: "In women's writing, as in modernist, there is an encyclopedic impulse, in which the writer invents a new and total culture, symbolized by and announced in a long work, like the modern long poem" (*PG* 17). To achieve this, the woman writer must engage in a constant, wide-ranging, reflexive process: "Any work is a strategy to resolve, transpose, reweight, dilute, arrange, substitute contradictory material from culture, from society, from personal life" (10). The second principle requires openness to both inward thought and dialogue with others: "Writers know their text as a form of intimacy, of personal contact, whether conversations with the reader or with the self" (5). This is not to be just a poetry of prosopopoeia, grabbing the attention of the reader of the lyric, or sending letters out to the general public, this is to be a poetry that reaches deep within to listen to the self while attentively listening to others too. In addition to establishing these personal axioms, the essay's very form also hinted at her future poetic style: its series of frequently discontinuous paragraphs anticipate an episodic structure for the poem. Indeed it has several other features that point to future poems: intermittent asides about everyday life; ambushing metaphors pushed to the limits (notably ovine ones—sheepishness, the golden fleece, the herd behavior of men, and the writer Woolf that might harry the sheep); unexpected aporias that leave loose ends; large shifts of register from scholarly summaries of feminist ideas to accounts of the author's dreams; and the pervasive melancholy created by comparing the situation of women's writing with that of the mysterious Etruscans whose unreadable texts survive to no avail. *Drafts* will try to answer questions raised by the essay: what kind of poetry is even possible to a woman poet in contemporary America, and what poems most need to be written? This very essay, it seems to say, may itself not be fully interpretable. DuPlessis would return to this preoccupation with the anguish of the illegible in "Draft 99: Intransitive," which looks as if a repressive editor has used a black marker to overstrike words and phrases, leaving a mutilated poem with the smallest traces of a few pendents just barely visible (seeing them for the first time, a friend wanted to peel back the blackout strip and see what the words had been).[2] "Draft 99" has become an Etruscan poem; by implication DuPlessis wants to avoid a similar silencing fate for other poems. How could she do this?

At the time DuPlessis began *Drafts*, literary and cultural theory could appear excessively dictatorial about language, telling everyone, including poets, in the jargon of the time, how they must comprehend the so-called signs and signifiers, divisions between voice and writing, roots into the unconscious (supposedly structured like a language), and the codes of postmodernity. I don't mean that Derrida, Lacan, Barthes, Kristeva, Cixous, and other French thinkers ever intended to impose a new set of dogmas on writers, far from it; they saw themselves as freeing up the writer. Speculations about language that began as spectacle in fierce yet playful Parisian intellectual debates migrated into the academic Anglosphere to be transformed by institutional requirements for professional validation into strict ontologies governed by rigid theories.

"Draft 87: The Trace" is a good example of how deeply DuPlessis has been engaged with the theory stirrings. The poem rummages among the many possible implications of the concept of trace, a key concept in literary theory since Derrida incorporated this Cheshire-cat grin of a noun into his announcement in his essay "Différance" of a new style of philosophy that would allegedly recognize the inevitable indeterminacy and inescapable ambiguity of language. As Matthew Carbery says, "*Drafts* deals with a provisionality in which inherited theoretical notions like Derrida's are themselves subject to the contingency of their application" (202). Other philosophers had tried to purify the language for philosophical reasoning; Derrida would work with its impurities of paradox, imprecision, and rhetoricity. In this famous essay, having introduced his signature paradoxical concept of *différance* (which my spelling program insistently corrects to *difference*), he adds in conclusion another concept, the *trace*.[3] He explains: "And to prepare ourselves for venturing beyond our own logos, that is, for a *différance* so violent that it refuses to be stopped and examined as the epochality of Being and ontological difference . . . we must allow the trace of whatever goes beyond the truth of being to appear/disappear in its fully rigorous way. It is a trace of something that can never present itself." DuPlessis is amused by this elusiveness: "Quick, to the side. Look! / There / was the trace. / But you missed it" (*PI* 88). Sarcasm is soon supplemented by both poetic allusion and thoughtful references to Blake and Roland Barthes: "Not so much the world in a grain of sand / but the grain of sand in the world / defines trace. // Not 'to express the unexpressible'—/ poetic posturing—it's wanting / 'to unexpress the expressible' / 'inexprimer l'exprimable'" (91). These phrases from Barthes's 1963 gloomy "Preface" to *Critical Essays* are meant to exemplify the literary critic's struggle to achieve any kind of originality: "The writer does not 'wrest' speech from silence, as we are told in pious literary biographies, but inversely, detaches a secondary language from the slime of primary languages afforded him by the world" (xvii).[4] (Barthes's choice of adjective for the discourses that make the world "full of language" translated as "slime" is actually "l'engluement," better translated as a mix of entanglement and stickiness, a meaning closer to how DuPlessis sees Barthes's "language that is always *previous*.") *Drafts* demonstrates a nuanced understanding throughout its immense network of poetic encounters with the traceries and excessiveness of languages in all their complexity, their pragmatics, their politics, their tangles, their histories, their textualities, and their absurdities.

    I have long been fascinated by what at first seemed a provocative idiosyncrasy of Rachel Blau DuPlessis's poems, a certain abruptness of interruption, a willingness to break the flow of a poem however beguiling it had become at that point, coupled with a refusal to let poetic music unite a poem. Harriet Tarlo describes this quality as ludic: "The playfulness of DuPlessis's poetry, a lightness of touch reminiscent of Gertrude Stein, drew me to her work from the start. It is a 'play splice' of word and letter slippage, the slip between letter and word; a love of the little word and the conjunction, a playing out of metonymic games, of punning, homophones and homonyms, an eager and 'errant' exposure of the unstable nature of language" (Tarlo). As a step toward delineating this feature of her poetic style, let's look closely at the handling of voice in "Draft 106: Words," and its role in the management of allusions to other poets, its references to theories of the lyric, its unusual modes of reasoning, and especially at its handling of interruption, its mysterious breaks in the sequences of poetic thought. Here is the first half of the poem and its conclusion.

    —swervswerve!
    but not as much as atoms.
    The main thing we have in common is "restlessness."

    Things do hold together, and
    so does meaning
    more or less.

    glyphs morse pebbles visionary long happenstance

    sing-song interlock other obdurate something memory

    really but also diagnosis ungainliness what never

barely shards thank you haunted between and/or

trace deeper equally where of midst

leaf syntax constitute unpick falsifies bumpy

Signs under impingement
great lists+ of seasons' days   +grids
swirling, davening
far beyond vagaries
and Open 24 Hours.+   +intermittently.

The main word we have in common is "hap."

There is a clacking sound,
a weedy ditch, a pre-war map.
Words are blacked out,
or
they evoke inarticulate things
or
they stick in your gut, unsayable.

Something's coming loose. There is scattering
and the snap out of blurriness.
             There is brightness, too, and no
genre enough for it, even for its sudden shifting
           even for its affect.+   +impact.
And there are words
that become tremendous mantras,
doing fieldwork in ordinary language,
inventing what one found needed to be said,
and they reverberate+ for a long, long time.   +pontificate

Though words establish no exact center, with
       some words inside intangible centers,
             so words declare the variable as such,+   +permanent
open what+ can never be scryed dependably.   +omens that

. . . .

And at 4:32 exactly
             the wind that's blowing fiercely

> hits such down swoops as a short-eared owl
> is like a night train with that longtime faraway hoo—.
> Nothing is stranger than life. Except, maybe, languages.
> With words, the world
> is more than is the case.
> How could it not
> be just that way.
> (*S* 83–87)

Things start to unfold not with a word but a punctuation mark, a dash that would normally indicate a switch away from the words that preceded this point to convey a shift of thought, perhaps parenthetic or qualifying, or simply a transition, a neat reminder that we always arrive belatedly in a world already overfull with language. Then the poem's first words collide in the truncated phrase, "swervswerve," a mimetic echo of Lucretius's theory that the world is composed of atoms whose *clinamina* ensure that we live in a world of constant change, a world with unending potentiality. The second line continues a subtext of the first, that words are the atoms of language, though with a hint that this analogy may require corrective adjustment. The third line comes close to abandoning the logic of the analogy, since if "the main thing we have in common is 'restlessness,'" then the similarity between atoms and words potentially includes a vast range of other experiences and phenomena. It will turn out that the main significance of this third line is to initiate a leitmotif in the poem, a series of similar statements about words or things that "we" share with the world, atoms, or other people.

By now readers have an intimation this poem will invite them to share in cogitations on the many roles of *words* in utterances, art, society, and the cosmos, a cue that is underlined by the appearance of a more explicit commitment to bold reasoning about these issues: "Things do hold together, and / so does meaning / more or less." Readers will recognize this as an antithetical position to Yeats's famous line "Things fall apart" (187), a neatly judged dismissal of a canonical modernist, as well as an allusion to perennial arguments about just how it is that matter, if it is composed of atoms, should be stable at all, given the amount of apparent space between the atoms and their potential to break apart. The conjunction's appearance of logical connection is deceptive of course, as the poem knows, since meanings hold together in a myriad of syntactic, sonic, historical, and associational processes unrelated, even analogically, to the fundamental, adhesive forces that keep the nuclear particles of physics in their place. DuPlessis is also pushing back against a form of once popular Anglophone post-structuralist argument that floating signifiers are always sliding against one another, that meaning is always falling apart, deconstructing itself. Instead, with the help of this seemingly authoritative analogy borrowed from the sciences, she proposes that linguistic meaning is less volatile, more cohesive, than modernist literary speculators have claimed.

Having made these crucial preliminary moves, she promptly counters this claim to verbal stability, giving us a six-by-six grid of words and short phrases that appear to have fallen apart, to have no hold on each other, lacking syntactic glue. The form of the grid itself is an allusion to Robert Duncan's poem "The Fire: Passages 13," which also begins with a matrix of words, hinting at a river landscape. It would be a mistake to treat this and other allusions in "Draft 106" as due to an anxiety of influence. They are much better understood as what Megan Jewell calls a "collaborative gesture" acknowledging predecessors, while recognizing that under new cultural conditions, especially a burgeoning feminism, formerly timely modes of poetry are no longer possible.[5] At first glance DuPlessis's matrix shows no such obvious semantic homogeneity as Duncan's, though on second glance we see that many of her thirty-six words and phrases could be interpreted as disparate images, metaphors, or descriptors for the pragmatics of words. The first six words of the grid could be successively ideas of the word as a visual sign, the word as a unit of code, the word rounded into shape by the forces of historical usage, the word as measurable in scale, and the word as a door to unexpected, serendipitous connections. Alluding to Duncan enables DuPlessis to make the tacit point that poets engage in radical investigations of the potentials of individual words and the role of the word in general.

Following Duncan's guest appearance, Emily Dickinson ghosts through the poem in another allusion based on form, this time the placing of words on the right-hand margin as variants to words to their left in the poem itself, matched up by a superscript plus sign. The sigil in the line "so words declare the variable as such,+" corresponds to the alternate word "permanent," whose replacement would give the line a considerably different character. This line also carries another formalist reference, as a tercet alluding to the variable foot William Carlos Williams developed in his late poetry. These nonstandard devices employed by Duncan, Dickinson, and Williams invite us to notice afresh how the ordinary, normative spacing of printed words sustains syntax, while their modularity invites poets to be linguistic inventors testing out radical ideas about altering the workings of language, and showing that dominant theories of language are only approximations, and may be on the way to replacement by new paradigms. A final formal allusion to yet another poet offers insight into the temporality of the poem. Frank O'Hara's occasional poems famously include the odd mention of the exact time ("It is 12:20 in New York a Friday"); here in "Draft 106," a specific afternoon moment of composition, "4:32 exactly," is apparently pinpointed.[6] DuPlessis's poems in *Drafts* are dated, not however with a single time or even day as might happen with a Philip Whalen poem; the paratextual dates of the poems extend over months or even years. Clearly *Drafts* cannot be said to capture a moment of composition, a moment of uttered speech, inner or outer, however extended. Language events extend across time.

After enlisting Dickinson, the poem openly shows its affinity to the verse essay, as it canvasses several canonical ideas about words: they can be marker buoys for stretches of the depths of sometimes unreachable inner life; they can be the product of manufacture evidenced by the noise of a typewriter; they can have the opacity of "a weedy ditch, a pre-war map"; and they can be vulnerable to illegibility. The style of this poem is now established, a style of interrupted thoughts that are not always readable as a coeval sequence, capable, at moments like this, of indicating a vestigial narrative. Here is a sense of expectation: "Something's coming loose," a something that turns out to be the thought that because some special words, such as mantras, can induce radical physiological and perhaps spiritual changes, there might be other types of words as powerful in different ways. Maybe, the poem speculates with charming absurdity, the cosmos has its own mantra that "pulses semi-translatable messages" across the plenum. By now we are becoming accustomed to the rapidity of improvisation, ideas giving way to others at the speed of thought rather than being assembled in cool afterthought into the interim conclusions we might expect of a formal essay.

About two dozen lines further on from the first part of the extract above, the poem pulls back from these transcendental reaches to a conversational tone, bringing even more firmly to our notice how the poem enacts arguments with itself, here incorporating compact representations of an inner monologue.

> Words matter, things are discussable.
> We cannot not think so.
> Alternative is unthinkable.
> Or worse still—thinkable it is. Suppose words
> do not matter.
> Then would we stop making them?
> And as best we can?
> No.
> The motivation?
> A wager so precise it makes Pascal's look petty.
> (*S* 85)

This halting, flat, anti-lyrical mode is deliberate. Reflecting on her practice in *Drafts*, DuPlessis writes that she did not want the sequence to depend on "the perfection of lyric, the separation of lyric, the selectivity of lyric, the purity of lyric" (*BS* 221), a decision evident in the avoidance of rhetorical elegance in such passages as this one. Near the end of "Draft 106" she summarizes her poetics in terms of a resistance to both music and *moralia*: "Not epigrams with a twist / of rhyme, nor lyric's / soaring+ soundings" (*S* 88). One consequence is that these poems don't offer the prosopopoeia that has been claimed as the foundation of lyric communication, and when they do have an address it tends to be to an inner forum. The resulting poems are likely to be heterogeneous, disjunctive texts, as the poem acknowledges with an instruction to writer and reader: "Let it all in, fissure, facture, and broken shard, let the mobile / in. Leap into this excess ripe and snide, the compost thick / with overlays of conjunction" (*S* 85). As "Draft 106" shows, DuPlessis wants a poetry capable of inclusiveness, of the trivial and the massively important, the minor fluff and major events, or as she describes it in an early essay on the project, "a deliberate intermingled generative midden of a voice" (*BS* 210). Bradley Fest describes *Drafts* as a "megatext" engaged in an ethics of salvage, an "ethics of debris" (152). In "Draft 106" this debris is everywhere evident in images of compost, and in middens of voice collected in "great lists," in a universe whose "every sociable part . . . pulses semi-translatable messages." This is the aural debris of inner and outer voices, a tumbling polyphony shifting between affirmation and quizzicality, of remembered poems, snatches of reasoning, interruptions, and a resistance to closure.

Reading sections of "Draft 106: Words" shows us that DuPlessis developed a poetics of voice that could become intensely self-dialogic, vigilantly interruptive, and conscious of the voices of the dead poets as well as the living culture around her. Most salient is the constant self-correction, the determination to adjust and deepen understanding without aiming for conclusions, a process so evident in the opening lines, where line two immediately qualifies the implication of the Lucretian analogy in line one, and line six mutes the assertoric force of lines four and five. Elsewhere are similar partial withdrawals of statements just made. The stuttering repetition of the negative in these two lines from later in the poem—"Words matter, things are discussable. / We cannot not think so"—marks hesitancies at the level of echolalia. Occasional residues of everyday slogans ("Open 24 hours+," "stick in your gut," and from later in the poem, "All of the above"), rhetorical small talk ("Something's coming loose," "And as best we can? / No"), and images of impurity ("a weedy ditch") all add to a sense that one laminate of the poem is taken from inner speech.

For help with understanding the role of inner speech in DuPlessis's poetic style, we can learn much from Denise Riley's influential essay, "'A Voice Without a Mouth': Inner Speech," which examines this familiar yet elusive phenomenon through recourse to personal experience and thorough attention to philosophy, psychology, and literary history. She founds her discussion on such observations as V. N. Vološinov's statement that "no conscious act of any degree or distinctiveness can do without inner speech" (83). Hannah Arendt's account of the internal dialogism of acts of thinking also provides support for Riley's discussion: "It is this duality of myself with myself that makes thinking a true activity, in which I am both the one who asks and the one who answers" (185).[7] Riley describes inner speech in eloquent detail, its value and shortcomings, its "rapid low-grade commentary without authorship" (72), its occasional "subcutaneous plotting" (82), and its "silent dialogue with yourself" (89) that helps you avoid "slipping into dissociation or incoherence, inclining you instead to live in critical harmony with yourself" (89). Inner speech is deeply intertextual: "The dead chatter away as the inner speech of the living" (71).[8] As a starting point for investigation, Riley provides a transcription of her own typical mental kibitzing: "Even my daily and amiably prosaic mutterings to myself tend to be polyvocal. As to how I inhabit my own inner speech, I'm probably more accurately described as talking with myself rather than to myself" (71). Several understated points are made here that will help us start investigating DuPlessis's recourse to the possibilities available through attention to one's inner speech: it is often "incessant small talk" (71); it is dialogic and sometimes polyvocal, a collaborative action happening *with* the self not *to* it; though it is companionable, it can also be confrontational, an interrogative process of explicitation, of drawing out implications, motives, and understandings; and all of this is silent, unvocalized (except in the occasional accidents of talking aloud to oneself), tucked away inside the person.

Let's take these one by one. Riley insists that "inner speech is no limpid stream of consciousness, crystalline from its uncontaminated source in Mind, but a sludgy thing, thickened with reiterated quotation, choked with the rubble of the overheard, the strenuously sifted and hoarded, the periodically dusted down then crammed with slogans and jingles, with mutterings of remembered accusations, irrepressible puns, insistent spirits of ancient exchanges, monotonous citation, the embarrassing detritus of advertising, archaic injunctions from hymns, and the pastel snatches of old song lyrics" (73). If inner speech was no more than this, the mouthings of an irritatingly clichéd homunculus ensconced in our heads talking over our finer thoughts, it might be best ignored. Fortunately its very "mobility" is its strength, and within it "fragments of a calculating reciprocity are embedded in the apparent spontaneity of inner speech" (83), enabling it to clarify issues through internal argument with an "inner companion" (72). Riley thinks of Ludwig Wittgenstein's later style as "done in a natural tone of quizzical meditation as if transcribed directly from a tape of his inner speech" (79). In general she portrays inner speech as taking place on a spectrum from midden to midrash (to use DuPlessis's own terms). Inner speech in the Wittgensteinian mode can therefore be active self-interrogation of beliefs and ideas from a wide range of sources. And inner speech is silent to the outside world, however loud and lively it may be on the inside, a paradox that would become a crux in twentieth-century philosophy.

Riley, herself a distinguished poet, does not say much about poets or poetry, though she does acknowledge Samuel Beckett as an "arch inscriber of inner speech" (95). Her two pronouncements on the potential contribution of inner speech to poetic composition both emphasize that the poet has to relinquish some control if they want to find inspiration in inner speech: "A poet's style is engendered from the style of his inner speech, which does not lend itself to control, and his inner speech is itself the product of his entire society" (77).[9] A poet who draws on inner speech must always be on guard, pulling out the quotations that count, the puns that might be constructive, identifying the ancient spirits still worth hearing, be altogether a beachcomber of usable flotsam from popular culture. This is not a process of automatic dictation; words from inner speech require curation. Inner speech may help the poet in another manner too, sharpening awareness of the exact weight of words: "Meditating on inner speech, far from drifting towards verbal ectoplasm, throws us hard back on the materiality of words, including the aural quality of the *sotto voce*" (95). Riley's observations about inner speech also invite questions about its relation to voice in lyric, not least because the prominent use of a personal, usually first-person voice in poetry has been a marker of sharp division between avant-garde or experimental writing and confessional, identity-based, and narrative poems. The assumption by the former has been that voice is normally a symptom of ego or a fixed subjectivity, a subject that is not *en procès*, that it is a theatrical performance of selfhood and probably a denial of the condition of textuality as language whose waves of signification are endless. Writers of the personal lyric, on the other hand, see voice as a guarantor of authenticity, a sign of sincerity, a rich space of emotional, psychological, and moral reflection on values and lived experience.[10] The poet who works nimbly with inner speech, as Riley describes it, will be neither producing a stage persona nor claiming authentic ownership of expression.

From early in her career as a poet, DuPlessis transgressed these tacit current dogmas of poetics. The dogma of voice insisted that a poem's expressiveness should be carried by a subjectivity affirming the authenticity of its perceptions; the poem was to be a place for affects, observations, occasional wisdom not extended argument. This dogma began to be challenged in the 1970s, after a couple of decades of dominance, by a new doctrine: the avant-garde espousal of writing, often drawing on versions of the *écriture* promoted by the Tel Quel group and the *écriture féminine* of Hélène Cixous and other French feminists.[11] In its American form, this dogma insisted that poems should not mimic speech, not pretend to be the voiced thoughts of the poet; they should encompass the entire universe of possible writing, however unsayable its most extreme, unsyntaxed verbal agglomerates might be. For many avant-garde poets this led to a deliberately intertextual collage taken from sources as diverse as advertising, medieval romance, political jargon, scientific discourse, and phrases derived from procedural or random searches. Ironically, given the importance these poets attached to polemic, theory, and philosophy, their poetic practice often entailed radically disjunctive structures not conducive to sustained argumentation.

DuPlessis's decision to break with the two dogmas and write a poetry of voice and inquiry, sometimes described by her readers as essays in verse, required courage and inventiveness.[12] What she calls her "creolized Jewishness" helped her create a viable poetic style: "These traits would be (but are not limited to) skepticism, a reverence for textuality so intense it moves into an antic quality within the seriousness, an exilic, nomadic sensibility, a certain kind of humor (Yiddish humor—the litotes of self-mocking/group-mocking fondness), a quarrel with the negative space some call God, a particular, actually somewhat skeptical, somewhat hopeful attitude to fulfillment and messianic hope" ("Midrashic Sensibilities" 210). As we have seen in "Draft 106," to achieve "a voiced text" DuPlessis would draw on features of inner speech that allow for a multiply dialogic reasoning, opening out ideas for intensive inspection on what she calls "vectors of 'querying'" (*BS* 242), while giving space to voices by turns antic, snarky, witty, aphoristic, rigorous, and doubting, voices usually divided from within, rarely projecting a single oral persona. Not just voice either; the poems would also insist on their simultaneously written status. The risks of this strategy are obvious: it has to avoid turning into a tape recording of the inner voice, and not allow introspection to become so self-absorbed it is incapable of addressing the scope of the political problems of language for the feminist poet of the contemporary world. Inner speech needs to be inner but not too inner.

In section two of "Draft 48: Being Astonished," a series of meditations on women's lives, we can see the pressures that her strategy would have to acknowledge, as she presents a breaking apart of the verbal texture of what are initially a series of confident observations on ideologies of femininity:

> whether these are thoughts
> they are what happened once
> love/l'oeuf
> eat please/ ee puppet   to avert
> pulp
> reprisals
> polyp   a diminished 7th
> revelatory

Here is the "the mouth(er)-eaten / writer" (*T* 183) that DuPlessis sometimes sees in the mirror of the text. Once the lacuna between *what* and *happened* has appeared, as if aphasia were forcing itself into the open, first we're presented with an awkward pun, then a voice that might have babbled up from Kristeva's *chora* urges a child to eat, and words are cut adrift from syntax.[13] Voiced poem has shifted into *écriture féminine* or a near pastiche of it (it is characteristic of DuPlessis's poetry that such irony is never far away).

How did recourse to inner speech help DuPlessis create a poetry that would acknowledge the gains of both voice-based open-field poetry (especially that of Charles Olson, Robert Duncan, Denise Levertov, and Robert Creeley), the objectivist nexus with which she has had a strong tie (she and Peter Quartermain claim that "all writers absorbing the Objectivist example consider the praxis of the poem to be a mode of thought, cognition, investigation—even epistemology" [*ON* 3]),[14] as well as the achievements of practitioners of anti-voice language writing such as Susan Howe?[15] One guide to a resolution of this dilemma came from her mentorship with George Oppen ("In a certain light everything I write is set against his uncompromising sign," she has said [*BS* 186]). His poetry was able to carry political affirmations without requiring an expressive psychodramatic subject position to authenticate them because of what Bernstein has called the "hinge" and what DuPlessis notes is his ability to use each line segment to "construct the 'sequence of disclosure' by 'separating the connections of the progression of thought'" (*BS* 209).[16] In practice this meant statements that, if embedded in a more conventional personal lyric, might sound like freestanding positions taken by the poet can be kept provisional, simply moments in an open "progression of thought." From this point it is possible to imagine a poetic form that represented sequences of thought or mental life at its largest, more in the spirit of William James's stream of consciousness than as a series of well-formed dicta. DuPlessis would find ways to open out this serious voice, allow it to be "open-throated," while tracing a sequence of disclosure by drawing on the neglected phenomenon of mental life, inner speech.

The concept of inner speech was not readily available as a heuristic until the twenty-first century despite a long history in philosophy and psychology. I am not suggesting that by drawing on inner speech DuPlessis implies some sort of determinism at work in her composition, as if to say that it was the inner speech that authored the poems, nor do I want to open the way to diminishment of her impressive achievement as a poet and author of one of the major long poems of our time, by appearing to endorse old stereotypes of feminine discourse as unreflective, or derivative of popular forms of expressivist poetics. What I am claiming is that across the range of practice that eventually crystallized into *Drafts*, and then continued with a series of recent out-of-system poems, she develops a strategy of inquiry that draws upon the resources of inner speech, while not simply mimicking or reproducing it verbatim, because a voice of open-ended inquiry can be based around the intelligent vicissitudes of inner speech. We might sum up by saying that DuPlessis's feminism, poetic allegiances, and inventiveness combined to make inner speech considered as "a form of intimacy, of personal contact, whether conversations with the reader or with the self" a guide worth hearing, in what she punningly calls "midrush," her form of midrash.[17]

The poetry critic Gerald Bruns explains midrash in terms that can help clarify DuPlessis's poetics of inwardness. This Jewish tradition of theological debate is primarily a collective practice of intensive, searching discussion whose source of authority is not doctrine but its communal nature: "The idea is that Torah speaks to a public, communal situation, not to the solitary, single-minded private reader. Under these conditions—which are very different from those produced by the printing press, and which led Luther to restructure hermeneutics around the individual reading subject—interpretation is bound to be many-sided and open-ended" (107). Bruns reminds us that midrash developed in a text culture that relied on oral debate and skilled memory, on holding sacred texts in one's mind and questioning them: "What seems to distinguish a scribal from a print culture is how narrow the analytical distance between text and exegete remains when the text exists in memory instead of in a small portable book" (110). Communal it might have been; it relied on inner dialogue too. Bruns also draws attention to another feature of midrash that is relevant here. At times "puns and parables and open-ended dispute are the rule rather than systematic closure or even decision by majority rule" (113). I notice this midrashic character in one of my favorite verbal zingers in DuPlessis's poems, from "Cosmos, a Nocturne": "The merger of two black holes forms / one binary black hole—is this really a thing?" (*PR* 14). When I heard her read this poem, I interpreted the phrase "a thing" in the current idiomatic sense, to mean something trending in social life and media, not noticing that it could be a literal question: in what sense could we describe a black hole as having thinginess, since it is apparently the antithesis of substance? My first reaction was, in other words, to hear an idiomatic rhetorical question; only later did I notice that she might also be asking for a reasoned response to these new entities. What sort of thing are they: negations of matter, metaphors, myths, nigredo? These shifting interpretations are what DuPlessis hopes for as she folds into her poems wit, silliness, comedy, puns, and other exuberances of low seriousness in order to push back against excessively dogmatic authority—poetic, philosophical, or sacred—while still giving voice to philosophy, knowledge of all kinds, and a sophisticated political consciousness.

She is as I say a poet of vigilant interruption, as is especially evident in the looser poetic forms of the post-*Drafts* collections such as *Poetic Realism* and *Late Work* (2020), where this feature of inner speech is sometimes strikingly evident. The poem "Adventures of the Book" is set out as a series of short sections separated by a sigil (a large otherwise nondescript printed dot), each ruminating on the vicissitudes of writing, the "failures of the writer," the "gaps and fissures" that striate the texts as they emerge from "the abyss of writing" (*PR* 18–22). From the start of the poem uncertainty prevails. Writing may stare into the abyss, but it is not an empty void, for in a reversal of the metaphorical image, it is more of a mountainside, "a downward with various leaps," an erratic space as if perhaps a scree slope requiring large bounds from the descending writer: "it is unreadsonable air / where maybe something . . . Not sure" (ellipses in poem). The neologism "unreadsonable" could be an example of the haste of inner speech that encourages shortcut amalgams of words, here "unreasonable" and "unreadable," when a decision between the two would take too much time. The break before "Not sure" also imitates the recoiling judgments of inner speech. Verbal exfoliation in "Adventures of the Book" is fast and disorganized enough to leave verbal debris behind in this abyss: "Sentences ignored, / fragments lined up and forgotten." At other times inner speech escapes onto the page: "Other words now, stunned / by escapade, / manifest electric desires." Maybe the best strategy is to give over control to these escapees: "I let the words demand their shape, and yes, / they did." Verbal inspiration has momentum.

To write with attention to inner as well as outer speech is to locate oneself however tacitly in a long history. Barthes's "middle voice," Derrida's *arche-écriture*, and Cixous's *écriture féminine* are defined in relation to inner speech, while a modernist literary legacy of suspicion about inner speech still lingers today. In 1923 T. S. Eliot wrote acerbically that "possessors of the inner voice ride ten in a compartment to a football match at Swansea, listening to the inner voice, which breathes the eternal message of vanity, fear, and lust" (Eliot 1975, 71), a hostile view that he radically amended several decades later, saying that the fundamental voice in poetry is indeed "the voice of the poet talking to himself—or to nobody."[18] Poetry starts with the inner voice; what matters is that this be a dialogue resulting from thoughtful questioning: "The most bungling form of obscurity is that of the poet who has not been able to express himself to himself" (Eliot 1954, 42). Eliot may well have been recalling W. B. Yeats's more aphoristic comment "We make out of the quarrel with others, rhetoric, but of the quarrel with ourselves, poetry" (29). These poets were aware that modern fiction had recently developed free indirect discourse as a means of representing the verbal twists and turns of inner imagination. Michael Gorra argues that Henry James sets the novel in a new direction when he recognizes in the pivotal account of Isabel Archer's long night of reflection and later in Maggie Verver's extended self-examination, like his brother William, that the stream of internal thoughts is not uniform, that no more than an actual river does it consist of, in William James's words, neatly separated "pailsful, spoonsful, quartpotsful, barrelsful, and other moulded forms of water" (235).[19] James was questioning the assumptions about introspective psychology made by the philosophers of his time. By the postwar world the idea was well-established. Gilbert Ryle extrapolates an important conclusion when he observes: "Much of our ordinary thinking is conducted in internal monologue or silent soliloquy, usually accompanied by an internal cinematograph show of the visual imagery. This trick of talking to oneself in silence is acquired neither quickly nor without effort; and it is a necessary condition of our acquiring it that we should have previously learned to talk intelligently aloud and have heard and understood other people doing so" (16). Inner speech is as much internalization as an intrinsic ability, and like other human abilities (for example, imagining the music as one sight reads a score) can be trained.

This history of the understanding of inner speech is a backdrop for DuPlessis's practice. Just as her poetry frequently inserts itself into the poetic tradition by allusions to earlier forms, quotations, and references to poets, it also inserts itself more quietly into the continuing tradition of speculation on the significance of our ability to talk silently with ourselves. At the time she began *Drafts* and for years afterward, the most salient of these speculations was Derrida's deconstruction in *La Voix et le Phénomène* (a title translated understandably, if misleadingly, as Speech and Phenomena) of Edmund Husserl's account of inner speech. Husserl centers his argument on the apparently uncontroversial observation that linguistic expressions "play a great part in uncommunicated, interior mental life" (191). In the wake of Derrida's books and essays on speech and writing, and his notorious claim that "there is no linguistic sign before writing" (Derrida 1976, 14) that appeared to downgrade speech to an epiphenomenon of writing, much Anglophone literary criticism abandoned voice as a viable heuristic concept, treating it as an old-fashioned irrelevance.[20] Derrida's concern was never directly with inner voice but with a metaphysical issue: by conceiving of the signifier that constitutes one indivisible half of the sign as a mental event, it might seem that this splinter of mind thrust into the sign had smuggled back in the very subjectivity that structuralists and post-structuralists hoped to eliminate as the first cause ascribed to all language and thought. With hindsight, this tendentious interpretation of Husserl and earlier traditions interested in inner speech misses the point, for as Riley says, "Among its convoluted qualities, the inner voice, however ostensibly silent, is still able to be heard by its possessor" (58). On the whole, despite his forensic attention to Husserl's arguments, Derrida does not show much interest in inner speech itself, leaving Husserl's incomplete portrait of inner language to stand for the entire curious and actually very diverse phenomena of inner speech.[21] DuPlessis's poems represent a significant, if tacit, rejoinder to this latest round of a long history of religious and philosophical attempts to link inner speech to ideologies of mind.

DuPlessis's project in *Drafts* is far larger in scope than a debate with post-structuralism, being a series of investigations of language in the broadest possible sense, one of whose main tools is inner speech, employed in a self-aware, reflexive manner that retains its sense of a subjectivity emerging out of desire and reasoning, while responding to all the shocks and politics that we are heir to. A late poem, "Angelus Novus," ostensibly about Walter Benjamin's famous reflections on Paul Klee's picture, is a good place to start to sum up this discussion of the role of inner speech in DuPlessis's compositional repertoire, because being a freestanding poem, it is not enmeshed with a larger framework, and its poetics of voice is sharply revealed. Fest describes the poem vividly: "'Angelus Novus' confronts the darkening tunnel of the twenty-first century: a world of climate change.... In the face of the catastrophe of the status quo, DuPlessis takes the risk of recommitting to poetry" (158). Here I want to dig into what in the poem's workings justifies us saying that in this poem DuPlessis "confronts" contemporary horrors and recommits to poetry.

"Angelus Novus" reprints the entirety of Walter Benjamin's mysterious paragraph about the Angel of History struggling against a meteorological and metaphysical fate, though only after launching the poem with several lines of skeptical irony and comedy. This is how the poem begins:

It's A Strange Angel!

A NEW & **improved** angel!

Chicken-footed claws and finger feathers,
a perfect poultry type.
Raglan sleeve-y wings
with a sigh-nage, hmmmm.
Him. Her. It. They.
Ange or angel-us.
An angular build,
spikes poke half-wise as its puzzle parts—
triangles, churches, knife blades
and/or mountains.

Tri-ages. A wire-line's the shadow
of its doubled halftone self.
It stands in clarity. It stands in blur.
Its face is a scroll, or maybe a lion
with intelligent snout.
You'd think, given strength and virtue,
things might just work out.
(*LW* 88)

The poem alludes to lines in Laurie Anderson's lyric, "Strange Angels," including "strange angels singing just for me," and "Big changes are coming."[22] Will the angels sing for this poet too? Skepticism rules at first. How can the poet take the newness, the freshness of this "angelus novus" seriously, noticing the unimpressive features of Klee's sketchily drawn angel, which looks, we are told, more like poultry than an exalted spirit, bestriding a landscape of "puzzle parts," a debris of knives and churches. DuPlessis starts to ask awkward questions. How does Benjamin know what the angel is thinking, or what he sees in human history; how does he know the angel wishes he could resist the gale that is driving him irresistibly into a future on which he has turned his back in order to stay in this moment long enough to "awaken the dead and make whole what has been smashed"? Readers of Benjamin tend not to ask this question about Benjamin's friendship with angels, his apparently godlike power to look inside their spirit thoughts, because he sets up the scenario through Paul Klee's painting, so that we are likely to tacitly assume that Benjamin is simply interpreting Klee's visual insights. In response DuPlessis asks these questions of herself. What does this storm elicit from her, and what does she imagine the angel is thinking? "Will the future be the same / as this wrecked past?" How can it be that paradise could be a source of destruction? DuPlessis responds to this thought with a flurry of awkward questions: "What does have the power? A storm. / A Power Surge. From whence. From // Paradise! And where is Paradise? Yes—ask?" (*LW* 90). In these lines DuPlessis balances the inner running commentary with the anchoring text from Benjamin, showing that one can ask difficult questions, that the respect in which Benjamin's text is held should not prevent us asking those difficult, midrashic questions. She continues in this style: "How can this be? Is every image wrong? / Is Paradise Malign? Is Angel powerless?" (*LW* 91). Accurate as Fest is about the wider context of the poem, and its confrontational attitude to contemporary history, his description needs to be augmented by analysis of the poetic strategy, which as I have been showing is a brilliant fabric of inner speech, poetic thought, and philosophical reasoning.

In conclusion I must repeat that as far as I am aware, DuPlessis never identifies her poetic practice as a working with inner speech. The closest she gets is in passing mentions of inner mental activity. In her essay on Barbara Guest, "The Gendered Marvelous: Barbara Guest, Surrealism and Feminist Reception," during a skillful close reading of feminist subtexts in Guest's poetic allusions to fabric, DuPlessis cites Guest citing Kandinsky on the "inner sound, the noise of the imagination" (*BS* 174). She also, especially in later poems, talks about the breaking forth of poetic speech in terms that suggest she does have inner verbalism in mind. "Draft 107: Meant to Say," a poem of retrospective assessment of the whole *Drafts* project, may be the closest DuPlessis comes to describing inner voice, as she reflects explicitly on the internal shifts and openings she has invited into her sequence, hovering around the phrase "meant to" linked to different verbs—list, note, erase, make, sketch, take, write, and more: "Meant to make the stitches more overt, patches and their overlap" (SP 247). As I pointed out earlier, she also comments on the possibility of the act of writing the poem startling herself.

It might seem that what I have been identifying in DuPlessis's poetics might be as well described as *thinking* in the way that Arendt describes it. As I said earlier, Riley brings Arendt into her discussion of inner speech to demonstrate that inner speech is not a bleak form of lonely self-alienation. Instead, says Riley, Arendt depicts thinking as a *splitting* of self into a dialogue "in which I keep myself company" (89). Arendt is interested in the risk that the empty mind may tend toward evil acts, and feels it is essential to make the following distinction: "Consciousness is not the same as thinking; acts of consciousness have in common with sense experience the fact that they are 'intentional' and therefore *cognitive* acts, whereas the thinking ego does not think something but *about* something, this act is dialectical: it proceeds in the form of a silent dialogue" (187). Thinking is a "silent dialogue," and for this reason it is misleading of Paul Valéry to say "Tantôt je pense et tantôt je suis," because to be thinking is to be alive in the world; thinking and being are not mutually exclusive, even if inward concentration may temporarily shut out the noise of the world. Arendt's image of the silent dialogue points us toward why it is insufficient to categorize all of DuPlessis's poems solely as acts of thinking, because as Riley emphasizes, not all inner speech is reasoned dialogue, though much of it can be.

DuPlessis's poetic thinking combines inner dialogue and outward-reaching communication by staying close to the abundances of inner speech, its spectrum from sludge to the sublime, light jokes to dialectical rigor. She tests imagination and coaxes judgment, without enlisting the compressions of lyric or practicing exclusions of register, where poets who avoid projecting a voice, poets such as J. H. Prynne, tend to strive for lyric compression, resisting asides to the audience. In such hands, lyric language itself can also be a mode of thought, a vector of inquiry.[23] In the American situation of the time DuPlessis was writing, however, these possibilities were largely occluded by political divisions centering on the legitimacy of such poetic forms.

By attending to inner speech, DuPlessis can trace acts of thinking while retaining traces of their embodied idiosyncrasies, following logic and outbursts, reason and expostulation, sense and absurdity. *Drafts* and her later poems are records of many acts of thinking, acts whose significance lies less in resolutions than in the acute attention to thinking itself, to its phonic, imaged, verbal, and conceptual character.[24] Staying close at times to inner speech enables DuPlessis to present a more accurate picture of the heights, vagaries, and slippages of thinking than if she had tidied it all up for conventional poetic form. It's noticeable that commentators on her work concentrate on the structure, register, scale, and ambition of *Drafts*, relying on DuPlessis's extensive paratexts (endnotes, talks, and essays) as much as citation from the poems, asking if *Drafts* is best described as a defense of poetry, a feminist manifesto, the poem of a life, a set of interlocking verse essays, a test of poetic forms, a metamorphosis of the American modernist long poem, or all or some of these? Although my discussion continues in this vein of largely descriptive criticism, directing our gaze to the poem's far-reaching critiques of the fraught debates about language and discourse at a time when several schools of thought clashed about the significance of the sign, the unconscious, cultural codes, economic determinism, the body, transcendental preconditions, ontology, and more, at the same time I hope that it does open a conversation about how poetic process and investigation coincide. A poetics that draws from inner speech is capable of achieving registers of cultural critique of our lives in and with language today not readily available to more formal modes.

Notes

1. Burton Hatlen points out that "had she never published any poetry, and had she never ventured into the intermediate genre that she calls the essay, DuPlessis would be a major figure in academic literary studies" (131).

2. The version of "Draft 99" published in *Jacket2* differs in having no such ant-like traces of letters showing.

3. Integral to his argument is the assumption that "trace" cannot be considered a concept, since the notion of concept itself is, in his view, metaphysical. My view is that the notion of concept is fine as long as we don't try to treat it as a logical entity of mathematical precision.

4. In her note on this poem, DuPlessis says she took her quotations from Jonathan Culler's book on Barthes, where he writes: "The task of literature, Barthes writes in the preface to *Essais critiques*, is not as is often thought 'to express the unexpressible'—this would be a literature of the soul—but 'to unexpress the expressible' (*inexprimer l'exprimable*), to problematize the meanings our cultural codes otherwise confer, and thus to unwrite the world as it is written by prior discursive practices" (129). Unwriting the world constructed by dominant political and gender codes—this was close to DuPlessis's own goal.

5. What Megan Jewell says of the allusions to other poets in DuPlessis's footnoted poem "Draft 33: Deixis" might be applied widely to *Drafts*, including "Draft 106": "She cites them not to invoke their authority, as that is not what she is seeking in this poem, but to collaboratively gesture to the ways in which their poetics have influenced her own working-out of the concept of deixis" (29).

6. I say "apparently," because this is not the first appearance of this precise notation of the time. It first occurs in "Draft 21: Cardinals" (*T* 139).

7. Not cited in Riley. Arendt argues that philosophers since Kant have paid little attention to "thinking as an activity," because thinking and intellect are different, and thinking and reason are inspired by the "quest for meaning" (15).

8. Riley is explicit about the role of inner voice in her celebrated elegy, "A Part Song," especially section xii. Her dead son's voice reechoes within her: "me being sung in by you / And being kindly dictated to. // It's not like hearing you live was. / It is what you're saying in me / Of what is left, gaily affirming" (Riley, *Say Something Back*, 10).

9. The disconcerting masculine pronoun is intended to indicate that this is Riley's paraphrase of Vološinov's ideas, although perhaps inadvertently the pronoun

underscores DuPlessis's argument that women's writing has been rendered illegible by patriarchy.

10. Writing in 1994, the poet Mary Oliver (winner of a Pulitzer, a National Book Award, and the Poetry Society of America's Shelley Memorial Award, among others) describes the "main style" of contemporary American poetry as "one of confidence, even intimacy . . . so there exists a definite sense of a *person*, a perfectly *knowable* person behind the poem" (77–79).

11. DuPlessis calls Hélène Cixous's essay "The Laugh of the Medusa," "one of the great twentieth-century manifestoes," an essay that is "millennial, apocalyptic, and filled with that interplay between political and spiritual energies often found in feminist essays" (*BS* 44). DuPlessis's poems also work between political and spiritual currents.

12. I'm conscious of DuPlessis's dry remark: "'There are two models of literary history' is where I stop listening" (*LW* 51). Libbie Rifkin uses the term "verse essay" to describe both "Draft 33: Deixis" and "Draft 52: Midrash."

13. DuPlessis discusses "baby melodies," echolalia, and child development in her learned, poetic essay "Language Acquisition" in *The Pink Guitar* (84).

14. Alan Golding cites this passage in his essay on DuPlessis's interrelations with Objectivism and goes on to argue that "*Drafts* begins with a questioning of Objectivist premises" (73).

15. DuPlessis says that in Howe's poetry, "word, gesture, memory and dream are all glyphs for an infiniating practice of decoding" (*PG* 126). DuPlessis also praises Howe's "resistance to smoothness and 'normalcy' of poetry" by using "deformations . . . (mis)spellings . . . line-breaks, page canvas" (133). These descriptions could also apply to prominent features of DuPlessis's own poetry, although her poetics is not centered on deciphering myths and legends projecting issues of gender and identity.

16. She is citing Oppen (26). Charles Bernstein, writing in 1985, when the concept of speech was still treated with great suspicion, argues that Oppen uses the line break as a hinge and, recognizing that Oppen appears to rely on a form of voice in his poems, feels compelled to add that "Oppen's achievement has little to do with speech or sight, but with speech as sight, site of the social" (192).

17. "Midrush" is a favorite pun of DuPlessis's. See "Draft 6: Midrush."

18. "The distinction between the first and the second voice, between the poet speaking to himself and the poet speaking to other people, points to the problem of poetic communication; the distinction between the poet addressing other people in either his own voice or an assumed voice, and the poet inventing speech in which imaginary characters address each other, points to the difference between dramatic, quasi-dramatic, and non-dramatic verse" (Eliot, "The Three Voices," 88).

19. Citing William James (16).

20. Peter Salmon offers a helpful summary of Derrida's indebtedness to Husserl in Chapter Three of *An Event, Perhaps*. See also Cisney.

21. Charles Ferneyhough points to evidence that there are people with silent

minds, no inner speech at all. His talk is available from the BBC at https://charles fernyhoughcom.wordpress.com/2022/07/29/the-silent-mind/. See also his book *The Voices Within*. There is an extensive technical literature on the diversity of inner voice phenomena by both psychologists and linguists.

22. The song narrates a journey in an open-top car, seeing "Millions of tiny teardrops just sort of hanging there," when the singer asks, "What next big sky? / Strange angels singing just for me?" I cite the lyric because the ironically depicted egotism is integral to DuPlessis's allusion.

23. Comparing Arendt's ideas about the activity of thinking with those of psychoanalysis, Kristeva says: "Thinking in such a way is a poetic activity in the sense that it is articulated like a work of poetry that seeks not to produce an object of beauty but to endlessly reveal dehiscent truths about the experience that takes place in the condensation that makes each word flourish and that the thinker proceeds to divide and expose" (195).

24. J. H. Prynne describes "poetic thought" as an intense struggle for realization: "To work with thought requires the poet to grasp at the strong and persistent ways in which understanding is put under test by imagination as a screen of poetic conscience, to coax and hurl at finesse and judgement, and to set beliefs and principles on line, self-determining but nothing for its own sake merely; all under test of how things are" (596). He mostly steps around questions about the precise innerness of this process.

Works Cited

Anderson, Laurie. "Strange Angels." *Strange Angels*, Warner Brothers, 1989.

Arendt, Hannah. *The Life of the Mind: Thinking*. New York: Harcourt Brace Jovanovich, 1978.

Barthes, Roland. *Critical Essays*. Translated by Richard Howard. Evanston: Northwestern University Press, 1972.

Bernstein, Charles. *My Way: Speeches and Poems*. Chicago: University of Chicago Press, 1999.

Bruns, Gerald. *Hermeneutics Ancient and Modern*. New Haven: Yale University Press, 2009.

Carbery, Matthew. *Phenomenology and the Late Twentieth Century American Long Poem*. Cham, Switzerland: Palgrave Macmillan, 2019.

Cisney, Vernon W. *Derrida's Voice and Phenomenon*. Edinburgh: Edinburgh University Press, 2014.

Culler, Jonathan. *Barthes: A Very Short Introduction*. Oxford: Oxford University Press, 2002.

Derrida, Jacques. *Speech and Phenomena and Other Essays on Husserl's Theory of Signs*. Translated by David B. Allison. Evanston: Northwestern University Press, 1973.

———. *Of Grammatology*. Trans. Gayatri Chakravorty Spivak. Baltimore: The Johns Hopkins University Press, 1976.

DuPlessis, Rachel Blau. *Poetic Realism*. Kenmore, NY: BlazeVOX Books, 2021.
———. *Late Work*. New York: Black Square Editions, 2020.
———. *Surge: Drafts 96–114*. Cromer Norfolk, UK: Salt Publishing, 2013.
———. "Midrashic Sensibilities: Secular Judaism and Radical Poetics (A personal essay in several chapters)." *Radical Poetics and Secular Jewish Culture*, edited by Stephen Paul Miller and Daniel Morris. Tuscaloosa: University of Alabama Press, 2010.
———. *Pitch: Drafts 77–95*. London: Salt Publishing, 2010.
———. *Blue Studios: Poetry and Its Cultural Work*. Tuscaloosa: University of Alabama Press, 2006.
———. *The Objectivist Nexus: Essays in Cultural Poetics*. Edited by Rachel Blau DuPlessis and Peter Quartermain. Tuscaloosa: University of Alabama Press, 1999.
———. *Pink Guitar: Writing as Feminist Practice*. New York: Routledge, 1990.
Eliot, T. S. "The Function of Criticism." *Selected Essays of T. S. Eliot*, ed. Frank Kermode. London: Faber & Faber, 1975.
———. "The Three Voices of Poetry." *On Poetry and Poets*. London: Faber and Faber, 1957.
Ferneyhough, Charles. *The Voices Within: The History and Science of How We Talk to Ourselves*. London: Profile/Wellcome, 2017.
Fest, Bradley J. "'Is an Archive Enough': Megatextual Debris in the Work of Rachel Blau DuPlessis." *Genre*, vol. 54, no. 1, 2021, 139–65.
Golding, Alan. "Macro, Micro, Material: Rachel Blau DuPlessis's *Drafts* and the Post-Objectivist Serial Poem." *Poetics and Praxis after Objectivism*, edited by W. Scott Howard and Broc Russell. Iowa City: Iowa University Press, 2018, 69–81.
Gorra, Michael. *Portrait of a Novel: Henry James and the Making of an American Masterpiece*. New York: W. W. Norton, 2012.
Hatlen, Burton. "Renewing the Open Engagement: H.D. and Rachel Blau DuPlessis." *H.D. and Poets After*, edited by Donna Krollik Hollenberg. Iowa City: University of Iowa Press, 2000. 130–62.
Husserl, Edmund. *Logical Investigations*. Vol. 1. Translated by J. N. Findlay. London: Routledge, 2001.
James, William. "On Some Omissions of Introspective Psychology." *Mind*, vol. 9, no. 33, 1884, 1–26.
Jewell, Megan Swihart. "Between Poet and (Self-)Critic: Scholarly Interventionism in Rachel Blau DuPlessis's *Drafts*." *Contemporary Women's Writing*, vol. 5, no. 1, 2011, 18–35.
Kristeva, Julia. *Hannah Arendt*. Translated by Ross Guberman. New York: Columbia University Press, 2001.
Oliver, Mary. *A Poetry Handbook*. New York: Harcourt Brace & Co., 1994.
Oppen, George. "Statement on Poetics." *Sagetrieb*, vol. 3, no. 3, 1984, 25–27.
Prynne, J. H. "Poetic Thought." *Textual Practice*, vol. 24, no. 4, 2010, 595–606.

Rifkin, Libbie. "Little Words and Redemptive Criticism: Some Points On *Drafts*." *How2*, vol. 1, no. 8, 2002, https://www.asu.edu/pipercwcenter/how2journal/archive/online_archive/v1_8_2002/current/forum/rifkin.htm.

Riley, Denise. *Say Something Back*. London: Picador, 2016.

———. "'A Voice Without a Mouth': Inner Speech." *Qui Parle*, vol. 114, no. 2, 2004, 57–104.

Robertson, Lisa. *Anemones: A Simone Weil Project*. Amsterdam: If I Can't Dance, I Don't Want To Be Part of Your Revolution, 2021.

Ryle, Gilbert. *The Concept of Mind*. London: Routledge, 2009.

Salmon, Peter. *An Event, Perhaps: A Biography of Jacques Derrida*. London: Verso, 2020.

Tarlo, Harriet. "'Origami Folds': Rachel Blau DuPlessis's *Drafts 1–38, Toll*." *How2*, 2002, https://www.asu.edu/pipercwcenter/how2journal/archive/online_archive/v1_8_2002/current/forum/tarlo.htm.

Vološinov, V. N. *Freudianism, A Marxist Critique*. Translated by I. R. Titunik. New York: Academic Press, 1976.

Yeats, W. B. *The Poems*. Edited by Richard J. Finneran. London: Macmillan, 1984.

———. *Per Amica Silentia Lunae*. London: Macmillan, 1918.

CHAPTER TWO

"First Feminism" in Rachel Blau DuPlessis's *Drafts*

"Draft 49" as Counter-Archive

MEGAN JEWELL

IN *BLUE STUDIOS: POETRY and Its Cultural Work* (2006), Rachel Blau DuPlessis, an established feminist poet-critic at its time of writing, devotes the first half of the book to discussing the influence of second-wave feminism on her critical work. She writes that "it is true that feminist criticism exists. That it came from the women's movement and is in a continual constructive dialogue with both the movement and others for social justice" (15). Grounding her feminist writing practices in the material reality of activist history, DuPlessis emphasizes the collective, rather than the "confessional" or individualistic, nature of her account, acknowledging the multiplicity of perspectives characterizing a contested movement (15). In *Blue Studios*, and throughout other writings and interviews, DuPlessis returns to her own on-the-ground activism with Columbia University's Women's Liberation in the late 1960s and '70s, citing this time as integral to her writing while also locating it as the forcefully generative collective practice behind not only her criticism but many of her poetic innovations in *Drafts*. The poem "Draft 49: Turns and Turns, an Interpretation" demonstrates the importance she places on a specifically collective self through its innovative engagement with the genres, discourses, and modes of thought that she identifies as necessary to understanding this period of her feminist activism. Importantly, DuPlessis's poem invokes the context-specific social engagement of the feminist 1970s while also resisting the ways in which the complex realities of the period have been misrepresented in historical accounts of US feminisms. Turns are important to DuPlessis's writing, and "Draft 49" is an important return to an era that DuPlessis characterizes as a turning point in cultural and her own personal history. It charts the multiple discursive turns involved in the representation of multiple feminist practices. In this sense "Draft 49" in particular serves as a vital counter archive for US feminist history.

In "Draft 49" DuPlessis returns to her experiences as a feminist activist in New York City in the 1970s. She begins by framing her entry into social activism as the tangible coalescence of the ways she had been previously thinking about gender: "Palpable, It appeared." (*P* 112). In uniform stanzas with irregular yet purposefully rhythmic spacing, she collapses the experience into a frenetic period of rallies and action: "Noveremember, decemb- manifesto after manifesto. What somber depths and quick decisions what exclamations leaping there were many / driving fast inside the array and we turned, we turned the wheel!" DuPlessis alludes in form and content to two poems, "A Supermarket in California" and "America," respectively, by Allen Ginsberg, putting his expansive poetic protests in dialogue with feminism.[1] Importantly, in this section, DuPlessis questions whether she is able to illustrate the "force of it"—in terms of both the communal energy and the sexism the women were up against (112). In the next stanza, to elaborate on the overwhelming multiple and discursive barriers to feminist progress, DuPlessis alludes to a photo from the controversial March 23, 1970, issue of *Newsweek*. Directly referenced in the poem's footnote, this issue's cover story is titled "Women in Revolt." The issue is an infamous representation of second-wave activist history: on the morning the issue came out, more than forty-five women on the staff publicly announced they were suing *Newsweek* for gender discrimination. Their lawsuit was the result of a secretly organized effort to take action against the difficulty women faced in rising up the ranks from "mail girls," secretaries, and sometime-researchers to writers ("Women"). Such a perfectly timed lawsuit on the very day of their own woman's revolt actualized the kinds of very calculated, analytic feminist activism that DuPlessis describes later on in the poem: "We took X-rays of each moment, bitterly, decidedly penetrating bone" (*P* 113).

Engaging with one of the issue's photos of women protestors, DuPlessis cites part of its caption: "Women's Liberation members demand full rights for the once frail sex" (112). The photo displays women fervently chanting at a rally. One woman holds up a sign that reads, "The American Dream is for Men Only," while another, photographed while she is shouting, takes up most of the right-hand side of the shot. Marching ahead, the women are made to appear completely unfeminine according to the American standards of the time. DuPlessis's eighth stanza reads:

> the rebuff, the clarity, in. "Women's liberation   members demand full rights
> for the once frail sex"   said Newsweek.   "Once frail" —a nice turn.
> Someone is photographed   holding a sign.   She is sneeringly "ugly"
> a fact we recognize and   are proud that some can garner   that level of slander.
> Or they said   this "feminism" is polemical—   or "we knew it already
> it is not   such a big revelation   no particular surprise.   Ho hum."
> (*P* 112)

DuPlessis cites the backhanded compliment "once frail" as a "nice turn" in order to expose its implication that the so-called weaker sex is now unattractive or mannish, like the ages-old but now commonplace caricature of the ugly feminist. The phrase "once frail" is a "nice turn," an ideologically infused invocation of sexist discourse perpetrated by the patriarchy. The phrase not only recalls to readers how the women are coming from a traditional position of weakness but also manages to convey how they are not ladylike, and thus signifies the benevolent sexism infusing similar terms (i.e., delicate, dainty, fragile) faintly praising women as the weaker sex. In distinct contrast, DuPlessis and other participants in the women's liberation movement of the 1970s saw ugliness and the fundamental disobedience it represents as a badge of honor, being able to "garner that level of slander" (*P* 112).

In an interview in 2015, DuPlessis succinctly states the importance of this first feminist period to her work reiterating the importance of the collective to recognizing pleasant and compliant behavior as forms of self-sacrifice: "Even with my excellent education and no obvious barriers to thought and achievement, the prevailing ideologies of minority, niceness, second-class citizenship, and service unto servility were so culturally ingrained in young [white, middle-class] women like myself that it took a social movement to blast through the smug, yet painful and limiting walls of accomodationist [*sic*] consciousness so that we could begin to face what the psycho-social repression of women really involved. *Will that convey the force of it?*" (Grogan; emphasis added).

Yet the section of "Draft 49" that I quote above not only highlights the photo's intentional selection by the editors at *Newsweek* to represent feminists as a willful threat to the social order but also recalls the renewed conservative misrepresentation of 1970s feminism beginning in the 1990s and extending past the first decade of the twenty-first century. In 2006, just two years after the publication of "Draft 49," Toril Moi refers to this distortion of feminist causes as a "feminism-bashing agenda" that relied upon "unspoken fantasmatic pictures of feminism" (1739). These might include "bra-burning lesbians on horseback, castrating bitches eating men for breakfast, or whining victim feminists crying date rape and sexual harassment" (1739). Citing several popular books, Moi locates in both conservative and liberal discourses a tendency to "start attacking feminism in general" by failing to account for its modes or forms (2006). I argue that the experimental features of "Draft 49" work against these forms of manipulation and the historical codification of second-wave feminist activist images by recognizing through formal innovation or direct citation the plurality of perspectives characteristic of the 1970s. DuPlessis's poetic return in 2004 to the *Newsweek* photo is particularly appropriate during a time of widespread distortions of actual feminist positions promoting the ages-old uninspired ideas that feminists "hate men," are "dogmatic, inflexible, and intolerant," and constitute "an extremist, power-hungry minority" (Moi 1741). As I address, the experimental semi-autobiographical form of "Draft 49" resists such visual and discursive categorizations. It is a densely allusive account of the numerous and volatile moments, perspectives, and discourses characterizing the feminist contexts that DuPlessis first encountered and that have since significantly influenced her feminist poetic and critical practices.

I. Continual, Constructive Feminist Autobiography

DuPlessis's most extended prose treatment of her feminism is in the essay "Reader, I Married Me: Becoming a Feminist Critic" (from *Blue Studios*), an autobiographical account of her activism and subsequent work as a feminist literary and cultural critic. In this essay, DuPlessis makes the compelling statement, "If I had not become a feminist, I probably would not have been able to write much or think anything especially interesting in any original way" (16). Grounded by the material conditions of social inequalities, her critical inquiries serve to politicize, along gendered lines, the production and reception of literary texts. She makes clear that without feminist activism and its critical frameworks she "would not be able to create the works that came through me and go under my name," noting that the "ferment of the 1960s exploding in the spring of 1968 and beyond was a combustible politicization" (23). She writes that "the idea that culture itself functioned as a political instrument and a social institution; that not only subject matter but also structural and formal choices were part of ideology; that language; hegemony, discourse, form, canon, rightness and wrongness, allowable and not allowable were historical, relativized, and interested concepts" (23). It was her activism and membership in a collective that actualized her subsequent feminist investigations of language, her work recovering modernist women poets in numerous articles and books, and the methods of social philological criticism that she employs in *Genders, Races and Religious Cultures in Modern American Poetry, 1908–1934* (2001).

In "Reader, I Married Me," DuPlessis writes about this critical feminist activist period, giving it the subject heading "First Feminism:1968–73: Consciousness-Raising and the Personal/Professional Project" (*BS* 21). Before DuPlessis begins her account, she asserts in the very first sentence of the essay that there is "no innocence in the autobiographical" (15). She expresses her wariness in taking up the genre of autobiography in which there is the implicit presumption of singular authority. DuPlessis explains she has a "suspicion of narrative in the first place," and "if I cull my journals from the eager, pressured past, that self with its 'experiences' is postulated as the authentic one. And this one as processor of that truth. Which is not true" (16). She is well aware of the ways in which an under-interrogated "I" is naturalized in lyric poetry and other discourses as a particularly gendered source of knowledge or, as she notes elsewhere, as the "sol(e) authority" around which all other perspectives orbit (*PG* 5). Therefore, before proceeding with her account, she acknowledges her position and the categories that intersect to create her "situated and socially formed" perspective: "I can be said to be an off-white feminist, resisting even 'enlightenment' Judaism, a radical but middle-class U.S. inhabitant in a professional job category. A person mainly gendered female, who maintains an imaginary bisexuality and a polygynous curiosity about the feminisms I and others have traversed. Who benefits from many world-economic interests that I abhor. I am a non-biological real mother. A heterosexual married property owner. Poet, critic, and essayist" (15–16).

The phrase "off-white feminist," along with the intersectional positions acknowledged above, resists potentially reductive characterizations of second-wave feminists. Critic Jackie Stacey, in "Feminist Theory: Capital F, Capital T," gives an overview of the negative assessments of 1970s feminism: "We are told that [it] was naively universalistic, it was anti-sex, it ignored differences among women (especially ethnic and national ones), it embraced experience unproblematically, it was humorless, it was anti-pleasure, it was homophobic and/or anti-lesbian, it was bourgeois, it was humanist, it was essentialist and it tried to speak for all women" (59). In contrast to one-dimensional portrayals, DuPlessis grounds her "I" in particulars so as to completely self-implicate and avoid what she refers to as the "seduction" of narration with its accompanying "judgment" and loss of detail (*PG* 16). DuPlessis will again disperse her autobiographical perspective in "Draft 49" in order to avoid the elision of multiple feminist perspectives. The essay "Reader, I Married Me" with its fully implicated "I" is structured according to the evolution of her feminism to emphasize the movement's fundamental influence on her poetry and criticism. The first section is titled "Way Before, or Up, to 1967: Inscribed Female (As Well as Other Things)." Beginning with the statement "Gee—I am living in a Patriarchal Family!," it is in this section where she discusses her family background, her upbringing in relation to Judaism, and her entrance into college at Barnard, where she identifies a "major contradiction" between "the culture's incessant (and our internalized) demand for instantly ratifying engagement and marriage and any sense of independence, self-definition, autonomy, social commitment" (16–18). To underscore the material conditions of women's lives at this time, their bodies still under patriarchal control—and leading to the "political arousal" that she will more forcefully depict in "Draft 49"—DuPlessis makes it a point to mention that access to birth control was legally restricted to married couples. She writes that "in those days (pre-*Griswald v. Connecticut*, 1965). . . . there were all sorts of furtive forays to find birth control—to find a gynecologist who would prescribe a diaphragm, for example, or an abortion that wouldn't kill you" (18). Subsequent periods that DuPlessis addresses in this essay trace from these origins her work in the academy as a critic, facing forms of career hazing (that she successfully contested) due to her status as a woman, as well as the very political choice in academe at that time to be a feminist critic. As she writes, her "risks were patent: I wrote both critical and creative writing in a new field. I worked with other women to build a new feminist journal; the field was 'political'—that whole story. But the cultural necessity of feminist work gave me the drive and the justification" (31). Her writing continues the force of first feminism.

In "First Feminism," DuPlessis narrates her first time realizing the cultural necessity of her feminist work. This section charts her initial activist involvement with Columbia Women's Liberation, which was brought to campus by fellow students *Sexual Politics* author Kate Millett and economist Harriet Zellner "from a mysterious 'downtown'" (21). DuPlessis was one of the first three women appointed as a preceptor in the Columbia College English Department. The very decision to hire a woman was itself a controversial one and would have involved an approval from multiple stakeholders. DuPlessis recounts the experience of her "tokenism" as a "deeply radicalizing" (*BS* 21) one for her. At the time also identifying with civil rights and anti-Vietnam War causes, she describes the environment of Columbia University leading up to her feminist activism as "a most vigorously fermented site with the issues of the increasing complicity of the universities in the military-industrial complex" (21). As DuPlessis continues to describe, these experiences led to her "Great [Political] Awakening" (*BS* 22; Gilbert, cited in Showalter). It was a "conversion experience ... a giant room filled up with women—many of whom were prepared to testify: brilliant, angry, articulate witnesses to overt prejudice, sexist remarks, invidious discouragement, hostile intellectual atmosphere, sexual suggestiveness, instructions to 'go home to your children,' charges of 'lacking seriousness,' prejudice in the awarding of financial aid or TA's—the whole gamut of sexual and gender discrimination and second-class citizenship 'despite' shining Alma Mater's light" (*BS* 22).

Her revelation: "'Woman' was a political, an economic, category" (22). The necessity of establishing this category enabled DuPlessis to passionately advocate for justice for women and not to be "sidelined or blocked by gender" assumptions accompanying internalized constructions of women as inherently inferior, the weaker sex (22). This realization, she notes, led her to participate in influential Women's Liberation projects such as the notable sit-in that took place in the *Ladies' Home Journal* offices in the spring of 1970 to protest the magazine's problematic images of women and lack of feminist content (Echols 195–96).

The poem "Draft 49" returns to this second-wave feminist period to emphasize the importance of that and other collective moments to the long poem's social justice origins. I cite instances of DuPlessis's first feminism as they appear in "Draft 49" as a way to underscore this era as a critical period in her development as a feminist poet-critic. I point to them to emphasize the formal ways in which these references allow readers important points of entry into the long poem project of *Drafts*. These autobiographical and other traceable moments of feminist history within the poem function as important moments of dialogic identification with readers. In the poem, these are grounded, contextualized moments that stand in formal relief to, yet also necessarily work in tandem with, *Drafts*' more experimental tactics of engagement and innovative formal elements. Formally, these innovations could be broadly characterized as forms of recursive heterogeneity allowing her to interrogate and avoid the linear reductiveness of the mythologies surrounding second-wave feminist activism while also incorporating important elements of her personal history. Ultimately, DuPlessis's return to the development of her feminism and participation in American women's liberation in "Draft 49" invites her readers to participate in a feminist collective reexamination of language and culture. The poem serves as a critical articulation of *Drafts*' early feminist influences and demonstrates the ongoing cultural relevance of DuPlessis's feminist poetic practices to current feminist aims.

Specifically, DuPlessis's return to first feminism in "Draft 49" and in subsequent "Drafts" throughout the volume serve as necessary reminders of the ways that ongoing examination of language and representation remains fundamental to feminist causes. The poem "Draft 49" is dedicated to Ann Snitow, with whom DuPlessis coedited *The Feminist Memoir Project: Voices from Women's Liberation* (1998), a collection of thirty-two first-hand accounts of individuals' experiences with feminist activism in the 1960s and '70s. In their introduction, DuPlessis and Snitow write that "amnesia about political movements is not only an innocent effect of general forgetfulness, it is socially produced, packaged, promulgated and perpetuated" (23). In other words, if they are not outright forgotten, constructions of feminist activism during this time are easily subject to mythologizing tendencies characterizing the second-wave feminist period as a nostalgic golden age of fervent dedication and progress or, conversely, as Stacey notes above, outdated in its various exclusionary or anti-intellectual middle-class perspectives. DuPlessis and Snitow, therefore, assert about the narrative accounts in their collection, "these stories are a political inheritance, but we intend no elegy. We seek knowledge of a collective experience, and we hope to link the passions stirred in this generation to a past, present, and a future" (24). As I discuss, "Draft 49" serves as a counter-archival form of resistance to the literal and symbolic misrepresentation of feminist action as exclusive, static, and irrelevant at a time when feminism collectivity remains necessary for bringing about social, and at this particular historical moment, reproductive justice. In their essay "Imagining the Feminist Seventies," Clare Hemmings and Josephine Brain view the "feminist seventies" as more than a discrete historical period, but an active part of imagining feminism in the present (11). In this sense, a return to DuPlessis's endless returns to it are vital. After the recent 2022 Dobbs v. Jackson Women's Health Organization US Supreme Court ruling that abortion is no longer a constitutional right, it should go without saying that there is once again a need for yet another return to the kind of forceful feminist collective action invoked by "Draft 49" in terms of a renewed recognition of the complexities of women's class and race privileges.

A poem in two parts, "Draft 49: Turns and Turns, an Interpretation," appears in *Drafts 39–57, Pledge* (2004). Constituting evidence for its insights about American US feminist history, the poem was published during the same year in the academic journal *Feminist Studies*. It is dedicated to writers Susan Stanford Friedman and Ann Snitow, two of DuPlessis's longtime collaborators with whom she has served as co-editor on prose collections and whose writings influence the ideas in the poem and are credited in its footnotes. These prose collections are major feminist undertakings: with Friedman, DuPlessis coedited *Signets: Reading H.D.* (1990), and with Snitow, as previously mentioned, *The Feminist Memoir Project* (1998). As DuPlessis and Snitow write in the introduction to the latter, "we asked our authors to focus on the initial burst of excitement and engagement that marked their entry into the women's movement" (3). Aside from its disrupted narrative and dispersed "I," DuPlessis might be said to have at least partially responded to her own editorial call for submissions in "Draft 49." The poem charts DuPlessis's very personal academic trajectory and its emphasis on the recovery of women modernist poets such as H.D. overlooked in terms of their contributions to early and mid-century innovative poetics. The dedication to Friedman and Snitow also represents the value she finds in both subjective and objective feminist discourses. Personal testimonies, in the form of memoirs, and academic criticism are two modes equally important to bringing about gender equality and are representative of the varying feminist aims of different genres.

Those who have written criticism about "Draft 49" have focused in various ways on its engagement with objectivism. In the poem's footnotes DuPlessis acknowledges Louis Zukofsky's "patent" influence on it, particularly his structurally similar poem "Mantis" and "'Mantis': an Interpretation" (1934). The poem's objectivist influences are present in terms of its seriality, lineation, word choice, and other literal and formal elements, and as the critics point out, are functionally compatible with DuPlessis's feminism. I additionally see in "Draft 49" non–mutually exclusive important feminist political discursive tactics that can be identified as working at one and the same time within DuPlessis's heterogeneous poetic practices, her distinct, feminist self-reflexivity that appears in the fold, and her midrashic return to each nineteenth poem. Alan Golding contextualizes this self-reflexivity in terms of a "post-Objectivist seriality" allowing an ongoing questioning of its own forms (8). Also, recognizing this poem as a "lineated essay," Golding emphasizes how the nature of DuPlessis's seriality "refuses resolution" (8–9).

The dangers of "resolution" are expressed in the epigraph of the poem's second part, "Turns, an Interpretation." A quotation from *Mimesis* by German critic Erich Auerbach, it reads: "or 'To write history is so difficult that most historians / are forced to make concessions to the technique of legend'" (*P* 119). Narrating political reality without mythologizing it is an ongoing concern throughout *Drafts*, a poem that is necessarily cautious about employing forms of representation that might also elide experiences. DuPlessis's particular form of recursive seriality—her turns and returns "refusing resolution"—are fundamental to her project. Legend is perhaps a necessary evil when recounting one's origin story, or entry into politics; the tropes of conversion, and awakening into a new visionary reality, can be programmatic at best and propagandistic at worst. Not to mention that so-called legendary stories usually center on male protagonists. As I address later, DuPlessis's innovations in form, including her seriality, promote ongoing inclusivity that resists the closure of gendered and other narratives formally reproducing unequal power relations and, conservatively for liberal causes, misrepresenting feminist history. Usefully, C. J. Martin writes that "Draft 85" and "Draft 49" are similar in the "directness with which these Drafts politicize authorship and perform a sustained feminist historiography." Again, this politicization of authorial stance is a necessary counter-archival gesture that resists the codification of feminism as a historical artifact, situating it as a viable active political movement. The "directness" of the poem's essayistic formal features has distinct importance with regard to the inclusive feminist aims and origins of the poem (Martin).

II. Essayistic Textures and Formal Collectivity in *Drafts*

> The essay is the form in which material sociality speaks, in texty texts, forever skeptical, forever alert, forever yearning.
>
> —Rachel Blau DuPlessis, "f-Words: An Essay on the Essay"

"Draft 49," in its lineated mostly chronological, forthright presentation and exposition of ideas with examples, can certainly, despite its formal difficulties, be referred to as "essayistic." Yet *Drafts* is in many ways an essayistic long poem given its exploratory, provisional nature, which I argue is important to collectivist engagement. Writing about the relationship between her three major modes of writing—poetry, criticism, and experimental essays—DuPlessis characterizes them as being equally generative to her feminist critical thinking. She writes, "Poetry propelled my criticism, criticism propelled poetry, and essays were originally born in a growth spurt between them. Essays then further incited my main critical book, and even my next one on H.D. The three genres I use offer (at least) three different and related subject positions, answerable to different social expectations and writing forums. But they were not separate tracks. Discoveries made in one mode led the way to work on another" (*BS* 30).

Drafts as an essayistic, non-lyrical long poem is a project that incorporates and engages with heterogeneous social discourses. As DuPlessis writes in "On *Drafts*: A Memorandum of Understanding": "*Drafts* could be described as heterogeneric, making allusive loops around and through concepts of genre that the poems both appropriate and disturb, genres such as midrash, elegy, ode, autobiography, and meditation. In texture they are heteroglossic—open to a range of voices, tones, verbal textures, social codes, and rhetorics" (215).

"Draft 49" presents the poet's encounters with discourses that are directly traceable to historical, documented events associated with women's liberation in the 1960s and 1970s. DuPlessis's choice to include examples of historical, essayistic, prose-like discourse in "Draft 49" connects to what I identify as the poem's political aims in generating collective activity; it is engaging to readers in its representation of grounded experience representing the exigency of feminist causes. Yet, importantly, essayistic form in this poem represents the ways in which prose, particularly a critically interrogated autobiographical and situated prose, is associated for DuPlessis with collective feminist action. As DuPlessis writes in "f-Words: An Essay on the Essay" (1996), "When a situated practice of knowing made up by the untransparent situated subject explores (explodes) its material in unabashed textual untransparency, conglomerated genre, ambidextrous, switch-hitting style—as if figuring out on the ground, virtually in the time of writing—that's it: f-words. The essay" (24–25).

DuPlessis's treatment of the genre of the essay in "f-Words" illustrates the relationship she sees between exploratory prose discourses, self-actualization, and collectivity. In this essay, which also addresses her experimental essays in *The Pink Guitar: Writing as Feminist Practice* (1990), DuPlessis defines the genre of the essay and surveys its various modes while engaging in her own characterization of essays as "acts-of writing-as reading" (17). She reads the historical development of the essay form as "impelled by the social and cultural forces of '1968'—and all that went before—as these forces and events coalesced and influenced 'reading'" (17). Or, as DuPlessis elaborates, essays are "works 'wrought,' a thinking that occurs through the material fabrication of language, a work and a working in language, not simply a working through intellectually or emotionally—language not as the summary of findings but as the inventor of findings" (19). The distinction between summary and invention is key to DuPlessis's understanding of the role of the essay in terms of politics given that invention entails a forceful form of collective self-actualization. Discussing various contemporary modes of the essay, DuPlessis observes a "particular kind of social autobiography in which the exemplary self comes into its own in a moment of particular palpability," the latter term echoing the term "palpable" in "Draft 49" of the palpable selfhood coming into being with DuPlessis's identification of a community of women, the "breathtaking space of the 'we'" (*PG* 20, *P* 112). As she later acknowledges, "many feminist essays from conversion and engagement also identify the moment of liberation through acceptance of a social identity" (*PG* 21). The use of essayistic prose in "Draft 49" is informed by this awareness of its various uses in feminist discourses and works to convey the key importance of the emergence of a collective self within women's liberation.

   Yet it is necessary to reiterate the importance of the dispersed "I" to her practices. Explaining the collectivity invoked by the shifting "I, DuPlessis writes, "My argument, abrupt, unregenerate, but somewhat willful and over-stated: the essay is transpersonal, collective, based not on I but on we and it and she and he (and others too) in peculiar and unstable mixtures. Its pronouns are unimaginably different, maybe even invented (as Cixous invents "hesheit") to intimate the social meaning of the form. Transpersonal—even when autobiographical, collective. And its tone, mode, open form, intimate sound is the sound of a we—of an I dissolving back and forth into a listening other. Real pluralism. Real desire" (*PG* 32). The first feminist experience in "Draft 49" with its autobiographical yet dispersed essayistic experience works to convey the necessary and vital link between self and self-actualization when being part of a collective. In this case, it is American women's liberation of the 1960s and 1970s, "a space breathtaking of the 'we'" and the actualization of a dissolved yet participatory self (*P* 112).

III. First Feminist Returns in "Draft 49"

> In a minisecond, far beyond drowning in the enormous sea of this, I lifted up as on a gigantic blue-green-gray wave. Riding the "second wave"? A long march through texts and institutions is more like it. Everything! Remade!
>
> —Rachel Blau DuPlessis, "Blue Studio: Gender Arcades"

The poem "Draft 49" is nothing if not a "a long march through texts and institutions" (49). The spaces between phrases and the poem's uniform stanzas produce a cadence that conveys the energy and rhythm of collective action, feminist marches (49). Importantly, DuPlessis prefaces *Blue Studios*, a book wholly concerned with poetry's relationship to material practices, with a quotation from poet George Oppen that invokes poetry, cadence, and the force of events: "Poetry is related to / music and cadence and therefore to the / force of events" (*BS* v). From the "Mind's Own Place," Oppen's line, often referred to as his statement about the political in poetry, appears at the beginning of DuPlessis's extensive writing on the cultural work of poetry, and, at the very least, it formally infuses the presentation of collective politics in "Draft 49." DuPlessis's first feminist awakening to collectivity, as briefly described at the beginning of this essay, appears in the first third of "Draft 49."

Yet, prior to this moment, the poem begins its long march by first taking on the gendered conventions of the Künstlerroman, a genre, like the quest or romance plots she addresses in *Writing Beyond the Ending: Narrative Strategies of Twentieth-Century Women Writers* (1985), usually depicting men's entry into mature, creative selfhood. DuPlessis recalls experiencing acutely that such literary conventions did not apply to women artists. In "Reader, I Married Me," her titular torquing of *Jane Eyre*'s ending, she writes, "I also kept on asking which was I, the woman or the artist, with a relentless and lacerating binarism" (19). DuPlessis acknowledges in her notes the importance to "'Turns" of *The Descent of Alette* (1992) by Alice Notley. Notley's text is an innovative feminist revision of epic poetry; her heroine encounters a world of subways and undergoes multiple transformations, not separate tracks from the moments DuPlessis depicts here. Elsewhere, DuPlessis refers to Notley's work as "a magisterial feminist work, making a critique of patriarchy and tyranny and of the internalized consciousness and external society that supports these forms of social control" ("Anne Waldman"). In the beginning of "Draft 49," the speaker is recognizing the ways in which society has shaped gendered consciousness and, as DuPlessis has frequently mentioned, the conflicts involved with internalized conceptions of the inferiority of woman-as-artist.

DuPlessis begins the first section of "Draft 49," which is called "Turns," as follows: "I was walking through the woods spring-strewn green sodden" (*P* 111). The first lines invoke mythological journeys and the poet's youth (111). This opening scene is dreamlike as the speaker emerges from the woods, and then possibly into a train station and on a train going into a tunnel. Trains, tunnels, and the general Freudian atmosphere here are allusions, perhaps, to poet H.D.'s *Tribute to Freud* (Bouchard). Disoriented while going deeper and deeper into a "Dark tunnel of an unusual train of thought," and prior to her dramatic entrance into collective selfhood, that "space breathtaking of the 'we,'" DuPlessis viscerally recognizes gender structures:

> Everything turned inside out.   Shifts so large got mapped   on contradictory coordinates   by sheaves of metaphor: hunger   blood   quilts & piecing   empty luminous books   silence and layers unspoken   glottal stops,   blocks in the throat   reflux revulsion acid Alimentary   (Engorgement and Overflowing)   Re-visionary Seeing   self-Birthing   Flying   Delivering   Cracking.   Participials parturient.
> (*P* 112)

In the notes to the poem, DuPlessis writes that "Re-visionary Seeing" alludes to Adrienne Rich's famous essay, "When We Dead Awaken," in which Rich emphasized the importance of women looking at the world with "fresh eyes" (*P* 227; Rich 18). As Rich writes: "The sleepwalkers are coming awake, and for the first time this awakening has a collective reality; it is no longer such a lonely thing to open one's eye. Re-vision—the act of looking back, of seeing with fresh eyes, of entering a text from a new critical direction—is for us more than a chapter in cultural history it is an act of survival" (18). The stanza and others depict the energy of revisionist feminist realizations that DuPlessis would have encountered and seen at the time through "fresh eyes" (*P* 18). Yet for DuPlessis in particular it ends in "participials parturient," or word forms about to give birth to new sociocultural meanings that would later inform her life's work as a poet and critic.

The poem proceeds by describing additional women's liberation contexts taking place for people embracing and resisting in various forms the performative, socially constructed nature of gender:

> turned on.   Pregnancy coupled   with dreams of my penis.   All genders. on stage half reversed.   Played "Transvestite Street Theater."   Outside hostile
> job-related putdowns   pre-clipped advice   from other women
> why don't you want   to be a woman   you need to play woman   You could look
> good   why do you want to look like   to act like   to dress like a man.   Conversely,
> they'll get you   so don't ever acknowledge   you're a woman.
> (*P* 113)

In addition to the not-so-subtle implication in the *Newsweek* photo I discussed earlier, women are bombarded with "pre-clipped advice from other women" (113). As Betty

Friedan writes in *The Feminine Mystique* (1963), representative magazine articles appearing in mainstream women's publications such as *Redbook*, *McCall's*, and *Ladies' Home Journal* include: "Are You Training Your Daughter to Be a Wife?," "Do Women Have to Talk So Much?," "Why GI's Prefer Those German Girls," "What Women Can Learn from Mother Eve," "Really a Man's World, Politics," "How to Hold On to a Happy Marriage," and "Cooking to Me Is Poetry" (71). At the same time, from the resistant women's liberation side, one might be told to downplay one's womanhood in favor of adopting male modes of power, to not "acknowledge you're a woman," the category synonymous, as those feminist circles would have recognized, with frailty and weakness (113). In terms of resisting mainstream codifications, DuPlessis represents in this section of the poem that people at this time were confronted, often in a no-win type of way, with conflicting discourses rather than a unified, or programmatic, agenda on what it means to be a feminist.

The following stanza continues with only one line break into the next that continues to chart DuPlessis's negotiations with multiple overlapping forms of mainstream discursive backlash while also commenting on the contemporary elision of women's contributions:

> words like that   wounds like that   and other careful   tricks of soured milk
> "Gals Squeal for Repeal."   Can choose   to investigate.
> Everyone grappled   through the deep wide open outspun.   "social and historical
> Dimensions   of our innermost selves."   Moved speechless.   Between each word
> I turn page upon page   look for "diagnosis" for   "justice"
> In the scintillating swirl and snarl   of mixed paths and junctures.
> (*P* 113)

As with "once-frail" in the *Newsweek* caption, the milk is "soured," and one's stomach turns at the headline "Gals Squeal for Repeal," referring to the 1969 feminist protest where members of the radical group Redstockings of the Women's Liberation Movement (WLM) disrupted the New York State legislature's "expert hearing" on abortion law reform and demanded a total repeal of the law. The "experts" in this hearing were fourteen men and a nun (Pollitt). As DuPlessis points out in her notes, Katha Pollitt has written about the ways in which feminist activists were not given credit for their work toward the legalization of abortion at this time (*P* 227). Pollitt writes that "these are the same women—New York Radical Women, Redstockings—who have gone down in history, inaccurately, as the notorious 'bra burners' at the 1968 Miss America pageant in Atlantic City, and whose slogan 'the personal is political' is now so widely ridiculed." Here, DuPlessis is well aware of the dangers of historiography to represent complex "mixed paths and junctures" (*P* 113).

This next stanza recalls the "analytic" identification of the multiple forms of injustice that were being pointed out by multiple feminist thinkers of this time and captures even more forms of feminist texts and actions:

> Here is something!   women propelled   with analytic rages every day.
> "Adventurous for him"   turns "careless for me."   "Prolific for him" comes to "facile for me."   He is opinionated   but I am hectoring;   he passionate, I strident.
> We see, we see, we see!   "We are demanding   an end   to hypocrisy!" (P 113)

Once again, DuPlessis takes sarcastic note of the manipulation, or *turning*, of language. DuPlessis cites in her notes a book by Elizabeth Swados, *Becoming a Composer* (1988), in which Swados writes: "What would be called adventurous for a man was careless for me; prolific for a man was facile for me; opinionated, passionate, strong for a man was schoolmarmish, hectoring, strident for me" (227). Swados's egalitarian-based "Second Wave" formulation demonstrates adjectives used to subordinate women. The phrase "end to hypocrisy" is taken from a fact sheet from the feminist sit-in at *Ladies' Home Journal* in 1969 in which DuPlessis participated and during which feminists not only protested the magazine's publication of "degrading" images of women but in which they also demanded racial and gender equity for all employees as well as day care (*P* 228; Echols 195–97). Defining analytic feminism in 1995, philosopher Ann Cudd writes that "analytic feminists distinguish themselves from nonfeminists by an interest in a wider variety of works by feminists: works that draw on other traditions in philosophy as well as work by feminists working in other disciplines, especially the social and biological sciences" (3). While diverse in disciplinary focus and modes of thinking, Cudd writes that "most important, analytic feminist work is characterized by the conviction that there is value in the pursuit of notions of truth, logical consistency, objectivity, rationality, justice, and the good, despite the fact that the pursuit of these notions has often been dominated and perverted by androcentrism" (3). Again emphasizing a plurality of approaches not unlike those represented in "Draft 49," Cudd writes that perhaps the only social or political position that analytic feminists can be said generally to take is that there is a sex/gender distinction, though they may disagree widely on how this distinction is to be drawn and what moral or political implications it has" (3). In "Reader, I Married Me," DuPlessis describes an analytic project to which she contributed: "With [art historian] Ann Sutherland Harris I counted up and sorted the percentages of female faculty at Columbia, adducing institutional prejudices. We made one of the first such reports in the country, and our dismal statistics made the *New York Times*" (article by Linda Greenhouse, January 11, 1970, section 1, 35) (22). Recalling analytic pursuits in "Draft 49," DuPlessis writes that they would "Turn text and stats to rips and jabs, with cartoon joy, the POW! the WOW. / Shaking" (*P* 113). The irregular punctuation and strong visual gestures toward Lichtenstein's pop art reflect the energy of the "upsurge of collective," the energy of the "we" (114).

The poem continues to chart DuPlessis's first feminist encounters with women's liberation groups and its multiple modes of feminist thinking while self-reflexively commenting on its form and gesturing to Zukofsky's concern with the sestina. Near its end, DuPlessis connects her first feminist experiences to her poetics. Throughout the poem, DuPlessis continues to invoke the importance of—while characteristically questioning and disrupting—any notion of unified collective feminism. She writes "I was angry at my sister; who is my sister." She also acknowledges the energy of the time "to be women breaking into / Woman as different women. Ethic of freedom!" in order to emphasize that her "Co-workers in gender" were individuals united mostly by the focus on women's freedom and justice. Near the end of the poem, she moves from the analytic concern with "to get the word male out of the Constitution" with a collective she now addresses variously as "you" and "we." She writes: "By turns reckless and careful, we are social conduits, given 'to imagine new forms of collective good'" (116). Such collectivity, she writes, leads to her desire to write a similarly resistant poem, as heterogeneous and grounded in material history as the women's liberation movement itself. DuPlessis writes: "I wanted to write an imploded poem of this. I wanted lines turning, / In linked gaps, on hinges as if from visible silence yet palpable / yearning. I wanted an imperfect artwork exhibiting striations / Of historical processes" (117). In the line "wanted to write an imploded poem of this," the referent is both collective action and the word "this" itself, a pronoun fundamental to her longtime interest in deixis, or the functions of words and pointing. With this close focus on pronouns and attention to discursive gaps and linguistic hinges of logic upon which discourses are constructed—but mostly with its inclusive heterogeneity—*Drafts*, like the participants in collective feminism, is purposefully "imperfect" and consists of irregular, material stretches and striations, their marks always resisting containment. "Gender issues," as she writes in "On *Drafts*," "suffuse the formal and discursive choices that underlie my resistance both to continuous narrative and to lyric" (215).

The notes for "Draft 49" give credit to the heterogeneous activists and writers who informed it and resist narrative codification as they illustrate the diversity of feminist thinking composing a movement. DuPlessis's characteristic heterogeneity is an inclusive feminist gesture: in an essay about poet Anne Waldman, DuPlessis states, "An encyclopedia poem is simply inclusive," and points out, in terms that could easily apply to *Drafts*, "An encyclopedic poem is simply inclusive. Although encyclopedias are generally organized by the alphabet, giving a non-teleological order to things, the encyclopedic long poem insists that anything and everything could, in principle, be included in any order, so it gives the feeling that no cultural censorship has taken place—no exclusions for false norms, for standards of elegance or fitness" ("Anne Waldman"). The encyclopedic nature of "Draft 49," along with its footnotes, serves as a counter-archive resisting "cultural censorship" ("Anne Waldman"). The many feminist and other political thinkers acknowledged covers on-the-ground activism and its subsequent academic permutations, including analytic feminism and gynocriticism, issues of women's representation and the male gaze, intersectional feminism, masculinity, and postmodern critique. Importantly, they represent the poem's emphasis on collectivity while acknowledging the intersectional forms of thinking. In "Draft 49" she writes that she "feel[s] polemical kinship / with many positions. Which is 'We' if 'I' is split? What is your class overview? 'Which men is it that women want to be equal to?'" The latter quotation, cited in the poem's notes, comes from bell hooks's 1987 article "Feminism: A Movement to End Sexist Oppression" (228) and represents intersectional considerations of class and race happening during the second wave (Stacey 59).

DuPlessis endlessly and of necessity returns to examine her accounts of feminism. She does so in the second part of "Draft 49" titled "Turns, an Interpretation." She also returns to it in the unnumbered "Précis," a summary of *Drafts* 1–57 appearing at the end of *Drafts 39–57, Pledge*. Other full and partial returns occur in subsequent drafts, both on, or in alignment with, or off the numerical fold. Ultimately, however, it is only this critical returning that remains. In "Turns, an Interpretation," and in the summative poem in "Précis," DuPlessis questions her own representations. Nevertheless, at this juncture, she seems to be mired within the stalled revolution feminists have identified since the mid-1980s and still identify today. At the end of "Turns," she asks, "Now what? So much damage need I resign myself?" (118). She does write that "this work cannot be 'unified' nor end on / literary uplift on satisfying readiness," signifying an acute awareness of the construction of feminist narratives. In "Turns, an Interpretation," she reflects again on her representation of first feminism, writing that:

> It is difficult enough even claiming
> a "political poem" given I am hardly
> writing "to program,"
> with any correct itinerary or
> conclusion.
> Could only propose
> gender justice in the context of social justice
> enacted in particular struggle or location
> Those six words (gender, justice, social, struggle, location, enacted)
> might trace through the poem, and be repeated there,
> but to use them as such was too positive, positivist.
> I did not use them.
> (119)

While the last line might express regret in not repeating or calling more attention to those six words representing importance to her work, in the end she is just, finally resistant to dominant narratives. Near the end of "Turns, an Interpretation," she writes, "O originary passion for justice and rectification," and acknowledges, "To capture éclat / to expose conviction" is "almost impossible" (125). The last two lines emphasize that "It is almost impossible / to tell of those enormous encompassing Turns." In other words, the Turns are at once historical moments of collectivity, the clarity and force of which are difficult to convey, but also are fundamental aspects of her seriality that are defined only by their being situated in practice and in time. In "Précis," DuPlessis's last assessment of "Turns" in this volume, she concludes:

> We turned some structures of gender
> beyond themselves
> collectively, desirably, hungrily,
> skeptically, furiously, mantically.
> We said women! this turned, too,
> to the sobering sense
> of everything that still remains to do.
> (217)

In this summative version, perhaps in compliance with the generic expectations of "Précis," there is a recognition of the progress of women's "turning structures of gender" (217). The collective "we" is also present. Ultimately, however, only the turns—closely attentive to particular histories—remain.

Note

1. The lines in which I read the allusions to Ginsberg are "What peaches and what penumbras!" from "A Supermarket in California," and "America I'm putting my queer shoulder to the wheel" from "America."

Works Cited

Bouchard, Daniel. "A Little Yod and a Rocking Enormity." *Jacket2*, 14 Dec. 2011, https://jacket2.org/article/little-yod-and-rocking-enormity.
Cudd, Ann E. "Analytic Feminism: A Brief Introduction." *Hypatia*. vol. 10, no. 3, 1995, 1–6.
DuPlessis, Rachel Blau, and Ann Snitow, editors. *The Feminist Memoir Project*. New Brunswick, NJ: Rutgers University Press, 2007.
———. *Blue Studios: Poetry and Its Cultural Work*. Tuscaloosa: University of Alabama Press, 2006.
———. "Anne Waldman: Standing Corporeally in One's Time." *Jacket*, 27 Apr. 2005, http://jacketmagazine.com/27/w-dupl.html.
———. *Drafts 39–57, Pledge, with Draft, Unnumbered: Précis*. Cambridge, UK: Salt, 2004.
———. *The Pink Guitar: Writing as Feminist Practice*. New York: Routledge, 1990.
Echols, Alice. *Daring to Be Bad: Radical Feminism in America, 1967–1975*. Minneapolis: University of Minnesota Press, 1989.
Friedan, Betty. *The Feminine Mystique*. W. W. Norton & Company, 1997.
Friedman, Susan, and Rachel Blau DuPlessis, editors. *Signets: Reading H.D.* Madison: University of Wisconsin Press, 1991.

Ginsberg, Allen. *Collected Poems 1947–1997*. E-book ed. New York: HarperCollins, 2006.

Golding, Alan. "Macro, Micro, Material: Rachel Blau DuPlessis' *Drafts* and the Post-Objectivist Serial Poem." Blackbox Manifold, https://blackboxmanifold.sites.sheffield.ac.uk/issues/issues-11-20/issue-16/alan-golding-essay.

Grogan, Kristin. "An Interview with Rachel Blau DuPlessis." *Oxonian Review*, 6 Dec. 2015, https://oxonianreview.com/articles/an-interview-with-rachel-blau-duplessis.

Hemmings, Clare, and Josephine Brain, "Imagining the Feminist Seventies." *The Feminist Seventies*, edited by Helen Graham et al. York, UK: Raw Nerve Books, 2003, 11–23.

Martin, C. J. "On 'Pitch,' with Special Reference to 'Hard Copy.'" *Jacket2*, 14 Dec. 2011, https://jacket2.org/article/pitch-special-reference-hard-copy.

Moi, Toril. "'I Am Not a Feminist, But . . .': How Feminism Became the F-Word." *PMLA*, vol. 121, no. 5, 2006, 1735–41.

Oppen, George. "The Mind's Own Place." *George Oppen: Selected Poems*, edited by Robert Creeley. New York: New Directions, 182.

Pollitt, Katha. "Abortion History 101." *Nation*, 29 June 2015, https://www.thenation.com/article/archive/abortion-history-101/.

Rich, Adrienne. "When We Dead Awaken: Writing as Re-Vision." *College English*, vol. 34, no. 1, 1972, 18–30.

Stacey, Jackie. "Feminist Theory: Capital F, Capital T." *Introducing Women's Studies: Feminist Theory and Practice*, edited by Victoria Robinson and Diane Richardson. New York: NYU Press, 1997, 54–76.

"'Women in Revolt': A *Newsweek* Cover and Lawsuit Collide." *Newsweek*, 2 Nov. 2016, https://www.newsweek.com/women-revolt-newsweek-cover-and-lawsuit-collide-514891.

CHAPTER THREE

Infinite History and the Mortal Body

Rereading the Unending Surge

AMBER MANNING

So too literature as a human institution is, baldly, organized by many ideological scripts. Any literary convention—plots, narrative sequences, characters in bit parts—as an instrument that claims to depict experiences, also interprets it. No convention is neutral, purely mimetic, or purely aesthetic.

—Rachel Blau DuPlessis, *Writing Beyond the Ending*

Once more out of darkness
Come the great green hills.
Wind plunges and lifts,
Jays plunge and scream overhead.
Slowly erupts up
Again the risen red.

—Alicia Ostriker, "Once More Out of Darkness"

I. Swallowtail(s)

Rachel Blau DuPlessis opens her collection *Surge: Drafts 96–114* by summoning the earth, the sea, the wind, and the biological. She writes,

    Pulses uneven, pushes
            surging air gusts, gusts plunge
                  horizontally, sweeping
  wings, its wings
        open and shut, balancing
            the swallowtail

gripping down.
          It snorkels as precariously
                   fast as it can.
(*S* 23)

In this opening stanza, both the reader and the swallowtail withstand the "pulses," "pushes," and "surging air gusts" that the poet constructs with both form—via the line breaks—and content. The butterfly tries desperately to survive the surging wind, which, at the end of the stanza, becomes surging waves: the insect is left "snorkel[ing] . . . precariously." In the next section of the poem, DuPlessis clarifies that this swallowtail is not the "*Parnassius mnemosyne*" but rather "just a swallowtail" (*S* 24). For the poet, this distinction means that the insect has neither "memory" nor "poetry" contained within it (24). Instead, the ordinary, common butterfly attempts to negotiate the surges of the world, trying desperately to breathe among the ever-threatening gusts. This butterfly, the *Papilio machoan*, is already a kind of warrior: the second half of its name references Machoan, the famous Greek warrior and grandson of Apollo. Our insect rides the waves of the wind in the here and now and recalls battles of a very distant past; the living body mediates the terror of the present moment without leaving history—with its violence and upheaval—entirely behind. As such, DuPlessis simultaneously presents the dangers of nature, the legacy of war, and a delicate swallowtail trying to survive.

    Although the swallowtail will not follow us all the way through the poet's collection, its legacy of guiding the mortal body through the surges—and the waves—of the past and the present will. We might, in fact, read *Surge*—the purported final volume of DuPlessis's serial poem—as crafting a way of being via the "tidal surge of writing" (*S* 145) and a way of reading. More specifically, the collection creates an equilibrium between unending sociohistorical movements and the mortal body by refusing to end, while showing the reader how to exist—via indexing and accumulation—in the eternal surge of history. Although *Surge* is composed of poems that reference particular social, cultural, and historic events from the very beginning of the twenty-first century, the collection brings even the distant past into a contemporary moment beyond the writing of the individual poems. And so, in the third decade of the twenty-first century, as one floats through a pandemic that just keeps going and going and going, DuPlessis's work offers us a glimpse of hope, a moment of reflection in times of crisis, and a strategy for moving forward.

II. Surge(s)

DuPlessis's choice to use *Surge* as a title points the reader toward a constellation of nature, history, and the body before they even encounter the collection's first poem. The word "surge" can, of course, be either a noun or a verb, and it holds meanings that include the base of a river, "a violent wave," "undulating" features of the natural world, a sudden increase, to rise, or "to toss on the waves" ("Surge"). Moreover, since the sixteenth century the term has taken on a more figurative usage, evolving to refer to a rapid increase in emotion, the escalation of social movements, or dramatic economic inflation ("Surge"). This evolution is not accidental; the relationship between the undulations of natural phenomenon like the sea and movements in history remains causal, coterminous, and undeniable (Connery 177; Braudel 17). Indeed, as technology advances, so too does the intimate relationship between nature and society, in both the literal and metaphorical sense; according to Max Horkheimer and Theodor Adorno, the progress of modernity only reinscribes the mirroring of social relations and the relationship between the humans and the natural world because these associations all rely on dominance and domination (?). More technology increases the efficiency for the development of the natural world and for the development of weapons that can, in the midst of war, cause immense environmental destruction. Technology makes crossing land and sea easier and easier while providing ways to use the ecological for the political; hence associations between what feels environmental and the advancement of society brace and strengthen. Therefore, the term "surge" brings traces of the natural world, the body that experiences it, and the society that manipulates it.

This constellation of nature, body, and the social has, of course, a rich poetic and cultural history. Although she doesn't use the word "surge," the writer H.D. deploys an oceanic metaphor to describe the apparently sempiternal global conflicts that erupted after World War I. In *The Gift*, a novel-memoir written in London during World War II (but published much later), H.D. confirms that surviving in the twentieth century creates a new lived experience of an eternal sociohistorical (and figurative) ocean; layering history with a marine metaphor, she simultaneously describes enduring world wars and childhood trauma: "The second wave! We could go down, we had gone down, the wave was breaking over us and if we came up to the surface again, there was only one certainty; there would be the third wave. Would the third wave be the last wave?" (218). The narrator (who, with the word "we," could also be the fellow survivor or the reader) bobs in the "waves" of history, in the tide of war-torn trauma. H.D.'s pronouncement "there would be the third wave" indicates a perpetual moment of waiting for a surge in violence, an eternal in-between that can only beg the unanswered question, "Would the third wave be the last wave?" In *H.D.: The Career of That Struggle*, DuPlessis herself notes that the twentieth century signals a radical shift in which bodies are directly threatened in moments of global violence: "The drowning of civilians in the sinking of the *Lusitania* signaled a profound change in the conduct of wars: women and children and other noncombatants were as vulnerable to fire-power and semi-legitimate violence as any soldier" (72). In other words, bodies—and life—become more at risk than ever as the twentieth century ushers in a new kind of warfare, creating an inescapable tension between the historical and the body, a tension the term "surge" always recalls.

The decade immediately preceding the publication of *Surge* (2013) brought even more unending waves of war, violence, and trauma. Writing in the wake of the 9/11 attacks on the World Trade Center (2001), philosopher Judith Butler notes that as the twenty-first century unfolds, particular kinds of trauma responses emerge, especially with respect to grief, mourning, and violence; she argues that after 2001, some lives are further constructed (by institutions such as—but not limited to—the United States government) as not grievable and even as "unreal" (33). When groups of people are rendered "unreal," Butler argues that this triggers a kind of unending violence against them, an "inexhaustibility" of the object that, in never existing, is also, paradoxically, never defeated (33). When coupled with the intense kind of public mourning for *other* lives (like what happened after 9/11 specifically), unending and even "permanent" war can be construed as justified (Butler xix). Butler's analysis certainly rings true in the years DuPlessis composes the poems that make up *Surge*; the War in Afghanistan, which began in response to the September 11 attacks continues until 2021, and the Iraq War, which began in 2003, continues until 2011.[1] Moreover, violence resurges in Gaza when a 2008 ceasefire ends and a century-long war wages on and on (Narea). At the same time as global violence continues, global temperatures also surge, and 2010 ties 2005 for the hottest year on record (Hansen). Theorist Ursula K. Heist notes that climate change really entered the "cultural imagination" in the 1990s and, as it continues, forces a rethinking of the planetary scale and a new understanding of temporality (205). And so, DuPlessis's poems enter the world in moments of inexhaustible waves of history, waves that weave the world, the social, and the body together.

But DuPlessis's title also manages to bring the future into this tapestry by prophesying a global phenomenon that unfolds more than a decade after the publication of *Surge*. In his 2022 *New Yorker* piece on the pandemic, writer and physician Dhruv Khullar meditates on what feels like a public-health crisis that will never end and apparently interminable possible variants of COVID-19; he quotes fellow physician (and professor) Robert Wachter, who says, simply, "We may be in this phase forever." But this "forever," the moment that stretches on and on, is not precisely a moment of stasis because, of course, COVID-19 cases increase and decrease; different variants emerge; medical technology advances new and more effective vaccines. In fact, the waves of pandemic—like those of the sea—undulate, swell, and recede. Beings across the world do their best to survive and to negotiate what experts call the swell in cases: "the surge" ("The Latest"). But, just as H.D. worries about how to survive the waves of war, the reader worries about how to survive the surges of a global pandemic. There is a strangeness in the notion that the very surges that kill bodies will outlive—and outlast—all the individual bodies that currently exist. And so, although the poet references an early moment of the century, the COVID-19 pandemic calls the reader to return to these poems, to reinvestigate the surge she is either anticipating or experiencing. DuPlessis's title is historical and prescient; we find, in these poems, the poet's moment and our own.

Indeed many of the poems in *Surge* meditate upon the individual body as it exists in relation to all different kinds of eternal—and historical—phenomena. In fact the poet deploys "surge" to illustrate how the everlasting can swell, how waves of time and history can, if not overwhelm, at least preoccupy us. Considering the many versions of herself—including "the leggy girl-self" and "Rachel of the longue durée"—DuPlessis interrogates how the individual relates to eternal forces. She asks, in "Draft 102: One-on-One," "What dramas did these characters propel / what toil of time / what surge of fate, / what bespoke selvedge, what diva borderlands?" (*S* 60). When the poet implies that "characters" can, in fact, "propel" a "surge of fate," "self" and "surge" enter a causal relationship. In other words, versions of the individual self do not simply have to ride a surge but can actually *affect* the surge, nudge it somehow. When this particular "surge of fate" also relates to a "toil of time," we find an exhausting eternal and a gesture toward the labor of just *being* in relation to the passing of time (which, of course, will never stop). Later, in "Draft 106: Words," DuPlessis links the temporal more explicitly to a kind of eternal, or at least to a kind of grandeur, by referencing the "out-flung surge of cosmic time" (*S* 84). Here, "cosmic time" feels transcendent but also graspable because the "surge" can be felt, or at least sensed, even if it is "out-flung." The surge, then, is one that brushes against the human being but also, being "cosmic," includes the universe, its potential, and its infinite existence in both space and time (Sagan 5). The poet's term "out-flung" recalls a movement of a limb, perhaps even a human limb, as if the "surge" that happens is simply the appendage of "cosmic time." The surge—in time, in history, in society—is bigger than the human, but this does not preclude the body and the surge from being inextricably and maybe causally linked. In both examples, DuPlessis presents us with a surge that is enormous, that is overwhelming, that feels transcendent but does not seem violently threatening in the way that a surge of water, of war, or even of disease might feel. As such, the poet hints at establishing a different kind of relationship to the surge, the waves, and the unending.

But sometimes, for DuPlessis, the surge can be dangerous. In "Draft 114: Exergue and Volta," the author directly exploits the polysemous "surge" but this time centers it in relation to the text and writing. She writes,

> From nothing to everything
> from desiccation to drowning:
> this
> is the tidal surge of writing.
> This is the way it is; how can it
> stop?
> (*S* 145)

DuPlessis's "tidal surge of writing" threatens to bring with it two different kinds of bodily destruction: the extreme lack of water and the complete envelopment of the body in an overabundance of fluid. In this moment, does the "tidal surge" take on the role of H.D.'s final wave? Because DuPlessis considers this surge in terms of the written word, the body is not directly invoked; indeed, the "desiccation" and "drowning" may be entirely referencing literary output. However, even if this is just figurative summoning, there is a relationship between using the body as a touchstone and the movement between "nothing" and "everything." Although the poet asks, "how can it / stop?" one might read this as really asking, what happens—what do we do—if it doesn't stop? How do we negotiate the unending of a virus, of a war, of a text, of writing when we know that the human frame must, and will, end? In other words, how do we survive *the surge*?

III. Enumeration(s)

For DuPlessis, negotiating the next wave—of history, time, violence, text, and more—means embracing unending and using textual indexing and accumulation to reconcile the mortal body and the infinite other.[2] While the poet models methods of indexing and accumulation, she also—via the text—engages the readers in this same work; the reader must, in order to keep up with the text, recall previous moments, find moments of textual layering, and unravel this seemingly limitless constellation of poet, text, history, and reader. And, from the beginning, DuPlessis makes the reader aware that this process will be unending. In the preface to *Surge*, she boldly declares, "*Drafts* closes without ending. I mean it—*Drafts* ends, but doesn't end. It is not teleological, but has many stopping places. Many. One can begin anywhere and read in any desired direction. It is both a constellation and a set with many series in it" (*S* 1). The author clarifies the way her serial work remains both finite and infinite by deploying a comma—just a pause—between the "ends" and "doesn't end." Hence, she asks the reader to see the closing of the last installment of *Drafts* as a place of pending, of waiting, of almost floating, an eternal liminal. Her "constellation" does not just involve the relationship between the historical and the textual, however; the poet weaves the human body—the emphatically mortal coil—into the text, gesturing toward the infinite history, the finite body, and the somewhere in-between-serial poem. More specifically, to encounter the surge, DuPlessis searches beyond the violence of the current historical moment to a space where time—like text—can be raveled and unraveled; she indexes, catalogs, and allows for the accumulation of living artifacts and texts; this embodied act, when performed on the page, leaves the reader in the nonending volta: anticipating another change (another wave) that offers hope—instead of simply terror—for whatever comes next (even death).[3]

Before nestling into the volta, DuPlessis exhumes the terror of unceasing history (and the body's mortality) in "Draft 112: Verge."[4] The poem opens with

> You know this story.
>
> *translation*
>
> First, "Horrible things happened
> and they were introduced to us
> as something good."
>
> *something*

>   Killings.
>   Uprootings.
>   Fissures and divisions
> between those
>   who considered they were as   *splits*
>   civic as the others,
> or had more right to act, but
>   at that punctual moment
>   and then for years after
> found they were, or were found as, not.
>   Certain atrocities   *borders*
>   registered. Then were forgot.
> Everyone, it seemed, had realigned,
>   criss-crossed,
>   double crossed.   *atrocities*
> Maps had scratches, ridges, edges
>   that the never before,
>   it seemed, had.   *crossed*

(*S* 126)

Directly addressing the reader in the first line, the poet indicates the enormity of the historical moment the poem gestures toward, and she also implies—with the right justified "*translation*"—that what follows is a kind of retelling of history, a new language for a never-ending tale. As the stanza moves through a generalized list of atrocities, line breaks and indentations seem to undulate, until they are cut through by italicized words that either clarify, correct, or define; in other words, the poem repeatedly weaves and unweaves itself, deconstructing the dichotomy of a rigid list and the fluid sea. In fact, these words feel like a kind of pulse or surge, a different voice that layers on the poet's narration. Despite the claim that atrocities "then were forgot," the italicized words punctuate reminders of war, separation, and (re)creation of nationalized spaces. DuPlessis's use of the past tense almost lulls the reader into thinking the atrocities are over—or have already been committed—but the italicized words function as a present, as a reminder of the ongoing-ness of the trauma.

The poet gets these italicized words (and uses the italics to denote citation) from Yiannis Papadakis's 2005 book *Echoes from the Dead Zone: Across the Cyprus Divide* (*S* 165). In this text, Papadakis narrativizes his travels (beginning in the 1990s) to Nicosia, a city that has been inhabited for more than four thousand years but is still occupied—and fought over—by both Cyprus and Turkey: it is a city that never ends with borders that are constantly redrawn—the finite and the eternal in one (Papadakis 1–9). Gestures toward the United Nations' "Dead Zone" in the divided city of Nicosia (Cyprus) are underscored and echoed later in "Draft 112," but in the opening,

DuPlessis allows the atrocities to be general, almost universal, and the injection of Papadakis's work—but in an abstract way—allows Cypriot turmoil to stand for and outside of itself. These atrocities—and the borders they necessitate—remain universal.[5] Moreover, they punctuate the reader's present, invade the text, and bring the violence directly before her eyes.

Amid this unending conflict, DuPlessis exhumes the human and the textual body. Indeed, the borders that emerge remain inscribed on the body; DuPlessis notes, in the next section of the poem "maps and lines are drawn over bodies" (*S* 126). The move to present tense indicates the continual drawing of lines but also the ways in which these lines are imprinted on the body: history is literally, to borrow from Jeanette Winterson, written on the body, or—in DuPlessis's clever double entendre—it is forged over the "bodies" of the dead. In either case, the tension between everlasting conflict and the mortal body hovers close to the surface of the poem, despite the rhythmic waves the poet crafts in the opening stanza. Later in the poem, DuPlessis returns to books that attempt to trace tragedy, noting in a prose-like section, "Twinned and tripled cataclysmic dreams bleed over all four margins down into the tight-sewn gutter of the page. The book tries to contain and present these bloody verges. It fails. Bad blood escapes" (*S* 131). The poet does not clarify whether "the page" comes from the aforementioned Papadakis text, her own literary or scholarly work, or another text altogether; however, she does make it clear that the textual cannot contain the vitality—either pulsing or waning—of "cataclysmic dreams" that can, like the body, "bleed." These "bloody verges"—these borders—highlight how the text fails to "present" them, to even tell their story. Nevertheless, the poet continues to engage with textual works, and maybe this is a way to resolve the paradox of the finite body and infinite history: the body can craft a text that will invite continuous—and interminable—engagement. DuPlessis closes the poem with another prose-like block of text, culminating with "Thanatos might take care of itself. It's desire that needs nurturing. 'Change or Die TPYING.' The P is Greek for how we would write R" (*S* 134). Here we get one glimmer of hope: the scrambled, playful "TPYING" that goes until one's death, the (un)ending serial poem, perhaps? If we cannot change the atrocities of history, should we die while typing them?

In another poem, "Draft 111: Arte Povera," the author offers ritual accumulation and indexing as a way of facing—if not resolving—cataclysmic history and an ever-precarious human body; for DuPlessis, this summons a Penelopian unending, a form of self-reproduction that guides us through the surge of history. She begins by connecting the messy human body to the sempiternal political event of creation: "In the world as such / DNA dumplings / (with skin wrapped around them) / spatter recklessly / (unwittingly? uncannily?) / because of randomized events in a politics of explosion" (*S* 120). The "politics of explosion" plays on the notion of the eternal by considering a cosmic explosion—like the Big Bang—in relation to the political: as if each mirror one another *and* affect the "spatter[ing]" of the "DNA dumplings" of humanity. In the next section of the poem, the author considers how to reconcile these "dumplings" with the eternal they're faced with:

> Suppose after all this, one just listed
> house, book, mug, window,
> daughter, dogs (gone), desk Apple™.
> Suppose it was budded tree limb, hair-thread fingers—
> the baby oak in spring, rain "heavy at times,"
> and the cleared branches of fall, suppose
> yellow gusting in a greeny-pinkish light,
> a dark red pear leaf blow into the room,
> suppose a salvaged shmoo-like basil plant
> eager, even in winter, to give pesto,
> or a fondness, a warmth, eros
> blue as the sky, could it be otherwise?
> the apt healing of a wound, even with
> its startling scar—
> unaccountable enumerations:
> the oddly glistening, the half-started language.
> (*S* 120–21)

DuPlessis's phrase "after all this" indicates that she'll be attempting to unravel the aforementioned "dumplings'" confrontation with the eternal; this unraveling comes in the form of listing organic objects, inorganic items, emotions, and even concepts ("eros"). Here DuPlessis's list feels almost like an incantation, a ritual, and, as a result, the everyday connects to the eternal, the list ritualizes into the "unaccountable enumerations." Although the repeated "suppose" implies uncertainty or tentativeness, the list continues in earnest and remains—somehow—present in the ongoing seasons; time passes, but the list lurks in the present moment, even as the world goes on. The poet reminds us of the biological body when she adds "the apt healing of a wound" to the list, as if, despite the "startling scar," there is alleviation in the listing itself, even when this list seems impossible. After all, the "enumerations" remain "unaccountable" and the language "half-started." The ongoing list emerges as a way to face the endangered body *and* the incessant "politics of explosion."

Clearly the accumulated index that DuPlessis begins cannot resolve historical conflict, nor can it save the body from an eventual drowning in endless waves; however, the poet offers the list as something that—in remaining *unfinished*—might actually be lasting. She wonders, in the next section of the poem, "Would this be enough? / What would be enough? / It is never enough. / The task is unfinished, / the persons, unfinished. / The structure is unfinished" (*S* 121). The list—like some serial poems—remains "unfinished" and, in this state, also remains unending, eternal, almost immutable. But, as the poet tells us, the "persons" are also unfinished—never fully formed but also never ended. And so, when the list goes on, creation goes on: a reconciliation between the body that must die and the political that must continue happens on the page in the form of another kind of suspension. The list cannot be reduced to the poem (according to DuPlessis, "poetry is not the goal") but wants "to be present to itself" (*S* 123); the list exists in its own matrix, functioning partway between the page, the body, and what the poet refers to as "astronomical despair" (*S* 123). More importantly, this accumulation is what offers a glimpse not just of reconciliation but of hope; DuPlessis continues:

> ... but still the stuff still shines.
> It accumulates scintillation.
> It is impossible to avoid
> fractions of joy.
> (*S* 123)

The repeated "still" offers a feeling of permanence to the "stuff" accumulated on the page, a "scintillation" of luminosity. More importantly, with this luminosity come "fractions of joy." Something, if not the body, goes on and on with the ritual—something that might match the ongoing history we cannot escape; part of that something, at least in this poem, is "joy." In fact, although poet and scholar Eric Keenaghan does not see explicit hope in DuPlessis's work, he finds openings to it in the textual accumulation of everything (political, historical) one mourns. He notes, "In the end, perhaps loss is where ethics intersects with politics, where hope becomes more realistic and grounded in the present." The list does not heal everything (DuPlessis later reminds the reader, "We have an unreckonable fleshy pile / of the damages" [*S* 125]), but it does craft a reconciliation for what H.D. views as the tension between the body and the waves of history; moreover, there may be some happiness—albeit in fractions—that comes from such a catalog.

But DuPlessis does not simply *write of* listing and accumulation. She allows the poems to accumulate and even to list;[6] the penultimate poem of *Drafts*, entitled "Drafts 113: Index," does both. The poem is literally an index: DuPlessis lists people, places, concepts, and more alphabetically, just as indices have done since the sixteenth century ("Index"). In some senses, DuPlessis reproduces the historical. Some of what the poet includes in her index appears to be an actual list of moments in poems: for example, she includes words like "Vectors," "Water," and "Volta" (*S* 142), all of which figure heavily in several volumes of *Drafts*. DuPlessis lists "H.D." (under "H," of course), showing the depth of the listing: H.D.'s presence haunts the entire work figuratively, H.D.'s *Trilogy* works itself into the preface ("the same—different—the same attributes, / different yet the same as before"), and Robert Duncan's *The H.D. Book*[7]—which itself discusses and quotes H.D.—comes up in the poems as well (*S*

138, 2, 165–66). Hence, even within DuPlessis's index, we find accumulation—of words as the list goes on but also of concepts within individual words. One entry, in this case, stands for a person, another text, a spectral presence, and direct quotations. DuPlessis deftly weaves her own being into the index by providing a kind of commentary on some of her entries; she writes, "Coffee" /   see also Tea (before 1990)" (*S* 136). The directive to "see also Tea (before 1990)" already indicates something about the poet's life, by implying that her relationship to imbibing tea (and therefore coffee) changed after 1990; or, perhaps, someone else's relationship to these beverages changed. In either case, there is no entry for "Tea" in the index, which means we know this reference points to something outside the text of this particular poem; we must "see also" beyond the page. Raveling and unraveling extend back and forth across the volume but also extend to other works, to history, maybe even to the sea.

In fact, what DuPlessis's "Index" is *not* doing—the ways in which the poem does not behave like an index at all—situates the text and reader in a space of ambiguity, fluidity, and unraveled expectations.[8] First, generally the index comes at the end of a book ("Index"), but DuPlessis's book goes on: she includes another poem after this one, "Draft 114: Exergue and Volta," "Notes" on the poems, and a table that shows all the texts in *Surge*. The poet's final entry in the list is simply a black bar, as if there is something underneath that the poet blacks out (*S* 143). The bar functions as a kind of a redaction; it removes the reader's access to the word without removing the spacing of the word or literally the space the word takes up on the page. DuPlessis's choice to redact the word with the censorship bar—as opposed to erasing it or crafting another kind of placeholder—immediately recalls the kind of censorship that happens in legal and governmental documents. The poem almost ends like a kind of legal narrative, with important—or specific—names, titles, or details left out. DuPlessis leaves the reader with a marking of what cannot be seen and what cannot be read; a trace remains that points to something, but we cannot be sure what the something is. So there is a final entry, in a sense, but it cannot be accessed, it cannot be read; it is both the end and, in the act of reading, not the end (we can't read it, and more text follows).

More importantly, the blacked-out section could function as an entry in the index because it harkens back to "Draft 99: Intransitive," the third poem in the collection. In this poem, which DuPlessis wrote after the 2009 death of the poet Robin Blaser (*S* 161), the reader finds more than *thirty* redactions of varying lengths. At one point in the work, DuPlessis gives a redaction followed by the lines "What marks to put in the world / and in what world?" and then another redaction (*S* 41). By wondering "what marks" could go into a world, the poet implies that some marks may exist outside the world; as such, words can exist outside the page, and a redaction serves as their placeholder, rendering a kind of absent-presence. The mention of "what world" draws the reader beyond the textual world of "Draft 99," particularly when situated before a censorship bar. After all, in a post-9/11 United States, censorship by the media and the government exploded in courtrooms, print journalism, conversation, and even classrooms (Savage, Staples). Here DuPlessis controls the censorship of self, but she also implies there is a world where the meaning behind the black bars still exists, a world where this language can be, if not accessed, at least understood. As such, in the tidal surge of socio-history—particularly in the twenty-first century—there is the possibility for literature to provide and deny access to language; the buck stops not with the government but with the poet, the text, and the reader. In this particular text, even the act of reading is unending because redactions beg us to continue looking for meaning, to connect broken sentences, and to wonder which world these words appear in.

DuPlessis's redactions also point to another poem in *Surge*, the aptly titled "Draft 106: Words." This poem, which also features a redaction, links the ways polysemous language illuminates the incomprehensible world (or perhaps a world beyond our access); the poet writes, "With words, the world / is more than is the case. / How could it not / be just that way" (*S* 87). The index can be itself and more than itself; it transcends its own boundaries and, in doing so, resists its own closure; the index might end on a particular page, but, in pointing outside of that textual confinement, it engages in the work of unending referentiality. One of the poem's epigraphs links the finite and the infinite by considering how words can reemerge and reengage in a post-1945 political world. The poet quotes Adorno's "Ernest Bloch's Spuren": "Words become heated up as if they were to start to glow again in the disenchanted world, as if the promise hidden in them had become the motor of thought" (*S* 135). Here, Adorno reads a kind of circularity in Bloch: words can "glow again," and this, in turn, triggers more thinking. So the index circles around, pointing to new words and crafting new thoughts; it does not end, just like words, even in the "disenchanted world." This disenchantment is for Adorno, and for Bloch, and—by extension—for DuPlessis, *always* political (Adorno 143). In fact, Bloch himself links the sociopolitical to the imperfect circularity of art; he notes in the masterwork *Traces*, "But now, what was the beginning? Was it not just as abrupt as complete, everything at once? What was meant in it does not easily return, yet always *surges* forward again, as a dawn that must become loud and clear" (68; emphasis added). DuPlessis's aptly titled *Surge* employs the listed accumulation, the index radiating outward as "everything at once": the political, the historical and the embodied. "Index" opens with a gesture toward words engaging with what Hannah Arendt refers to as "the violence of wars and revolutions and the growing decay of all that has still been spared" (vii); and the list, the index, pulls through this unending, refusing to end and continuing to point forward, backward, and in circles. In a sense, DuPlessis unravels the index, time, conclusion, and her own poem; the surge is not in complete control, the poet is.

DuPlessis closes this volume with "Draft 114: Exergue and Volta" and allows her accumulated serial poem to refuse ending by folding back on itself, via the text, the body, and the reader. She weaves a narrative that never has to be interrupted and specifies how a text performs this balance, noting,

> Thereupon it will resolve, yes,
> stubbornly to begin once more.
> Resolve to re-assess
> yet not repeat,
> reordering its wayward line.
> A book therefore
> is not like time;
> one can go differently,
> reread, remember
> pursue another pleasure.
> Frottage, fricage, penetration, touching.
> (*S* 147–48)

In the first two lines, the poet implies that the end will be the beginning—but a new beginning. Just as her index points in all directions and all throughout time and space, so too the serial poem will constantly "re-assess" and be moved through multidimensionally. The accumulated text can be "reread" "differently," as if every body has the potential to encounter the accumulation anew, from different angles, beginning at different points and rebeginning somewhere else. Here the eternal manifests, but it is not fully outside of control—one is not drowning in these waves but rather negotiating the "wayward" textual line. Indeed, as Ron Silliman notes, DuPlessis's work here "may be the first anti-teleological long poem." The "book" is not the same as political,[9] but—in the serial form—it can be similarly immutable, and it offers a chance for a kind of "resolve." So the swirling constellation of accumulated texts offers the possibility for a new kind of eternal but one that is never removed from the body (after all, DuPlessis says that "*one* can go differently").

DuPlessis underscores that "one" is not just some disembodied being with the line "Frottage, fricage, penetration, touching." Here, the poet gives four ways of thinking about *touch*, beginning with a synonym for rubbing. According to "Notes to *Drafts 96–114*," DuPlessis gets the word "fricage" from poet Kate Lilley's "Starry Messenger" (*S* 166). Lilley actually uses the word "fricatrice," which she in turn notes means "lewd woman" but comes from *fricre*, to rub. Here DuPlessis's reference indicates a kind of sexual touching but one that is not likely to end in biological procreation, just textual reproduction; the body in the text gestures back and forth as the text itself accumulates.[10] Ending the line with "penetration" and "touching," DuPlessis indicates that the moving back and forth through (in this case) the serial text is embodied, ongoing, and even (in her words) a form of "pleasure." So we find in the unending closure of the serial a little relief and even joy in the body and the eternal; our body engages in a ritual of pleasure via the text.

IV. Volta! Volta!

In the last section of "Draft 114," DuPlessis continues to accumulate textual references as she encourages the reader to consider how the folding of the serial work negotiates the unending and the mortal; this accumulation provides fortitude in the face of the surge. A folding becomes a radical way of unthinking ending and finality; in fact, for philosopher Gilles Deleuze, "the fold is always double, always in two directions or levels at the same time," which means that a folded accumulation looks forward and back, incorporates the social and the embodied, and includes the potentiality of the future (Grosz 158). As writer Patrick Pritchett remarks, "The imminent ending of *Drafts* is as enticing an aspect of the poem as any since it challenges us to rethink the question of how poems end." DuPlessis initiates this rethinking in her closing section:

> That this began
> that this ends
> that this refused to begin
> (though it started)
> that it refuses to end
> (though it is folding itself up)
>
> We offer a full spectrum of services
> going round
>
> "*into an imagined 'endlessness'*"
> endlessly overwritten.
>
> The page is stamped in saturated black
> in which
>
> the last lines herein placed
> are thus unreadable
> hidden within a glossy square of ink:
> it is
> finished but it is
> not complete
> Is black all colors?
> Or was that white?
> "*I am not sure that this is not the end*"
>
> so that....
> or simply "*So...*"

> going backwards
> through the work's own vibrato.
>
> it's 4:32 AM exactly
> in the wind that's blowing fiercely.
> There are so many tasks. To start.
>
> Up. Again.
>
> Like this. The is, the it.
>
> Id est:
>
> So vector the crossroads once again!
> Volta! Volta!
> (*S* 159–60)

The poet once again elides a true ending by claiming that the poem is "folding itself up," as if the lists and accumulations refold on to each other, crafting something that goes back to itself again and again (though without repeating). Similarly, because "the last lines" remain "unreadable," there is no true last line, just as the previous index occludes its final entry. As a result, the end may not be read, may not be experienced; hence, for all purposes, the end is not reached. Even in the process of the "finished," DuPlessis reaches outside her text and time; she brings quotations from serial works such as Robert Duncan's *Ground Work I* ("*into an imagined "endlessness"*"") and Nathaniel Mackey's *Whatsaid Serif* ("'So . . .'") into the fold, and the poem points outward from itself while closing in (*S* 168). Nevertheless, unlike the body floating in unending waves, the (un)folding poem offers a place for the body—or at least the mind—to go and questions to explore ("Is black all colors?"). Importantly, the body is not left out of the fold either; feminist philosopher Elizabeth Grosz reads "the fold" in the work of other theorists (namely Gilles Deleuze and Gottfried Wilhelm Leibniz) as a concept that *always* conjures "the material and the ideal" together, doubling body, time, philosophy, and more together (159). So "the folding itself up" is a work of the text that goes on and on, but it is also a way for the body to feel less fleeting and maybe less precarious.

After all, DuPlessis ends the poem with a directive about change: "So vector the crossroads once again!" Here "vector" feels like a verb, giving the impression that one must direct the crossroads, or at least point toward them. However the verb's etymology comes from its noun, which means a direction, "an ordered set of numbers," "a sequence of consecutive locations in [computer] memory," and even an organic being that "carries a pathogenic agent and acts as a potential source of infection" ("Vector"). The set, the sequence, parts of memory, and even types of body come to the crossroads, giving the agent who vectors multiple ontological possibilities. And so the text, the accumulation, the index, and the being can keep going, keep looking forward (or backward). DuPlessis's double exclamatory "Volta! Volta!" is a textual turn but not a closure; and the excitement of the exclamation lends, in its own way, a glimmer of optimism, an anticipation of eternal change.[11] The poet weaves an unending only to move to quickly unravel even the concept of ending, the concept of conclusion. Instead she leaves text and reader in a space of ambiguity, almost floating in a liminal sea of back and forth, of past and present, of what was/is/might be. We simply float through foldings that emerge like reproductions of potentiality, that find a space for the contemporary politicized body in what the poet Joseph Donahue refers to as "*the sweetness / of the fruit that will be*" (45).

As for the surge, a blueprint has been laid out. The next undulation—of writing, of war, of disease, of the climate—feels inevitable. However, by the culmination of this collection, one finds that indexing, accumulating, and listing transforms the surge from an overwhelming and even threatening wave into the volta. In this volta, one might find a moment of peace in the reconciliation of the finite body and forces that feel everlasting because, as DuPlessis's collection implies, the unending can be pleasurable. Reading the unending of *Surge*, we find moments of joy in floating and in waiting, and proof that agency can emerge even in the surge; the swallowtail may still find itself in precarity, but something more hopeful does exist. DuPlessis writes in "Drafts 103: Punctum,"

> The city sparrows zoom around this
> corner now, their staging place
> that new, well-growing pear.
> We planted it.
> We watered it.
> We cared for it.
>
> The detail
> is a spiritual instrument.
> (*S* 69)

So, during our reading and hopefully after, we shoulder our "spiritual instrument[s]," accumulate the "detail[s]," and courageously turn to face the unending, the volta, and even the *surge*.

Notes

1. DuPlessis notes that she wrote "Draft 99: Intransitive" in 2009 and that she wrote the collection's preface between June and July 2012 (*S* 161, vii).

2. DuPlessis, writes of creating an ongoing poem, "the notion of One Poem, coterminous with One Life, turns on the authority of the author-figure to establish a heterogeneous unity, or at least purpose and drive, in that oeuvre" ("Puzzles" 4). The deceptively simple phrase "One Poem, coterminous with One Life" indicates that Poem and Life share boundaries; they occupy and emerge from the same space. "It's a life work," notes Nathaniel Mackey, "it extends beyond my life, the community of lives [in] our work in poetry and in other media and modes and vocations and occupations" (Interview).

3. According to Ian Baucom, the sea and the concept of accumulation work perfectly together. He writes of the Atlantic Ocean, "time does not pass, it accumulates, and as it accumulates it deposits an ever greater freight of material within the cargo holds of a present that is, in this, sense, eternally after the Enlightenment present" (325).

4. The sociohistorical is always on our poet's mind. According to critic Bradley J. Fest, DuPlessis's serial work always engages with the specific as well as global political: "[her] activity in the long poem over the past thirty-five years highlights how form might inhabit and address the neoliberal era, the era of big data and financialization, globalization, climate crisis, the forever war, and the ongoing immiserations of late capitalism" (146).

5. Papadakis generalizes the seemingly eternal historical moment too when, at the end of his text, he invokes a spectral James Joyce: "Will the Dead Zone keep haunting us? 'History is a nightmare from which I am trying to awake,' mused Joyce's protagonist" (251).

6. Harriet Tarlo insists that Rachel Blau DuPlessis continues to keep "form and content closely engaged" ("The page is slowly turning").

7. For DuPlessis, Duncan's *The H.D. Book* does more than simply haunt the pages of *Surge*; it is also a monumental work that muses on gender, sexuality, and poetics while defining Duncan's legacy. DuPlessis notes in "Polymorphous Poetics": "However, in [*The H.D. Book*], in a forceful critical move, women are granted co-equality and co-temporality in artistic and institutional struggles and can claim and be acknowledged for their powers. This is what Duncan achieved with *The H.D. Book*. So *The H.D. Book* is a beautiful but awe-ful work. Summarizing even some of its findings (inevitable here) violates the flashes of insight that accumulate via the dredged and repetitive accounts that Duncan offers. This book is overwhelming, pressured from within by the force of its rapturous, intent rhetoric" (661–62).

8. The *Oxford English Dictionary* notes that the word "index" first emerges as "the fore-finger: so called because used in pointing" ("Index"). The word's anatomical meaning circulates more than a century before "index" refers to words in a book, meaning it is the finger—the literal body—that allows a list to list, and even be named ("Index"). Some part of the body—some trace—remains in the "Index," somehow transcending its temporal limits to keep pointing forward and back again.

9. DuPlessis herself hedges back and forth on poetry and the political but does acknowledge "there are many ways in which it would be appropriate to claim that *Drafts* has a feminist implication" (*S* 9).

10. In fact, Lilley's poem already does a little accumulation of its own; the title is a reference to Galileo's *Siderius Nuncius*—Starry Messenger—the first treatise written after using a telescope; in the work, Galileo describes (among other things) discovering the moons of Jupiter (Lilley).

11. For more on how DuPlessis's post-*Drafts* works "turn . . . toward something else" while still considering the serial, see Fest's "'Is an Archive Enough?': Megatextual Debris in the Work of Rachel Blau DuPlessis," 155–58.

Works Cited

Adorno, Theodor. *Notes to Literature*. Edited by Rolf Tiedemann, translated by Shierry Weber Nicholson. New York: Columbia University Press, 2019.

Arendt, Hannah. *The Origins of Totalitarianism*. New York: Meridian Books, 1960.

Baucom, Ian. *Specters of the Atlantic: Finance Capital, Slavery, and the Philosophy of History*. Chapel Hill, NC: Duke University Press, 2005.

Bloch, Ernest. *Traces*. Translated by Anthony A. Nassar. Redwood City, CA: Stanford University Press, 2006.

Braudel, Fernand. *The Mediterranean and the Mediterranean World in the Age of Phillip II*. Translated by Siân Reynolds. New York: Harper Collins, 1992.

Butler, Judith. *Precarious Life: The Powers of Mourning and Violence*. New York: Verso, 2004.

Connery, Christopher L. "Ideologies of Land and Sea: Alfred Thayer Mahan, Carl Schmitt, and the Shaping of Global Myth Elements." *boundary 2*, vol. 28, no. 2, 2001, 173–201.

Donahue, Joseph. *Terra Lucida*. Hoboken, NJ: Talisman House, 2009.

Duncan, Robert. *The H.D. Book*. Berkeley: University of California Press, 2011.

DuPlessis, Rachel Blau. "Polymorphous Poetics: Robert Duncan's *H.D. Book*." *Contemporary Literature*, vol. 55, no. 4, 2014, 635–44.

———. *Surge: Drafts 96–114*. Sheffield, UK: Salt Books, 2013.

———. *H.D.: The Career of That Struggle*. Bloomington: Indiana University Press, 1986.

———. *Writing Beyond the Ending: Narrative Strategies of Twentieth Century Women Writers*. Bloomington: Indiana University Press, 1985.

Fest, Bradley J. "'Is an Archive Enough?': Megatextual Debris in the Work of Rachel Blau DuPlessis." *Genre*, vol. 54, no. 1, 2021, 139–65.

Forché, Carolyn. "H.D. after H.D." *H.D. and the Poets After*, edited by Donna Krolik Hollenberg. Iowa City: University of Iowa Press, 2000, 255–64.

Grosz, Elizabeth. *The Incorporeal: Ontology, Ethics, and the Limits of Materialism*. New York: Columbia University Press, 2017.

Hansen, Kathryn. "NASA Research Finds 2010 Tied for Warmest Year on Record." NASA Global Climate Change: Vital Signs of the Planet, 11 Jan. 2011, https://climate.nasa.gov/news/467/nasa-research-finds-2010-tied-for-warmest-year-on-record/#:~:text=In%202010%2C%20global%20temperatures%20continued,Credit%3A%20NASA%20GISS.

H.D. "Writing on the Wall." *A Tribute to Freud*. 3rd ed. New York: New Directions, 2012, 3–114.

———. *The Gift*. 1969. 3rd ed. Gainesville: University of Florida Press, 1998.

Heise, Ursula. *Sense of Place and Sense of Planet: The Environmental Imagination of the Global*. New York: Oxford University Press, 2008.

Horkheimer, Max, and Theodor Adorno. *Dialectic of Enlightenment: Philosophical Fragments*. Translated by Edmund Jephcott. Redwood City, CA: Stanford University Press, 2002.

"Index." *Oxford English Dictionary*, 2020, https://www-oed-com.proxy.lib.duke.edu/view/Entry/94372?rskey=e3hTKE&result=1#eid.

Keenaghan, Eric. "Openings: Some Notes on the Political in 'Drafts.'" *Jacket2*, 14 Dec. 2011, https://jacket2.org/article/openings-some-notes-political-drafts.

Khullar, Dhruv. "Will the Pandemic Ever End?" *New Yorker*, 23 May 2002, https://www.newyorker.com/news/daily-comment/will-the-coronavirus-pandemic-ever-end.

"The Latest on the Coronavirus." Harvard T. H. Chan School of Public Health, 2022, https://www.hsph.harvard.edu/news/hsph-in-the-news/the-latest-on-the-coronavirus/.

Lilley, Kate. "Four Poems." *Jacket*, vol. 10, 1999, https://webarchive.nla.gov.au/awa/20000228130000/http://www.jacket.zip.com.au/jacket10/lilley-4poems.html.

Mackey, Nathaniel. "A Long Song Log: Ten Entries on Seriality, to the Accompaniment of Charles Mingus' *Black Saint*." *Ways of Hearing: Reflections on Music in 26 Pieces*, edited by Scott Burnham et al. Princeton: Princeton University Press, 2021, 160–66.

———. Interview with Josiah Luis Aldrete and Fred Moten. City Lights Live!, YouTube, 26 May 2021, https://www.youtube.com/watch?v=eD8IteCcbco.

Narea, Nicole. "A Timeline of Israel and Palestine's Complicated History." *Vox*, 19 Oct. 2023, https://www.vox.com/world-politics/23921529/israel-palestine-timeline-gaza-hamas-war-conflict.

Ostriker, Alicia. "Once More Out of Darkness." *Once More Out of Darkness and Other Poems*. Berkeley: Berkeley Poets' Workshop and Press, 1974.

Papadakis, Yiannis. *Echoes from the Dead Zone: Across the Cyprus Divide*. London: I. B. Tauris (Bloomsbury), 2005.

Pritchett, Patrick. "Drafting Beyond the Ending: On Rachel Blau DuPlessis." *Jacket2*, 14 Dec. 2011, https://jacket2.org/feature/drafting-beyond-ending.

"Redact." *Oxford English Dictionary*, 2022, https://www.oed.com/dictionary/redact_v?tab=meaning_and_use#26344799.

Sagan, Carl. *Cosmos*. New York: Random House Books, 1980.

Savage, Charlie. "Judge Stops Censorship in Sept. 11 Case." *New York Times*, 31 July 2013,

Silliman, Ron. "Un-scene, ur-new: The History of the Longpoem and 'The Collage Poems of Drafts.'" *Jacket2*, 14 Dec. 2011, https://jacket2.org/article/un-scene-ur-new.

Staples, Jeanine. "'Do You Remember': Confronting Post-9/11 Censorship through Critical Questioning and Poetic Devices." *English Journal*, vol. 97, no. 5, 2008, 81–87.

"Surge." *Oxford English Dictionary*, 2022, https://www-oed-com.proxy.lib.duke.edu/search?searchType=dictionary&q=surge&_searchBtn=Search.

Tarlo, Harriet. "'The page is slowly turning black': Rachel Blau DuPlessis's 'Torques: Drafts 58–76.'" *Jacket2*, 14 Dec. 2011, https://jacket2.org/article/page-slowly-turning-black.

"Vector." *Oxford English Dictionary*, 2020, https://www-oed-com.proxy.lib.duke.edu/view/Entry/221825?rskey=WPZW1R&result=1#eid.

Winterson, Jeanette. *Written on the Body*. New York: Vintage, 1994.

PART II

Materialities of Making

Collage, Detritus, and Waste in *Drafts*

CHAPTER FOUR

Intertexuality as Collage, Text/Textile Interstices, Layering

Art Practice as Embodied Feminist Philosophy

MARIA DAMON

I. Open Up!

The following meditation addresses, broadly, Rachel Blau DuPlessis's "mediations/interventions in form and in poetry and visual text: rubrics of handwriting, footnotes, collage, page, line, seriality, grid, essay, concept of book" (Mossin) insofar as these formal questions and tropes are touched by Jewish cultural traditions and feminist practices, and also manifest a particular affinity for the "handmade." Taken as a whole, DuPlessis's oeuvre manifests a porous yet rigorously selective intertextual sensibility that potentially refuses nothing and that draws on techniques of improvisation, layering, fragmentation, juxtaposition, recycling/sampling, and dense intra-, inter-, and extra-referentiality that renders flexible otherwise rigid divisions between affect and analysis, past and present, vernacular and academic discourse. This intertextuality finds resonance in metaphors of failure and iteration, and in a practice of recycling tropes, language, citations, and, in the visual work, literal materials. A poetics and poesis that includes everything offers ultimate permission to readers and imaginers.

All of DuPlessis's work is characterized by a strong resistance to closure, evidenced not only by the duration of the *Drafts* project but by the internal formal properties of each (fragmented or incomplete sentences and thoughts; self-interruptions; the iteration, many pages or even volumes later, of material, form, or content) and the values espoused in thematic treatments, to the degree that one could say there is an ethics or even a politics (as well as, of course, a poetics) of anti-closure afoot here, a strong disinclination to relinquish any cause, word, or concept as having been definitively played out. Reflecting a particularly salient version of second-wave feminist scholarship and art that seems to be finding rebirth in the emergent field of "textile studies," familiar motifs in materialist histories of "traditionally feminine" survival activities—quilting, darning, mending, laying up "preserves"—find easy application to DuPlessis's intellectual preoccupations and their verbal embodiments. As if to underscore the point, a material practice of collaging—iterative layers of materials—accompanies, subtends, and thrives adjacent to this restless language-making, and has most recently merged with it in books such as *Numbers* and the forthcoming *Life in Handkerchiefs*.

II. Artisanal Cosmologies

Tucked into the final paratextual pages of her 2018 book, *Numbers*, Rachel Blau DuPlessis's enticing phrase "artisanal cosmology," used to describe the foregoing volume, emphasizes and encapsulates the handmade and traditional, the haptic neurointelligence of nonverbal touch—and yet simultaneously the systemic and ambitious scope of her various projects as they take on enormous concepts—here, specifically, the concept of numbers and numbering in all their dimensions: mathematical, spatial, temporal, and geometrical; mythological, cultural, historical, and mystical/occult (*N*) The two words comprising the phrase "artisanal cosmology" move in productive and seductive tension with each other: "artisanal" promises the highly individualized eccentricity and yet homespun utilitarianism of the "handprints of the potter cling[ing] to the clay vessel" (Benjamin 92) that signal both authenticity and craft rather than high art, while "cosmology" suggests a grandly ambitious artistry on the scale of Dante, Bosch, and the great intellectual scaffolding subtending world religions as well as sciences and pseudo-sciences, all of which offer a comprehensive hermeneutic "Theory of Everything" (Livingston).

Writ large, the phrase "artisanal cosmology" works to capture metonymically DuPlessis's entire corpus, in that it holds together form and improvisation, the cozy and the highly wrought, the local and the global, and a host of other antinomies of that ilk. Her major life work to date, *Drafts*, a decades-long series in the spirit of Robert Duncan's *Passages* or Nathaniel Mackey's *Songs of the Andoumboulou*, for example, holds everything in restless place and urgent play, iterating and reiterating most of the major modern Western philosophical and cultural themes through its cyclical structure. This sensibility, of joining the fragmentary, contingent, and minute with the "grand picture," is also carried forward in the current series *Traces*. There are, furthermore, freestanding works like the aforementioned *Numbers*, unincorporated into series, which also fit this capacious description. She has also written scholarly works of literary and cultural analysis that focus on the "social poetics" of modernist poetry, books of visual art (collages), and so forth. Indeed, any one piece or fragment of DuPlessis's oeuvre, in which I include the visual art, is metonymic for all of it. You can see the whole in the shard, and the whole is an endlessly refractive and (re)generative shambles of shards—in other words an unbounded verbal prism, if such a thing exists. The simple image of the "prism" is perhaps too neatly structured and too neatly envisioned: DuPlessis's work, though likewise rigorously structured and cosmologically/comprehensively envisioned, does not claim or aim for clean lines and smooth surfaces. Delighting in contrasting textures and counterintuitive juxtapositions, its cosmology is not one in which every metaphysical detail is tethered inexorably to its one and only physical counterpart in clean, deterministic lines of correspondence. Perhaps, then, a "twisted, fractured" verbal prism.

It's not unusual, in an ambitious serial or epic work spanning decades in its composition, to weave into later sections thematic, imagistic sonic or conceptual threads that have appeared earlier. Often, as DuPlessis does, the methods of incorporation and reiteration are deployed in recurring, schematic patterns that enhance the density of the cosmological and aesthetic texture of the whole. Think, for instance, of Dante's elaborate "terza rima," a three-line verse structure and rhyme scheme invented for the *Divine Comedy* to exalt and fully explore a trinitarian universe, in which each of three books invites comparisons between its corresponding thirty-three cantos (with one extra at the end to perform the excess and exalted nature of the divinity in which the work finds resolution). Canto I of *Purgatorio* echoes and reworks Canto I of *Inferno*, and both in turn are revisited in Canto I of *Paradiso*; within these three books of thirty-three (and thirty-four) cantos there are subdivisions of reiteration as well, a kind of constant folding back and forward that creates complexity, history, memory, and texture within the text, as well as exhaustively alluding to extra-textual historical events, personages, literary works, and so forth. In DuPlessis's *Drafts*, the cycles are nineteen poems/cantos in duration, with "Draft 1" serving as the primary (but not exclusive) "donor draft," as she terms it, for "Draft 20," "Draft 2" "donating" material for "Draft 21," and so forth. However, unlike Dante, and more akin to her contemporaries Duncan and Mackey, DuPlessis's restless series are marked not by a drama of loss and then resolution but by an abiding, ongoing skepticism, which she herself marks as an element of her Jewishness, as Paul Jaussen has astutely cited in an essay on *Drafts*' debt to midrashic practice as method and cultural/intellectual inheritance, "a kind of self-skepticism and praxis, not an iconic object" (DuPlessis, "Midrashic" 220; Jaussen 126). Her sense of her Jewishness consists "not the least in my skepticism, resistance, intuitive exilism, and quarrel with that curiosity called God. And in my deep commitment to the book and to textuality" ("Midrashic" 210).

III. Donor Sidebar (Digression)

DuPlessis is, as far as I know, unique in using the term "donor drafts" for the earlier poems in the series from which she draws intratextual material for subsequent ones. This particularity is a provocation worthy of investigation. In intertextual practices such as citation, the typical adjectives used for the precedent text are "earlier," "source," "antecedent," or "primary." In translation, likewise, an "original" text is referred to as the "source," written in the "source language," destined for a "target" language, the language into which the translator is transforming the poem. The word "donor" has specific and exceptionally fruitful but also anxious resonances in the context of modern (medical) and feminist practices, especially in those that conceive of a feminist cultural project as at least partially embodied and corporeal.

The fruitful aspect of the metaphor of a body as donor is obvious in the context of DuPlessis's work—namely, the long history of the association of women with embodiment, including through writing, most usefully perhaps captured late twentieth-century theorists like Hélène Cixous, whose "The Laugh of the Medusa" threw down the gauntlet in challenging women writers and intellectuals to write "from the body" not just in spite of the possibility but precisely because it would terrify and baffle the phallocentric male cultural order, the legacy of Western thought and art (Cixous). The notion of life as a cyclical series of unfoldings in which prior life forms "donate" their material to the emergence of new forms is one that corresponds to attention women poets have paid to the material, the embodied, the domestic, and so on. These cycles take the form of daily minutiae such as preparing meals from leftovers or turning a basketful of worn-out work clothes into a fanciful and utilitarian quilt or rag rug—as well as metaphors such as the uterus "shedding its lining" monthly in the reproductive process—to grander conceptions of fallen "mother trees" nurturing saplings or, expanding still wider, to Joni Mitchell's imperative that humans as "stardust" need rematriation to a ("the") garden. Likewise, Audre Lorde's stories of only speaking poetry in her early childhood years of language acquisition because she needed to feel physical certainty at some elemental core (Lorde). In an exploration of a body of poetry that thematizes and practices repetition, cyclical development, and so forth, it is pertinent to point out the element of bodily awareness that enriches the relationships between breathing, speaking, singing, poetry, and bodily pulsations of all kinds (the most facile of these tropes, proliferating in bygone classrooms of English literature, is the claim that iambic pentameter is "naturally" mimetic of the heartbeat; perhaps "nationalistically" would be the more appropriate adverb here). A cursory internet search of "poem as body" yields a cross-section of trauma literature, poetry and poetics, theories of embodiment, and any number of references that risk pulling such an inquiry into banality, not to mention unmanageability (another long digression). But the specificity with which DuPlessis uses the figure of the donor is matched by the rigor of method by which her intra-series donations take place.

And the notion of organ/body donation is anxious because, of course, the most common use of "donor" in relation to bodies is in the context of postmortem organ donation, organ "harvesting," and the like, which suggest cutting, disembowelment, and highly medicalized processes that challenge notions of holism possibly suggested by a facile association of feminist writing with "the body," "natural life cycles," and more, or even worse, assumptions about women as "givers," donors by nature, whether through their own generosity or through exploitive extraction. "Donor drafts" conjures suggestions of the excision and replacement of bits of language or conceptual units as organs that can be transplanted by a skillful surgeon, consent of the body itself notwithstanding.

The concept of "donor drafts" from which later drafts draw is one of recycling, not only in the sense of literary intertextuality but also in the realm of the material: it is an acknowledgment of the long life of things, fruitfully explored by anthropologist Tim Ingold, who has eloquently analyzed the long life of a thing from, say, its organic primordial form (a tree) through its encounter with the human and the changes that entails (planks, a table), and then its slow march toward a different form of material (firewood, fire, ash, gases, mineral detritus). But for a materialist poet, the "things" of greatest interest are those that inhere in words (iconically asserted by poet William Carlos Williams: "no ideas but in things"—and extended by Robert Creeley: "no things but in words") (Williams, line 17; Creeley). The extensive endnotes for each "Draft" refer to its structural ancestors as "donor drafts" to acknowledge their status as source texts thematically, sonically, and formally. I address below the ways in which titles of individual poems within the series often, though not always, echo each other or embed each other's syllables (and syllabuses, in the etymological sense, a compendium of contents), just as the poems echo and evoke or embed each other's content, obliquely as well as overtly. In counterpart to a Steinian repetition-with-a-difference, one could call this project's partial mission an exploration of difference-with-a-repetition, a changing same that is overtly more changing than same but contained nonetheless in a loose, formally diaphanous membrane (a "negligee"; that is, a forgotten garment) that permits and indeed encourages freedom, evolution, maybe even revolution. Structurally, then, the grid in the front matter and the "Notes" in the back bookend the poems with explanatory material that holds, without fixing in place, their motility and internal self-difference within a logically coherent system.

Medically, the practice of "donor organ"—and organ transplantation—was initiated in 1954, when a man donated one of his kidneys (oh, that fetal-looking little creature) to his twin brother (https://unos.org/transplant/history/). Noteworthily, donation is historically coincident with transplantation; at least in the official medical histories, there are no accounts of involuntary organ confiscation for the purposes of transplantation, though one can speculate that this must have been the case under some circumstances—"organ harvesting" is the preferred term for such abusive practices and is often featured as a charge leveled by oppositions or political enemies at oppressive regimes or institutions. Relevant here is that despite the fraught ethics swirling around the practice of organ acquisition in the medical world, in DuPlessis's artisanal cosmology, the individual "Drafts" are willing and eager participants in their own "cannibalization," (a term that DuPlessis rejects but one that is positively associated with particular modernist avant-gardes, especially in Brazil), and they do not have to perish to see their legacies continued. (This seems to be an important facet of the long duration of language as a thing>object>thing in Tim Ingold's sense, that it has the potential to survive millennia of revision, evolution, even violence [Ingold 2010].)

IV. The Fold

Drafts 15–XXX, The Fold (1997), an obvious nod to Gilles Deleuze, features as its cover photo a gathered swirl of white or light gray fabric—perhaps, guessing from what appears to be its heft, a hand towel—the soft folds of which suggest the folds of a rose in full bloom, similar to Jay DiFeo's *The Rose* (1966), a radiant white monolith of impastoed oil paint that suggests the sublime. It also suggests the "rose is a rose is a rose" of Gertrude Stein (an important literary ancestor for DuPlessis) in which the rose lives again for the first time in English literature in a hundred years; the line also appeared in circular form above the bed Stein shared with her life partner Alice B. Toklas, an instance of spatialized text that leads one to realize the "eros" behind the "rose" ("Sacred"). "Rose" is a noun that Stein "caressed completely caressed and addressed" ("Poetry"). The rose is a fold, an interface between external and internal. For Robert Duncan, another one of DuPlessis's antecedents, the "rose(bud)(hip)" is a clenched anus anticipating relaxation in the joy of penetration and a portal between inner world and its extrusions, a poetics (3). And the rose/fold, suggestive of so many internal organs, particularly suggests, in this photograph, the brain with its outer layer, the cerebral cortex ("gray matter") a mass of folds, crenellations, and convolutions, an organ of subjectification as it assimilates and processes externalities, converting them in the process into "consciousness" much as the gastrointestinal organs, crimped-up tubing with florid peripheries, assimilating new materials constantly, produce "fuel for the body." The organs are folds, the body a series thereof, as well as an encasing of organ within organ (the skin), a series of inter-flickerings, simultaneities, or oscillations—or better yet, a condition of greater or lesser porosity between internality and externality, between subjectification and objectification. The book of poems, thus, is an artifactual body made of intra- and intertextuality. One poem ostensibly housed within one book in the series becomes a "donor" to a future poem, just as organs can outlive their hosts and live on in another body through the social program of "organ donation"; intertextuality becomes a festival of giving. Poems themselves are but "drafts," provisionally drawn (draught) breaths that mark existence into the next moment.

And since the textile-adorned volume entitled *The Fold* contains the first "fold," that is, the first reiteration/donation—"Draft 20: Incipit"—of "Draft 1: It," it makes sense to subject a few moments of this poem within this volume to particular attention, using it as a focal anchor from which to explore DuPlessis's engagement with the trope and practice of handwork, bricolage, collage, textual and material rag-picking, and Jewish hermeneutics, most notably the Talmud, whose techniques of reading, rereading, and verbal embroidering via commentary fit right into the paradigm of a text/textile axis. *Drafts*, and within it, *The Fold*, is not only intertextual with regard to a wide canon of DuPlessis's literary, historical and philosophical concerns, enfolding all manner of allusions to texts, ideas, and writers into their capacious embrace; but the series is also, by virtue of this donating technique of antecedent poems in the same series, a palimpsest of intratextual intertextuality. Throughout *Drafts* and other of DuPlessis's works, historical, theoretical, social, and aesthetic problematics unfurl, twist, evolve, and mutate dialectically and dialogically, bouncing off each other in collision or play, interlocking in agonistic intensity or affectionate rapprochement.

Although all discussions of *Drafts*, including those by the author herself, center this folding and "donating" technique, the *Drafts* volumes as gatherings of consecutive poems decenter the folding sequence—note that *The Fold* begins not with "Draft 20," the first instance of the iterative pattern, but with "Draft 15," and runs through "Draft XXX." Thus the first fold does not even fall in the center(fold) of the book, which would be "Draft 22.5" (predictably, no such poem exists). We can therefore see that the structure of *Drafts* is both centered in regularity and decentered, marked by stochasticisms, like bodily rhythms that are both "regular" and "arhythmic" without necessarily being aberrant signs of ill-being, or like art practices in which pattern is deliberately marred, however slightly, by error or distortion. This element of positively inflected randomness or unpredictability points to a quotient of improvisation, a word whose roots in *improvisus* ("unforeseen, unexpected") have strong relevance to a diasporic, Talmudic, and feminist sensibility and history with its need for quick thinking, resiliency, and the ability to expand limited resources out of necessity, a need to quickly respond in the face of impending loss, displacement, or domestic catastrophe.

"Drafting" is, among many other usages, a spinning term, meaning to draw a few strands of "roving" (carded—meaning, combed-out—but unspun wool) and feed it into a rapidly turning spindle, which turns it into thread. "Drafting (or simply "spinning") from the fold" means to fold a few threads of the unspun material ("roving") over your index finger and feed it to the spindle from there. The trick with drafting from the fold is to hold not too much not too tightly in that loop over the index finger—precisely the same concept governing DuPlessis's formal concerns: not too much formal control, enough flexibility to guide the spinning/writing forward and backward across the whole *Drafts* series, sampling, revising, refuting, realigning previous phrases, notions, threads of logic or association, moving forward by moving as a spiral in a spinning gyre.

Turning to "Draft 20," we note that its title, "Incipit," is an expansion-from-inside of the title of "Draft 1," its "donor draft," "It" (*TR* 86–95; *TF* 28–31). "It begins." But it doesn't—it began nineteen poems ago! If something begins here, it begins not as its first or final manifestation but as one of many serial iterations. What begins here is not the poem but the folding, which, as noted above, is one of the poem's central defining characteristics. When does life begin? When does an "it" become a being in the world? Politically fraught questions are nestled in this womb of a word, "it," with its inner potential ("ncipi") expanding and increasing in complexity at every iteration! Autopoiesis! Poem as parthenogenetic entity! In "Draft 1: It," we find:

> Silences are the reaches of discourse
> (rich incipit's big initials)
> There is a yes and a no walled/welled up
> (*TR* 95)

–hidden in the s/well/ing (pregnant) parentheses, the word "incipit," tantalizingly both emphasized with its "rich"ness and "big initials" and diminished by its coy placement in its sotto voce womb of parentheses—it's both a yes and a no, both inhibited (walled up) and threatening overspill (welled up). Just as "silences" are both the structuring element and the obverse of "sound," enabling and disabling (silence=death vs. silence is golden), so silence borders discourse as an emphatic frame and at the same time threatens discourse with negation. Poetry, that play of black and white on the page (which is silence? which sound?), is both urgent and opaque—and has been characterized as "anti-discourse," not in the sense of obliterating discourse but in the sense of defining it through its adjacency thereto. It is a body yet to be born and also its enveloping body that is both threatened by and enhanced by the "life inside," if life i(ncipi)t is.

"The fold" is a feminist trope: a pleat, a plait, a plaint, a plea. The Deleuzian fold is an EVENT, namely the process of subjectification through folding internal and external, surfaces becoming depths, and so on, as in collaging, layering, the laying of one element on top of/athwart/in relation to another, in complementarity/juxtaposition/resonant difference. The individual, for example, assimilates external stimuli, folding it into their consciousness so that it becomes internal. These thousands of folds come to constitute the subject itself (O'Sullivan). As Luce Irigaray has pointed out (with specific reference to the labia, an obvious element here), folding is also an erotic practice owing to the intense intimacy that comprises such internalization. It is a bodily caressing of stimuli that transforms them, as an anemone devours and transforms a curious organism. Through *Drafts* and other exploratory workings that foreground inquiry and process, the poet infolds and creates her subjectivity from the remnants gathered from her textual, sociohistorical, and material environment, and invites us to do the same as we internalize (by reading) her words. We draw them from an external surface (the page or screen) into our consciousness; we interiorize them and recreate them in our own images. It's clear how these rhizomatic relations resonate with a practice of collage, appliqué, bricolage, and so forth, layering, juxtaposing, and fixing (through sewing, gluing, nailing, and more) pieces of material on top of each other to create either a functional object, a picture, art object, or all simultaneously. Moreover, in a comment that seems to perfectly sum up DuPlessis's ethos and method, architecture critic Greg Lynn observes of the "folded architecture's" ability to resolve opposites—typical of the baroque era—that "if there is a single effect produced in architecture by folding, it will be the ability to integrate unrelated elements within a new continuous mixture" (Lynn, Livesey). We can think of poetry as a body whose organs are enfolded therein.

The Fold, which gives its name to "Drafts 15–XXX," comprises the first ten of the reworked poems, as the folding-over process DuPlessis envisions starts with "Draft 20" revisiting "Draft 1," "Draft 21" revisiting "Draft 2," "Draft 22" revisiting "Draft 3," and so forth. The fold is not only, as noted, a rich theoretical concept introduced into the post-structuralist philosophical canon by Gilles Deleuze. It is also an exceptionally useful trope for all kinds of material and conceptual doublings, layerings, and other processes that are important in textual and textile process, bookmaking, alphabetic writing, collaging. It is, needless to say, a highly gendered trope (think of many depictions of rich folds of female flesh enrobed in or partially disrobed from rich folds of fabric that dominate many periods of Western art and of the terms in which genitalia are described). In short, many of the practices and guiding principles that mark DuPlessis's creative career are wrapped up in, held in netful suspension in, and, yes, enfolded into this capacious coziness.

Another form of folding is the works' constant self-referentiality; from "Draft 52: Midrash":

> an impossible draft of half-built, half-crumbled
> all-suspicious poetry.
> (*P* 156)

From *Surge: Drafts 96–114*: "Draft 104: The Book":

> There is no actual book, but it does exist.
> ....
>
> *The book, traveling backward, holds a smaller book, which it is reading.*
> ....
>
> A door is a hinge. A book is another.
> Opening a book is like tripping over a threshold
> A book is one gloss of the book.
> (74)

From "Draft 51: Clay Songs":

> 7. I am hot floating
> Calligraphy. A running script
> on the raging subject.
> 19 columns of impacted writing...
> (*P* 135)

Such examples could proliferate ad, possibly, infinitum.

V. *Numbers:* The Obvious Analogy Is with Quilting, Felting, Weaving, Collage, Intertextuality

In "Piecing and Writing," a fairly well-known text from the golden era of second-wave feminist literary scholarship that has been rediscovered under the rubric of an emergent "textile studies," feminist literary critic Elaine Showalter proposes quilting as the most appropriate metaphor for a "Female Aesthetic" and critical practice, drawing on now-familiar tropes of reuse ("upcycling" in current conservational jargon), community rituals (quilting bees), antihierarchical processes (a valorization of the small pieces that are successively assembled into larger units in either traditional or inventive—or both—patterns and designs), and distracted composition (piecework allows meaningful amounts of material to be assembled in any unit of time, no matter how small, typical of women's multitasking daily routines), and the blurring of domesticity and creativity, art and life, or more specifically, "high art" and random artisanal, functionally oriented bricolage, a make-do aesthetic chore with occasionally remarkable results ("The New Feminist"; "Piecing"). Showalter cites DuPlessis's "For the Etruscans" in an early observation that, though we would now most strenuously object to phrases such as "a pure women's writing"—the phrase is Showalter's not DuPlessis's—and indeed the notion of a simple category that conflates "female" and "woman," these phrases could be said to forecast the ways in which her poetics developed in *Drafts*. The word "drafts" has multifarious uses and finds equal frequency in the textile worlds (in spinning, the process of pulling strands of material into the force field of the rapidly rotating spindle, thus creating thread or yarn out of the mass of fluff—earlier mentioned is the process called "drafting from the fold," which gives a special structure and texture to the yarn; in weaving, pattern creation through drawing charts; in sewing, the process of transferring bodily measurements onto a paper pattern, etc.) as it (the word "draft") does in the writing world, where it primarily indicates a first, second, or any nonfinal effort at an undertaking, be it a poem, an essay, or a book. In quilting, the term usually refers to a direct process of "intertextuality," as it were, of copying a quilt design by tracing one block of a presumably repeating-pattern quilt and transferring it to another surface for the purpose of either changing its size or transposing it to another context—such as a new quilt with different colors or other alterations—where it can be redesigned or used as the basis for new pattern. In the cited passage, Showalter attributes to DuPlessis the notion that a "pure women's writing [the phrase is Showalter's] would be 'non-hierarchic . . . breaking the hierarchical structures, making an even display of elements over the surface with no climactic place or moment, having the materials organized into many centers.' In the 'verbal quilt' of the feminist text, there is 'no subordination, no ranking'" ("The New Feminist" 274). While contemporary feminist literary scholarship has left behind the concept that there is one "women's tradition" that has essential characteristics in either literary or textile production, it cannot be denied that this nexus provided a powerful set of tropes that has carried over to the current emergence of the centrality of "material culture" in the humanities in general and in poetry and poetics more specifically. In that turn to materialist studies' intermeshing with literary and language studies, DuPlessis participates with other artists such as Cecilia Vicuña, Elaine Reichek, and Francesca Capone, and scholars such as Tiya Miles, Megan Sweeney, Julia Bryan-Wilson, Elizabeth Barber, Victoria Mitchell, Amy Elkins, and many others—see the recent proliferation of conferences, panels, and gallery and museum exhibitions whose titles prominently include the words "text," "textile," "line," "thread(s)," and so forth.

The language of women's textile culture finds another particularly poignant textual counterpart in the notion of "sampling." In the textile world, the "sampler" is now an artifact of the preindustrial European girl's achieving both semi-literacy (knowledge of the alphabet, numbers one to twenty, and a few prayers or domestically themed maxims such as "home is where the heart is") and the ability to execute simple stitches that will thenceforth adorn her household linens with monograms and basic shapes: flowers, birds, hearts. It is a display of both semi-mastery and subjection—that is, of knowing just enough to be able to do one's job. In the literary world, the term "sampling" has migrated from the hip-hop world to simply be a synonym for "intertextuality," meaning, dropping a reference to a previous work into one's own to give it depth, texture, semiotic intensity, historical context, and so forth—to construct a map of one's artistic ancestors within the work itself—and also to talk back, to alter the narrative. It is a way of displaying mastery and erudition, of drawing one's authority from familiarity with precedence. From the PIE root "em"—to take or distribute—"sampl[ing]" is an instance of enfolding—taking and distributing—extant work into the construction of a new work, and placing or interlacing it throughout. DuPlessis's work engages both inferences in its refusal of an overbearing, over-serious mastery at the same time as it displays intimacy through its deft deployment of hints of the vast range of texts and histories with which it converses.

And the history of collage itself is generally offered as emerging in the nineteenth century as a genteel women's hobby—scrapbooking—that was an acceptable way for women to express their creativity: a process of assembling, with scissors and adhesive against a dark page, bits and pieces from greeting cards, printed musical or theatrical programs, any kind of prepublished textual or visual artifacts whose consumption reflected their tastes and pastimes as class and gender markers. The works were not intended for publication and indeed were considered private, visual analogs to, for example, a written diary. Only in the era of high modernism did the practice become one of high art and, predictably, migrated to the mostly male art world, only to be reclaimed by a select few women artists (prominently, Hannah Höch and Mina Loy from the Dada era, then Lee Krasner and Nancy Spero, and more recently still, many more including Kara Walker, Mickalene Thomas, Wangechi Mutu, and Lorna Simpson) as they are claimed or reclaimed from obscurity over time. As Joanna Fuhrman points out, "Collage appeals to feminist artists like Martha Rosler because it's talking back/recontextualizing 'mainstream' culture/taking and reframing. Lots of poets might do something equivalent." DuPlessis sees herself in both high-art modernist and women's popular—if not quite populist cultural—traditions, antihierarchically refusing those very distinctions. One could say that collage is a practice of "sampling"—"selection and combination, like . . . pretty much . . . anything else," to use Nada Gordon's words—from among the overwhelming tsunami of visual, digital, and textual detritus swirling around us at every moment.

Intertextuality, which formed the bedrock of the protracted philosophical and historical inquiry that comprised *Drafts*, takes another permutation, another fold, in *Numbers*, a volume that belongs neither to *Drafts* nor to *Traces* (DuPlessis refers to these nonserial books as "interstitial"). For many years a collage artist in her "nonprofessional" life, DuPlessis has long seen her visual art practice (aside from exercising great control over her books' cover images) as distinct from her writing, both her poetry and her scholarly essays. This has started to change; in 2013 we conducted a mutual interview about our respective relationships to our manual/visual practices compared to our relationships to our writing practices, which she titled "Desiring Visual Texts: A Collage and Embroidery Dialogue"; in 2018 she published *Numbers* with Materialist Press (about which more below); moreover, a crowdsourced project in which she collected old-fashioned handkerchiefs, created collages from them, and wrote poems to accompany them, has been published as *Life in Handkerchiefs*, also from Materialist Press (2023). If collage is a form of intertextuality, then intertextuality is likewise a form of collage, as well as quilting, appliqué, enmeshment, felting, overwriting, and so on. Textual practice is genealogically and materially—not merely etymologically—indebted to textile practice (to give just one simple example, the same raw materials are used to create paper and cloth, and the latter still plays a large role in the creation of the former). Referring to older texts, embedding them in a current text, is an upcycling or a reuse that is not so much on trend as traditional, endlessly present into human prehistory. Conversely, by collecting delicate scraps from a variety of acquaintances, locations, and temporal moments (souvenirs, etc.), DuPlessis extends, in the handkerchief book, the notion of intertextuality to include one's social, affective, familial, and professional networks, enmeshing us in each other's lives through potential representation in a printed book with color illustrations—not whole, but in pieces, subjected to the author/artist's excisions, recombinations, and repurposings.

There's a wonderstruck quality to *Numbers*, as there is in most of DuPlessis's poetry, at both the rational/coherent/"cosmological" and the irrational/random/"artisanal" elements of the presence of numbers in our lives—a Kabbalistic logic interexists with a sense of contingency and accident. (To take just one instance, the irrational number pi turns out to be the crux—or rather the center around which her enchanted puzzlement circles—that solves a number of crucial—"real life"—geometrical questions.) This sense of wonderment is encapsulated in the two phrases—"artisanal cosmology" and "one-woman collage Kabbalah"—that I've selected for special notice and is further borne out in the remarkable and endearing acknowledgment, in the "Background" section of the paratextual "Background and Notes," that "mathematical discussions on Wikipedia were incredibly valuable, even when (after their first paragraphs) I could not understand any word in certain statements except for the word 'the'" (*N* 107). There is a gutsiness in admitting that one is using numbers not functionally but as elements in a symbolic system whose cultural resonances are ultimately more important than their utilitarian purposes; it instantiates a switcheroo of the more standard line taken on "pseudo-sciences" like astrology, numerology, tarot, mythologies, religious trappings, and beliefs of all kinds: that they are significant not for their truth value but for the marvelous cultural institutions and hermeneutic activities they enable. Symbol systems, even those of arithmetic and mathematics, are there to be used, informed, reformed, and deformed.

Published by the aforementioned and appropriately named Materialist Press in 2018, *Numbers* explicitly ties DuPlessis's collage practice to her poetry. Ariel Resnikoff, one of the founding editors of Materialist Press, describes the press as

> an intermittent press, publishing when we have the means extremely high-quality material objects as books, often hand printed, handbound. The name of the press, if I remember correctly, comes from a play or extension (expansion) on the Objectivist Press, started by my cousin, the elder [Charles] Reznikoff, and also signals our interest in providing a specifically material-oriented space for publishing as a constituent to the rich and vibrant digital publishing realms. In this sense, the term materialist is not oppositional exactly, but co-operative and our notion of materialism becomes a way of seeing (thinking of Rezzy) and a way of being, through physical making, as much from the side of poetry as from the textility of printing and book arts.

The "textility" of DuPlessis's collages is, for the first time, featured as diegetic material in *Numbers*, in addition to adorning the cover; moreover, the book is bound by hand-stitching in a limited edition of two hundred. Thus, there has been movement over the last decade or so toward integration: in our 2013 conversation it seemed the collage work was envisioned as separate, if alimentary and supplementary, to the writing. In *Numbers*, however, the collages are presented alongside poetry, and indeed it would be difficult to determine which, if either, is primary or anterior and which secondary or ancillary—whether the language illuminates the collages or vice versa (Damon and DuPlessis).

There is, of course, another strand of cultural tradition that feeds into DuPlessis's generative matrix of influences beside that of women's and feminist concerns, and which cannot be neatly separated from it—namely, the aforementioned weight of Jewish culture or cultures with its or their sacred and secular, orthodox and mystical, colloquial and exalted histories, languages, and sensibilities. The concept of the "fold," for example, can refer equally to the processes of Midrash or Talmud, elaborations of commentary upon/beside/behind/around commentary, as it does to the erotics of subjectification. In the back matter alongside the generative "artisanal cosmology," we find an equally rich and idiosyncratic phrase wherein DuPlessis refers to *Numbers* as a "one-woman collage kabbalah," an epithet that functions as a kind of synonymous and yet internally antonymous counterbalance to the aforementioned descriptor. And, like "artisanal cosmology," the vivid phrase also works as an overdetermined DuPlessisism, a gendered manifesto that announces a twinned aesthetic (collage) and cultural/religious (Kabbalah) agenda/practice/ambition. Seizing control of the Kabbalah back from the exclusive male world that has traditionally comprised orthodox Kabbalah scholarship, and putting her highly individualistic stamp on a cultural and hermeneutic tradition of centuries-long (if not millennia-long) standing, DuPlessis announces her collage practice as a method of interpretation. Collage is not merely an artistic practice of recycling that brings aesthetic and haptic pleasure but a hermeneutic that generates meaning as well as material—that is, "creative" and "analytical" practices are not temporally or disciplinarily separate activities but co-foundational and simultaneous.

That creation of meaning starts, like the creation of genesis, with chaos and darkness. The first poem to appear is "Dark Matter," out of which comes color, language, form. The second poem is still prefatory to the ground zero of the book, as it were, "PREFACE/to a book," and concludes by invoking, in a defiant rhyme, the opposite of a divinely ordained cosmology:

> ... For failure is a definite part
> of the endless debris
> and practices of art.
>
> (*N* 4)

The zestful embrace of failure and failed material (debris) that precedes and colors a project that takes on the world of numbers, the Jewish mystical tradition, and the modernist domain of the collage is thoroughly characteristic of DuPlessis's fearlessness. Acknowledgment of failure not as a glitch but as a feature of aesthetic practice goes hand in hand with a palpable pleasure in thinking-in-language that defines DuPlessis's engagement with the world.

VI. (Anti-/In) Conclusion?

During the course of the writing/compiling/collaging/piecing-together of this essay, I undertook a weeklong, durational performance not intended as such. In trying to salvage an enormous, moth-eaten, tangled mass of silk yarn I had inherited from a friend who no longer weaves, I turned it, over the course of several stages and days that involved soaking it overnight and hanging it to dry, into a ball, or clew (from which comes our word "clue") of yarn that could be repurposed for a new project. I turned it and turned it, creating an ever-larger sphere. I didn't want to be doing anything else. What is it that is so satisfying about this process, a mindless and not especially productive one? After all, the moths had ensured that no single strand of the tangle was more than five yards long or so, and many fragments were just a few inches (I discarded those shorter than a foot and a half but later salvaged these thrums from the waste basket for their own little pile). It was a process of unfolding (the tangle) and refolding (the wound ball of yarn) in which my fingers passed over every inch of the material. I realized it was completely analogous to DuPlessis's project of salvaging every shred of detritus of our human life and consciousness and folding it into a spiraling sequence. Moreover, what I'm generously calling this "durational performance" came to a climax in the late afternoon of Yom Kippur, a day in which, while I fasted, I gave myself the liberty of terming this salvaging process a spiritual practice. Shaky and delirious, with pulsing black rings around my vision, I saw myself suddenly as a figure in a fairy tale or myth, a crone in a cave winding an endless clew with equally endless metaphoric possibilities. With the simultaneous grandiosity and humility that can accompany such mental conditions, I realized—or imagined—I was, like DuPlessis, engaged in a miniature process of *tikkun olam*, "healing the world," in an impossibly infinite task, and one marked by both self-delusion and skepticism (i.e., optimism of the will, pessimism of the intellect) My recognition was prompted by the fact that I was making a sphere, a globe—the earth, the "world," our orb, with bits and tatters hanging off it, each strand held on by the successive strands binding it to the core—like a poem or like an essay in which there are countless digressions and unintegrated aperçus. I saw in my obsessive activity the sense of possibility, doggedness, joy that bespeaks DuPlessis's feminist diasporic resilience, based as it is in a historically pragmatic faith in reuse (possibly metonymic for "redemption?" but always with a question mark), and yet with sustained Sisyphean skepticism and self-irony. Forgiveness and atonement—of self, of other, of the human mess—in the form of a making-better, an upcycling, a salvage. I learned later that the great anthropologist Mary Douglas has hypothesized that "according to the illustrative cases from Leviticus, to atone means to cover, or recover, cover again, to repair a hole, cure a sickness, mend a rift, make good a torn or broken covering. As a noun, what is translated as atonement, expiation, or purgation means integument made good; conversely, the examples in the book indicate that Atonement does not mean covering a sin so as to hide it from the sight of God; it means making good an outer layer that has rotted or been pierced" (117–18).

These were exactly my circumstances with the moth-eaten yarn that had been intact and become corrupted, pierced, and rotten, something holey in need of being made holy—something that however also (always) has been continuously holy. Douglas goes on to argue that, though the book of Leviticus appears to be "disorderly, repetitive," and "scattered" in its obsession with the topic of defilement, this shambolic repetition is in fact a careful way of rhetorically structuring the central significance of atonement. This creative feint, the valuing of a disorderly surface in service of a greater intellectual honesty and clarity, the deliberate engagement of repetition that risks the appearance of "dithering" or obsession, the willingness to "think aloud" to address difficult historical and cultural wounds, these all characterize DuPlessis's work. (Not accidentally, the book of the Pentateuch that follows Leviticus is Numbers, the title of DuPlessis's hand-stitch-bound volume that, as mentioned, centers the poet's visual collage work, collage also instantiating the process of gathering and remaking shreds and torn bits into a new whole.)

This study by Douglas, the modern ethnographic expert on "purity and impurity," does not address the aesthetic element of the book (any book), the pleasure of rhetorically or otherwise constructing a text or making something (anything), its poiesis, be it a foundational cultural text like Leviticus, a serial poem, or a ball of yarn that is merely an early step in some future and as yet unknown project. The why and how of the pleasure of it I will leave to phenomenologists and neurobiologists, but *Drafts'* literary text/textile nexus and its interfoldings, both intricate and simple, smooth and chaotic, linear and fractal, reverberate in our leisure/labor. And dare I suggest that this combination of pleasure and labor, in DuPlessis's work, instantiates a feminist practice? Artisanal cosmology in text and in textile, fully encircling a multi-arts lifework.

Works Cited

"Art Exhibits." Mina Loy: Navigating the Avant-Garde, https://mina-loy.com/galleries/. Accessed 3 June 2023.

"Audre Lorde." Poetry Foundation, https://www.poetryfoundation.org/poets/audre-lorde/. Accessed 5 June 2023.

Barber, E. J. W. *Prehistoric Textiles: The Development of Cloth in the Neolithic and Bronze Ages with Special Reference to the Aegean*. Princeton: Princeton University Press, 1992.

Benjamin, Walter. "The Storyteller." *Illuminations*, translated by Harry Zohn. New York: Schocken, 1968, 83–109.

Bryan-Wilson, Julia. *Fray: Art and Textile Politics*. Chicago: University of Chicago Press, 2017.

Capone, Francesca. Francesca Capone, https://www.francescacapone.com/. Accessed 5 June 2023.

Cixous, Hélène. "The Laugh of the Medusa." Translated by Keith Cohen and Paula Cohen. *Signs*, vol. 1, no. 4, 1976, 875.

Damon, Maria, and Rachel Blau DuPlessis. "Desiring Visual Texts: A Collage and Embroidery Dialogue." *Jacket2*, 25 Mar. 2013, https://jacket2.org/article/desiring-visual-texts.

"Cecilia Vicuña." Cecilia Vicuña, http://www.ceciliavicuna.com/. Accessed 5 June 2023.

"Collages." Lorna Simpson, https://lsimpsonstudio.com/collages. Accessed 5 June 2023.

Creeley, Robert. Lecture. 7 July 1977, Naropa Institute.

Deleuze, Gilles. *The Fold: Leibniz and the Baroque*. Translated by Tom Conley. Minneapolis: University of Minnesota Press, 1993.

DiFeo, Jay. *The Rose*. 1958–1966, Whitney Museum of American Art.

Douglas, Mary. "Atonement in Leviticus." *Jewish Studies Quarterly*, vo. 1, no. 2, 1993, 109–30.

Duncan, Robert. "Sonnet 4." *Bending the Bow*. New York: New Directions, 1968, 3.

DuPlessis, Rachel Blau. *Life in Handkerchiefs*. Cincinnati, OH: Materialist Press, 2023.
———. *Numbers*. Cincinnati, OH: Materialist Press, 2018.
———. *Surge: Drafts 96–114*. Cromer Norfolk, UK: Salt Publishing, 2013.
———. "Midrashic Sensibilities." *Radical Poetics and Secular Jewish Culture*, edited by Stephen Paul Miller and Daniel Morris. Tuscaloosa: University of Alabama Press, 2009, 199–224.
———. *Drafts 39–57, Pledge, with Draft, Unnumbered: Précis*. Cambridge, UK: Salt Publishing, 2004.
———. *Drafts 15–XXX, The Fold*. Elmwood, CT: Potes & Poets Press, 1997.
———. *Tabula Rosa*. Elmwood, CT: Potes & Poets Press, 1987.
———. "For the Etruscans." *New Feminist Criticism*, edited by Elaine Showalter. New York: Pantheon, 1985, XX.
"Elaine Reichek." Elaine Reichek, http://elainereichek.com/. Accessed 5 June 2023.
Elkins, Amy. *Crafting Feminism from Literary Modernism to the Multimedia Present*. Oxford: Oxford University Press, 2022.
Fuhrman, Joanna. Facebook response to a "social experiment" in outsourcing research, 30 Oct. 2022. https://www.facebook.com/maria.damon.3/posts/pfbid02wYfNS8E5X6qSPFZzd8fb8gwLEHymKmrVBwqBwScBppSy2NFUcgxk3idBUXjEaLLSl.
Gordon, Nada. Facebook response to a "social experiment" in outsourcing research, Facebook, 30 Oct. 2022, https://www.facebook.com/maria.damon.3/posts/pfbid02wYfNS8E5X6qSPFZzd8fb8gwLEHymKmrVBwqBwScBppSy2NFUcgxk3idBUXjEaLLSl (page discontinued).
"Hannah Höch." Museum of Modern Art, https://www.moma.org/artists/2675#works. Accessed 5 June 2023.
Ingold, Tim. "Bringing Things to Life: Creative Entanglements in a World of Materials," workshop at the Institute of Advanced Study, University of Minnesota, 1 Apr. 2010, http://eprints.ncrm.ac.uk/1306/1/0510_creative_entanglements.pdf.
Irigaray, Luce. "When Our Lips Speak Together." Translated by Carolyn Burke. *Signs*, vol. 6, no. 1, 1980, 69–79.
Jaussen, Paul. "The Poetics of Midrash in Rachel Blau DuPlessis's *Drafts*." *Contemporary Literature*, vol. 53, no. 1, 2012, 114–42.
"Kara Walker." Kara Walker, http://www.karawalkerstudio.com/. Accessed 5 June 2023.
Livesey, Graham. "Fold and Architecture." *The Deleuze Dictionary*. Edinburgh: Edinburgh University Press, 2010, 109, https://anarch.cc/uploads/adrian-parr/deleuze-dictionary.pdf.
Livingston, Ira. "Poetics as a Theory of Everything." Poetics Lab, 2015, http://poeticslab.com/works/1_poetics_as_a_theory_of_everything/.
Lynn, Greg. "Architectural Curvilinearity: The Folded, the Pliant and the Supple." *Architectural Design*, 1993, 3–4.

"Mickalene Thomas." Mickalene Thomas, http://mickalenethomas.com/. Accessed 5 June 2023.

Miles, Tiya. *All That She Carried: The Journey of Ashley's Sack, a Black Family Keepsake*. New York: Random House, 2021.

Miller, Nancy, editor. *The Poetics of Gender*. New York: Columbia University Press, 1986.

Miller, Stephen Paul, and Daniel Morris. *Radical Poetics and Secular Jewish Culture*. Tuscaloosa: University of Alabama Press, 2009.

Mitchell, Victoria. "A Marketplace in Miniature: Norwich Pattern Books as Cultural Agency." Textile Society of America Symposium Proceedings, 2008, https://digitalcommons.unl.edu/cgi/viewcontent.cgi?article=1221&context=tsaconf.

Mossin, Andrew R. E-mail to the author. 10 June 2021.

Mutu, Wangechi. "Resonant Surgeries: The Collaged World of Wangechi Mutu." *Bordercrossings*, Feb. 2008, https://bordercrossingsmag.com/article/resonant-surgeries-the-collaged-world-of-wangechi-mutu.

"Nancy Spero." Museum of Modern Art, https://www.moma.org/artists/5564. Accessed 5 June 2023.

O'Sullivan, Simon. "The Fold." *The Deleuze Dictionary*. Edinburgh: Edinburgh University Press, 2010, 108–09, https://anarch.cc/uploads/adrian-parr/deleuze-dictionary.pdf.

Resnikoff, Ariel. E-mail to the author. 15 Aug. 2022.

Rosen, Marianna. "Lee Krasner, Collage Paintings." Fine Art Globe, 12 Apr. 2021, https://fineartglobe.com/artists/lee-krasner-collage-paintings/.

Showalter, Elaine. "Piecing and Writing." *The Textile Reader*, edited by Jessica Hemmings. London: 2012, 157–70. Originally published in *The Poetics of Gender*, edited by Nancy Miller. New York: Columbia University Press, 1986, 222–47.

———, editor. *The New Feminist Criticism*. New York: Pantheon, 1985.

Stein, Gertrude. "Poetry and Grammar." *Lectures in America*. Boston: Beacon Press, 1985, 207–46.

———. *Four in America*. New Haven: Yale University Press, 1947.

———. "Sacred Emily." 1913. *Geography and Plays*. Boston: Four Seas Co., 1922, 178–88.

Sweeney, Megan. *Mendings*. Durham: Duke University Press, 2023.

Williams, William Carlos. "Paterson." Internet Archive, https://archive.org/stream/PatersonWCW/Paterson-William_Carlos_Williams_djvu.txt.

CHAPTER FIVE

"daily politics, weird shit"

*Feminist Weak Resistance and Waste in
Rachel Blau DuPlessis's Later Work*

ERIC KEENAGHAN

> But who cares about your little life except
> you, a family few, a friend or two
> given
> the politics of "our time"
> the politics of space and resources sexual politics
> race-laden
> politics
> the politics of agency   the politics of no agency protective
> politics
> proactive politics   water, water, water
>
> daily politics, weird shit,
>
> encrypted politics, complicity and loss—
>
> —Rachel Blau DuPlessis, "Summer Poem"

I. "daily politics," or Weak Resistance and Poetry

How can we do politics today? What is "the politics of 'our time,'" as Rachel Blau DuPlessis phrases it in "Summer Poem" (*LW* 108)? Such questions assume we know what politics *are* or that assigning politics some categorical definition *matters*. We all can name forms of recognizable political activity, sanctioned and legible and public: punditry, direct actions, labor strikes, electoral campaigns, grassroots organizing. Most self-identified activists usually participate in at least one, even several, of these forms. At times, just not *all* the time, though, simply living, being visible or heard in other ways functions as another kind of politics. We minoritized Americans—women and queer folk, racial and ethnic minorities, religious cultural minorities, the undocumented and refugees, the disabled—we know that not only is living itself a struggle but *how* one lives can prove an engine for smaller-scale change and transformation. Despite criticisms like Murray Bookchin's reproach of "lifestyle declamations" as "socially innocuous" and "narcissistic anarchism," the visibilizing and revaluation of what is unseen, discounted, or pushed to the margins *can* positively change others' attitudes, their perceptions, and even their ways of living (Bookchin 25). The legitimization only of the old ways of doing politics or activism obstinately clings to certain preconceptions that, as Situationist Raoul Vaneigem once warned, merely supply "the illusion of being together" (39). As he goes on to note, "Real community remains to be created" out of the micropolitical and microsocial experiences of everyday life (39).

Feminism, particularly, has been attuned to the need to count as activism less spectacular, less visible activities. Institutional or systemic change might not arise directly from minoritized people's and populations' living examples or experiences. Nonetheless, what emerge are the jumping-off points for change, materials one can work with, immediately, to refashion how life is lived and understood. A quarter-century ago Nancy Fraser argued for "the broadening of that designation [of the political] to encompass issues classically viewed as 'cultural,' 'private,' 'economic,' 'domestic,' and 'personal'"; and she added, "The question about the limits of [what constitutes] the political is precisely a *political* question" (6; Fraser's emphasis). More recently, Sara Ahmed has noted that merely posing such questions is disruptive, challenging the status quo. "Feminism is sensational. . . . We learn about the feminist cause by the bother feminism causes; by how feminism comes up in public culture as a site of disturbance" (21). Such disturbance is sensational in a second sense of the word too, for an inclination to question the established order of things originates in one's singular perceptions. "Feminism begins with sensation: with the sense of things" (21). It begins as "a sensible reaction to the injustices of the world, which we might register at first through our own experiences" and through "the failure to be habituated to a gender system" (21, 55). "I am suggesting feminism is homework," Ahmed contends; it is a pedagogical lesson, often beginning with, and continually reconducted in, one's home "because we have much to work out from not being at home in the world" (7). The resulting willfulness, persistently resisting the mere possibility of injustice in both private and public settings, so often felt becomes "a style of politics," not merely the sorts of politics of style disapproved of by Bookchin and other leftists (Ahmed 82). "How easily willfulness is confused with, and reduced to, individualism" by those who oppose feminist change, Ahmed writes. "We need to resist this reduction. The reduction is how willful subjects are dismissed" (83). It is how the change feminists argue for, via their dishabituated everyday interactions and their lived unlearning of gender and other social roles, is discounted. But such a willful political style, in actuality, does produce community and collective legacy, traceable in and discovered through small, often unrecorded exchanges like personal conversations and, as Ahmed models, through literature like Toni Morrison's *The Bluest Eye* (1970) or Virginia Woolf's *Mrs. Dalloway* (1925).

Teaching, writing, working in our communities, modeling good citizenship for younger generations, simply existing *as if* we could live openly with our desires and values are inherently politicized forms of living. The verb participles at the start of my preceding sentence suggest that this sort of life politics is a doing, that it exists *in* or *through* the doing. As such, politics really are not a category of activity. Instead they are *the activity itself*, encompassing the thinking and the working out of the theories in the doing. Anarchists call this prefiguration, an antipolitical politics that "rejects standard universalist, rationalist, naturalist versions [of knowledge production and political action]" and instead prioritizes the idea "that knowledge is generated through practical activities, and it is through these that objectives are identified and realized in social practices" (Franks 32). Ahmed's term "sweaty concepts" is apropos here, in how her idea designates a sense of how "concepts are at work in how we work, whatever it is that we do" and how "concepts are in the worlds we are in," rather than some metaphysical plane of abstraction (12, 13).

Prefigurative, sweaty conceptual work constitutes an expressionistic and passional micropolitics, positional or situational. It is not a sentimental kind of personal politics rooted in fixed identifications and illusions of community or self-expressive personal interiority. Quite the contrary. Life-based activism, like what one finds in writing and the lives of writers, dynamically emerges out of transformative processes of *becoming*, rather than grounded in identifications and pretenses of static *being*. "The problem is not that of being free but of finding a way out, or even a way in, another side, a hallway, an adjacency," Gilles Deleuze and Félix Guattari theorize about what they call minor, rather than minority, literature (8). Such political writing, as an active searching for a way of living, is no longer based on representation but instead constitutes "a materially intense expression" of new possibilities, rooted in the substance of the writing itself, language pushed to and testing its limits (19). "Language stops being representative in order to now move toward its extremities and limits" (23). For minor literatures, "everything in them is political" and has "a collective value" (17). Elsewhere Deleuze differentiates such collective expressionism from self-expression. Expressionism, his preferred term, is rooted in singular bodies and their passions, which give rise to what he, following Spinoza, terms "joy." That affect, in turn, stimulates a conceptualization of, and feeling for, commonality. "When we encounter a body that agrees with our own, when we experience a joyful passive affection, we are induced to form the idea of what is common to that body and our own" (Deleuze, *Expressionism* 282). In political contexts, we might call such a feeling "solidarity."

Joyful, solidary feeling and activity are modeled by a form of positional, everyday micropolitics Polish antifascist feminist Ewa Majewska dubs "weak resistance." Don't let the word "weak" fool you. Majewska's term suggests "an interesting shift from the patriarchal heroic vision of agency" predominating public sphere and political theory (128). Rather than treating political agency, especially resistive and protesting agencies, as residing in strong, solitary leaders and organizers, those who practice "exceptionality and heroic gestures" in the legitimated political field, she prefers to think of "genuine politics" as "requir[ing] persistence and everyday life strategies" (135). Politicized counter-publics emerge through everyday sociality happening in the margins, often unnoticed. In these spaces, forgetting, making mistakes, and learning through trial and error constitute the experience of developing new political imaginaries and new senses of social relationship. It's a messy affair, this meaning-making. Solidarity and commonality between otherwise distinct groups can grow out of such positive (as in, *acting toward*), rather than negative (as in, *acting against*), active configurations of resistance.

This is all to say, activism—particularly feminist activism—can and does happen on the microscale, through small, often unnoticed activities and experiences in both the private and public spheres that people, no matter their identifications or affiliations, can relate to. It's the stuff of poetry. In contrast with the New Left personal politics of the 1960s, contemporary micropolitics of weak resistance, by pointing to *shared activities* and *shared experiences*, better foreground connections across usually divisive or categorizing lines of identification. Perhaps the more quotidian the experiences the better, so long as the social actors can infuse those activities with new meanings. Recognizing others as doing similar things can be a start for such resignification. "Today we witness the growing popularity of alternatives to the classical, Western, masculine, white, individualist, straight and heroic subject of political agency, where the multitude of ordinary, weak, feminine, queer, trans, Black, ordinary subjects produce historical changes through their differences—but also through their commonality" (Majewska 140). Weak resistance is a starting point for solidarity, out of which grow imaginaries disrupting heteronormative patriarchy. "Comrade relations are relations of a new type, relations that disrupt the confines of the family, heteropatriarchy, and binary gender," Jodi Dean argues in relationship to the egalitarian bonds between activists (64). It is "a relation that cuts through the determinations [i.e., identity constructs] given by the present"; "identity has nothing to do with comradeship—it's about work, the work of building socialism" (66, 67). Or we might qualify that idea: it's about the work of world-building and -transformation, regardless of any ideological markers that might motivate some to take up such labor.[1]

Rachel Blau DuPlessis's work, especially since the start of the millennium, demonstrates much consciousness—and self-consciousness—about how the writing and reading of poetry are sites of weak resistance, or what she calls "daily politics" (*LW* 108). Such literary exercises entail both "the politics of agency" and "the politics of no agency," as they entail choice and will, and they can prove subjectively transformative but rarely produce immediate institutional, social, or systemic change (*LW* 108). Furthermore, the doing of poetry—reading and writing it, as well as reading while writing it—is a participatory exercise. Following the work of Jonathan Culler, though extending his theory beyond its exclusively lyric focus, I would argue that DuPlessis approaches such poetic doing as a performative activity. Her writing calls into being new subjects and relations through its ability "to create effects of presence" and depends on readers to complete the experience, "that the reader be not just a listener or an audience but also a performer of the lines—that he or she [or they] come to occupy, at least temporarily, the position of speaker and audibly or inaudibly voice the language of the poem, which can expand the possibilities of his or her discourse" (Culler 37). When the poems have a material dimension, as in DuPlessis's paradoxically collagist lyric, which I discuss in the next section, that interactive performance and performativity becomes all the sweatier, all the more embodied, as the poet's and readers' attentions are drawn to the materials of the poems, to the material world and social conditions from which they originated.[2] Doing poetry as DuPlessis does transforms readers' subjectivities, which, as a consequence of doing a lot of preliminary work on themselves, calls into existence new collectives, thus "inventing a people who are missing" (Deleuze, "Literature" 4). Or, if one's eye is not as fixed on the horizon as are the eyes of some, one could liken it to excitable speech, a risky kind of rhetoric spoken by a "subject who speaks at the border of the speakable [and thus] takes the risk of redrawing the distinction between what is and is not speakable, the risk of being cast into the unspeakable" (Butler 139). In DuPlessis's poetry, such excitability, such political performativity and related world- and people-building, often happens on a smaller, more intimate, weaker scale. As Majewska notes, "The revolution of the everyday is in fact the revolution of the ordinary and common, of the nonheroic and the weak" (141).

I am not as committed as Majewska to the rhetoric of "revolution," even in a weak sense. And neither is DuPlessis.[3] Nonetheless, Majewska's return to the idea of the "ordinary" nature of said revolution is worth underscoring. If there is anything revolutionary about weak resistance, it is only in the sense of a revolving, a cycling back, an orbiting. Some minoritized political poetry might be conceived as "revolutionary" in this entirely ordinary, unexceptional way of moving around and around. Its authors are consciously committed to doing politics, to offering weak resistance. They are unafraid of the ordinariness of both their politico-aesthetic activity and the materials such activity draws on, unafraid of how life enters their artmaking and their art. It's not life in the abstract, as some ontological or metaphysical force entering their materials and works. It's the stuff of *their particular lives*, which have been judged worthless, less than human or even nonhuman, by the dominant public sphere's social, cultural, and political standards. To insist on this stuff's value is inherently political. It calls on others to recognize it. Little beacons flash: *There is life here. Come.*

DuPlessis, throughout her career, has been preoccupied with a resistive politics emerging out of ordinariness and the dailiness of writing. Her proclivity for fastidiously dating her poems is just as important for orientating her readers toward their source—including the dailiness of her own life and writing practice—as are her notes, which assiduously document the cultural and social origins of her poems' ideas, language, and citation. Since the completion of *Drafts*, DuPlessis's concern with resistant writing's ordinariness has been especially pronounced, emerging explicitly and thematically in many of her collections since approximately 2010. But it would be mistaken to understand her as asserting a fixed political agenda or politicized poetic program. As I've written elsewhere, her work evinces more of an essaying, a trying out and experimentation to see what, if anything, sticks (Keenaghan, "Openings"). Such a modality of trial and error accepts the risk that not everything will succeed. And with micropolitics—emphasis here on the prefix—there are no assurances that the attempt will even be seen. Doubts infuse DuPlessis's recent poetry. Take the first line of my epigraph, from "Summer Poem" (2016–2018). Having been begun in the summer prelude to the Trump administration and constituting DuPlessis's ars poetica on her art's political life, this poem deserves closer scrutiny. Privately, she has called it one of the "serious" and "bigger juicier denser" recent poems (E-mail to the author, 24 Feb. 2022).[4] Yet, at the start of this major piece, DuPlessis wonders, "But who cares about your little life" (*LW* 108). Lacking a question mark, we ought to presume her clause is not a query. No answer is expected. Instead, she is merely making a point, colloquially, to register serious doubt. Who is going to care enough to read a poem, much less a poem about any one person's life?

Those who care. Whoever they are, and whatever "caring" means. Or maybe no one will read such a poem. Or care. Or care to read it. *Caring* is circumscribed by the realm of the personal, those who are willing to be personally engaged with the poems, to be touched by the author and her work, regardless of whether they know the author.[5] Those inclined to be DuPlessis's readers are exceptions defining the rule. "But who cares about your little life *except*" (*LW* 108; emphasis added). Those exceptions are atomistic entities, individuals, monosyllabically rendered, whose tight-knit connections surface as a quick series of internal rhymes: "*you*, a family *few*, a friend or *two*" (*LW* 108; emphases added). Using the rationalist and proceduralist word "given" as a springboard, on its own line, DuPlessis's exasperated statement jumps immediately outward from that small bound circle of intimates to "the politics of 'our time'" (*LW* 108). History is stripped of material historicity and reduced to ontological constancy, a quasi-metaphysical platitude lacking teeth as we can see in the scare quotes around the phrase "'our time.'" The word "politics" might just as well be in scare quotes, too, since this kind of thinking of generational or epochal time is neither transformative nor consequential. But the *idea of politics* has too much weight and far too many consequences to warrant scare quotes. "Daily politics, weird shit"—encompassing everything from concerns about water, personal agency, protection of the vulnerable, human rights—all that minor, quotidian stuff that makes life survivable has been pushed to the margins and defined by the dominant political order as "apolitical" or even "unpolitical" issues. We are interpellated by that political system, believing in and constructed by its judgments. In "Summer Poem," what is deigned "weird shit" is just a half-stop away from "encrypted politics, complicity and loss" (*LW* 108). In the end, weak resistance might be premised upon obscuring one's own beliefs, to the point of resisting not only weakly but also ineffectively. So much so that our resistance backfires. We might become complicit. We could lose the battle.

Despite immediate appearances, there is something refreshing about regarding poetic politics as run through with doubt, with admissions of complicity. By orientating herself and her readers toward caring and its private sites—family circles, friend groups, even the solitary pleasures of reading and writing—DuPlessis underscores the effects of how her kind of politics, a minor feminist micropolitics of weak resistance, is an ongoing effort to move outside "the politics of 'our time.'" Perhaps that effort does not wholly succeed. Who knows? (Who cares?) But it does sound a resounding note, signaling the one object strongly opposed through weak resistance: *DuPlessis's work rejects triumphalism*. It is an ironic strength, or a strength born out of irony. All I know for certain is that I cannot know anything for certain. Thus DuPlessis willfully and unhesitatingly spurns the attitude enabling American exceptionalism and all its associated recidivist ideologies—patriarchalism and misogyny, neofascism, militarism, imperialism, ecocide, white supremacism, xenophobia, homo- and transphobia. All the "weird shit" that's surfaced, a return of late modernity's and American democracy's repressed. The cesspool backing up.

But doubt about the most fundamental of political questions—*Who are the "we" in this collectivity?*—springs precisely from DuPlessis's move of rejecting doubtlessness. Due to the flux of day-to-day existence and power's vagaries and instability, one cannot enjoy, even for a moment, the triumph of a resistant victory or the comfort of even knowing who else is in one's collective:

> Who are the we?
> Who cares—WE are here, WE
> have declared ourselves.
> There was ad hoc leadership
> delivery of the necessary
> services; it was a triumph.
> Yet the commons change.
> The mood changes.
> ("+59," *ATW* 75)

The fact of triumphalism's and fixed collective identity's impossibility is especially driven home when resistance assumes a recognizable form, "after the demo" ("+59," *ATW* 75). The street demonstration doubles as a demolition. Hopes are both built up and torn down in the ephemerality of the protest-gesture. In such a climate, the answer is not to repeat the gesture, in an ever-iterated irruption of excitable speech. Instead the impossible must be achieved: "spontaneity . . . / must be fashioned into longevity" (75). The present must be dilated, to be inhabited and felt differently. It is not just a mostly forgettable blip on the way to the future from the past—whether that past is traditional or revolutionary or resistant. No, the present is, potentially, an always-space, an integral moment, a cosmos unto itself, which opens to all ways, depending on how one lives and what one does. A single day can provide a space for moving through, for momentarily occupying, eighty worlds.

Embracing strength through failure is one way of moving toward a future political horizon. More needs to be said though about the "weird shit" making that horizon imaginable. That phrase for DuPlessis does not just mark the political repressed, the bad shit and the dark side of the returning or resurfacing of the supposedly vanquished undemocratic elements from the twentieth century. There is another order of shit—what is actively suppressed by the powers that be as valueless. DuPlessis's postmillennial work focuses not only on the dailiness of feminist micropolitics but on revaluating the effects of the dominant political system's construction of such dailiness as shit, refuse, the refused and the rejected: that's the "weird shit" that *constitutes* the stuff, the doing, of feminist politics. The dominant political sphere, in embracing ontological vacuity, has emptied itself of history, more specifically of the material and the raced, gendered, sexualized, and otherwise marked bodies that help make history. But history has not gone away; it's just been pushed aside. Working through and with her doubts, DuPlessis rediscovers history among everything else that's been pushed out of the range of visibility and into those invisible or unrecognized spaces where all the caring happens. She searches amid what is misjudged as the muck of life, in what is recorded by those smudges and traces some of us keep insisting, to others' confusion, is the stuff of poetry.

II. "weird shit," or the Poetics of Waste and the Politics of Collagist Lyricism

Other readers have remarked on how the ethico-political dimensions and open form of Rachel Blau DuPlessis poetics are related to her poetic deployment of waste, particularly to bits and pieces of linguistic materials. For instance, Paul Jaussen notes how "the scraps of language" in DuPlessis's glosses contribute to an emergent poetics informed by her simultaneously culturally Jewish midrashic and materialist sensibility (138). Similarly, Alan Golding locates her in a post-objectivist lineage, with her work exemplifying "the test of a woman's sincerity," in Louis Zukofksy's sense, whereby "an ethos and an ethics emerges from the writer's attitude toward materiality—that of the object world and of language," particularly the "mark, jot, tittle, gap, space," the little things on the page (71). I would underscore that the thinginess of language and the poem's materiality are significant because those linguistic scraps and signifying marks point back to their origins in a dailiness, which cannot and should not be wholly aestheticized or mistaken merely for poetic devices. So much of these materials' scrappiness, or their resistant potential's being tied to their fragmentariness, depends on the fact they are waste and always will be read as such, extending traces of the undesirable, non-beautifiable material conditions from whence they were disposed. In "Summer Poem," DuPlessis links politics and waste as a cupola—"daily politics, weird shit" (*LW* 108). I read her use of the word "shit" as not merely colloquial. The word's coarseness, uncharacteristic for much of this long poem's diction, forcefully calls to mind its literal designation. If we read the comma as signaling apposition rather than serial conjunction—and as my essay's epigraph shows, DuPlessis's second comma, following "weird shit," suggests the phrase, indeed, is appositive—then shit itself is congruent or coterminous with dailiness. Shit is the waste and refuse, as well as the refused, constituting the everyday stuff of feminist weak resistance.

Power and politics lie beneath shit and sanitation. According to Marxist historian Dominique Laporte, the rise of modernity, capitalism, and urban infrastructures also entailed "the *domestication* of waste" and its "privatization," or the construction of individuals' waste as their own and the management of it as their responsibility (28; original emphasis). The necessity of tending one's garbage and sewage rather than letting it flow freely in public streets and gutters "played a role in the emergence of the family and familial intimacy" (28). Centuries ago, policing waste was a heteronormative and patriarchal technology, contributing to the emergence of a modern private sphere closely aligned with the individual, isolated modern subject, a sense of privacy that we have inherited. "The politics of waste," Laporte argues, "branded the subject to his body, and prefigured, not so insignificantly perhaps, the Cartesian ideology of the *I*" (31). I shit (and hide the evidence of my shitting), therefore I am. Of course, those who are recognized as subjects are those who best sublimate—that is, control and invisibilize—their waste. Thus they become all mind, no body. Laporte closely aligns "the policing of language and the politics of shit" (9). The more aesthetic language is, "ridding it of waste, saving it from weight, giving it its weight in gold," the more the politics of shit has succeeded, with its consolidation of the modern disembodied subject, a synecdoche for the heteropatriarchal head of family and state (9).

Women writers have long understood that much creation comes directly out of not only the stuff of life but also of a specific, gendered experience, which quite usually begins as what's neglected, devalued, and castoff. Poet Muriel Rukeyser, an influence on DuPlessis, makes that point clearly in "Many Keys" (written 1957, first recovered 2018), an unpublished early feminist tract suppressed by the same male editors who commissioned it.[6] "There *is* waste in nature, waste in art, and plenty of waste in the lives of women. Waste is an influence [on women's poetry], and the making of poetry works against waste.... To the work on the making of forms must be added the work of the individual on himself [*sic*]" (238; original emphasis). Rukeyser here seems to encourage fellow women artists to engage in the sort of aesthetic alchemy Laporte believes is poetry's role in modernity's politics of shit, turning waste into gold and in the process giving oneself a recognizable shape. As she goes on, though, she argues that to fully succeed in performing such poetic magic would be impossible, for the work is always rooted in one's life ... and a woman's life is culturally devalued, equated with waste. Women writers' responsibility, then, is to apply pressure, continuously and repeatedly, to available forms, to change the definition of the aesthetic and poetic. "To use the possibilities so that life is allowed and nourished; the life also of the forms. To make the forms so that experience is seen to include the world, so that all things of daily life are seen in their essential and full vitality ... to understand the withdrawals before experience, when they are made in generalization, in the impersonal and anti-sexual, and when they are made for the sake of more life" (241). Because open form poetics like what Rukeyser theorizes and DuPlessis practices extend the social field, the practice of such poetics is yet another site where heteropatriarchy's constraints and oppressions are felt. Still, in the aesthetic space, one can actively and consciously work organically with form, infusing it with what's deemed waste from one's life, to produce objects, poems, which cause the rest of us to look aslant at the world.

DuPlessis would not have known of this lost Rukeyser piece until its recent recovery. Nonetheless, as her early critical essay on Rukeyser, Denise Levertov, and Adrienne Rich demonstrates, she has long appreciated how her predecessor's mythopoetic lyric shifts "the consciousness of women and the sets of expectations in society and culture about women's feelings, acts, possibilities," thus disrupting external factors that "inhibit the work of the imagination and inhibit perception itself" ("Critique of Consciousness" 206). DuPlessis's more recent poetry and poetics suggest a felt affinity for what Rowena Kennedy-Epstein has called Rukeyser's exposition of "the gender politics of waste," not just a relegation of waste and its denizens to the margins but also of marginalized artists' need to embrace "the embodied, chaotic, and commingling materials of making in the wreckages and pleasures of our world, of the process that we are all born from, and that we create in" (6, 162). The theme of the waste of women's lives is common to feminist literature, and the same is true of queer literature. Waste's eternal return, and the ongoing attempt to use art to render meaningful the shit of our lives, is also theorized by gay poet Robert Duncan in *The H.D. Book* (1961–circa 1985, recovered 2012), a work anticipating much later queer and feminist poetic theory. DuPlessis has written of his project as modeling "a polymorphously perverse textuality," the effect of Duncan's irrepressible same-sex desire and cross-gender identification with matriarchy and *écriture féminine* ("Polymorphous" 657). For Duncan, existences and material relegated to the social and aesthetic margins consist of the queer and feminine detritus of civilization, the uncontainable dreams, imagination, and eroticism (and homoeroticism) relegated to out-of-sight, subterranean depths. To realign social power asymmetries, poets must recoup this rejected material through their embodied and desiring work on poems. "The underground uprises into the place of what is seen as above-board. Justice demands it" (Duncan, *H.D. Book* 127). Justice! Duncan is so rarely unequivocal in characterizing poetry as an activist process. Consequently, "margin *becomes* center in a happily perverse reversal" (DuPlessis, "Polymorphous" 657; original emphasis).

Such repositioning recomposes how we see the world and what we see in it by bringing squarely into the present what Gertrude Stein, in "Composition as Explanation" (1926), called "the history of the refused in the arts and literature" (522). The refused and refuse are closely linked, perhaps synonymous. "What does progressive politics mean if not the taking-into-account of the excluded?" asks theorist and curator Nicolas Bourriaud (xi). Any art that counts the excluded must plumb "the world of waste," to recuperate what is invisibilized "in the name of the Ideal" (xi). "The central political task of contemporary art . . . is to bring precarity to mind," Bourriaud explains (43). "Art exposes the world's non-definitive character. It dislocates, disassembles, and hands things over to disorder and poetry," and thus "underscore[s] the intrinsic fragility of the standing order," a fragility hegemonic forces veil to maintain their own power (43). The art that most effectively disrupts perceptions of a power culture's order is predicated upon "the aesthetics of *evidence*, cutting through historical and ideological falsification," and doing so by "exhum[ing] what has been cast away" (61; original emphasis).

DuPlessis ought to be counted among the "excavators of the minor," those who "present singular genealogies cutting through layers of history" (Bourriaud 60). She, like Rukeyser and Duncan before her, helps us articulate what it means for women and for queer people to *speak* or *sing* the stuff of waste. DuPlessis's poem "Mackle, Shard, and Trace," from *Late Work*, closes on what this all means for our sense of what poetry is, how it upsets prevailing understandings of the literary art's essence:

Poetry is not the poetic.

Poetry
       is something smaller, with
          "an unlikely smattering of themes."

A kind of Singing Smudge.
       Erasures, excavating slightest blurry trace.
       Recoveries within Effacement,

Mackled bits of Being
smatter smatter smatter.
(87)

Such enunciation of the "Singing Smudge" entails DuPlessis's struggle to sift through traces to recover and thus open a space for political voices, thereby authorizing herself and others in the social margins to speak in an intimately known language. When we, the marginalized, speak, sing, and write, it is nearly incomprehensible, irrational, for we're denied the imaginary space of so-called public rationality. We recycle the minutiae and refuse of commonplace goings-on to produce "encrypted politics," as DuPlessis puts it ("Summer Poem," *LW* 108). The recovery of the excluded and the recentralization of the margins produces work that's so encrypted, though, she and likeminded artists and critics don't know if sifting through the refuse means we're full of shit. Is this work political? Or is it ethical? What's the difference? What kind of future is this work going to produce if all that's seen is the social *refuse*, rather than the poet's *refusal*?

To come to terms with the relationship between *refuse* and *refusal*—between evidentiary art and the weak resistance of making such art—we first must take a step back and ask: is it even art? "Poetry is not the poetic," DuPlessis writes about the smatter and smudge she deals in (*LW* 87). If it's not poetic, then what is it? Her new long poem, *Traces, with Days* (2017–present), has struggled openly from its inception with this question. While struggling to begin the successor to *Drafts* (1986–2013), in *Days and Works* (2017) DuPlessis wonders, "So what if I am having an aesthetic crisis. Who cares?" (5). There's that word again—"cares." The resolution, or attempted resolution, to that crisis entails finding "the texture of actual time," opening from the private and personal out into the historical world and sifting through its debris (12). Fragments of newspaper clippings, scanned into the text, embody traces of that exterior world, manifest in its waste. The first is about neutrinos (1), and from there we get snippets of other items—a story on the fraudulent pyramid scheme of investor Bernie Madoff (5), a piece about tracking sewage's contamination of freshwater by tracing artificial sweeteners in it (13), a feature about a man's kidney transplant that feminizes him and remarks, "She's peeing like a racehorse" (17), among other odds and ends. Each bit is a soundbite about literal waste (sewage, urination) or metaphorical waste (lost finances, humanity's criminal dregs). In digital culture, we'd call it a meme. Hip-hop and musique concrète would call it a sample. But such traces' wasteful nature—the waste literally constituting our everyday lives as social beings—is reinforced by how DuPlessis works with these bits, literally clipping and scanning fragments from print newspaper items. She refuses the current modes of information dissemination—RSS feeds and digital echo chambers. Instead she goes old school, reaching for the refuse—the physical newspaper, a vestige of a dying industry. Collage begins here, not in merely sorting the Benjaminian wreckage of history, a grand ontological task, but instead by rummaging in the bin.

Collage is an exemplary aesthetic means of moving the margin to center. In *The H.D. Book*, Duncan passingly describes theosophist Madame Blavatsky's writings as collections of phantasmatic waste and repressed antisocial desires, "midden heaps where, beyond the dictates of reason, *as in the collagist's art*, from what has been disregarded or fallen into disregard, genres are mixed, exchanges are made, mutations begun from scraps and excerpts from different pictures . . . to form the figures of a new composition" (135; emphasis added). This passage recalls an earlier moment when Duncan, speaking of Ezra Pound, asserts: "The great art of my time is the collagist's art, to bring all things into new complexes of meaning, mixing associations" (58–59). What he appreciates about collage is its lack of control, its ability to produce new, unexpected relations, and thus new meanings, by giving space to elements otherwise repressed, rejected, refused. Forget Pound's idea that "the book shd. [*sic*] be a ball of light in one's hand" (55). Concentrate instead on the collagist nature of his *Cantos*, their juxtapositions and citations. Just don't forget the political, ideological, and hateful origins of many of that project's constitutive sources. Fascism, racism, antisemitism, misogyny, homophobia, too, are all so much waste, the repressed and rejected underbelly of capitalist and democratic society. Pound tried too much to sublimate that fact, to make his songs, his cantos, luminous and thus appear—what? A heavenly mandate? But as DuPlessis's singing smudge evinces, what I would describe as her collagist's approach to lyricism, to her willingness not just to show but to point to the seams, are more shit than shine. Poetry's political function depends on such shit, even if we find a poem's politics—as in *The Cantos*—reprehensible.

At the heart of it, the collagist's art is one of salvage, not just recycling or hoarding. Literary critic Scarlett Higgins has argued that, since the advent of modernism and the subsequent privileging of poetics of juxtaposition and fragmentation and thus a formal and content-based cultivation of "anti-narrative" texts, collage has been "the end-game of literature" (2, 1). While I would argue that these literary aspirations of collagist poetics are more seeped in uncertainty and perhaps antiliterary objectives (i.e., a rejection of the claims of literariness), I agree with Higgins's assertion that because collages "tend toward disrupting genre-specific boundaries and causal narration," these forms are "peculiarly favorable for the transmission of political critique" (2). Not every collaged text must "*look* like it has been cut up, rearranged, or stitched together"; instead, its "juxtapositional quality . . . has everything to do with context, syntax, and the expected relation between these two aspects of written language" (21; original emphasis). The act of sifting through linguistic and discursive discard, selecting and saving some to juxtapose and create new meanings, is transformative of self and world. Elsewhere, in "Wallace Berman: The Fashioning Spirit" (1978), Robert Duncan writes of his and his extended circle's contributions to their eponymous friend's collaged mail art magazine *Semina*. "We began to see ourselves as fashioning unnamed contexts, contexts of a new life way in the making, a secret mission" (*Collected Essays* 347). The resulting new context owed partly to the community built by the publication and by its contributors' exchanges. But it also stemmed from the assemblages and collages they built and made, "the redemption of trash in the recognition of devotional objects, emblems and signs rescued from the bottom in the art of a new context" (351). Such trash could be physical garbage, and, following Higgins's lead, it might also be textual, socially devalued linguistic content, the debris of everyday discourse.

In "Of George Herms, His Hermes, and His Hermetic Art" (1972), Duncan referred to his moment as the "Renaissance or Recycling of Riches," and its collagists and assemblagists were the "little company of Artists of the Reassembly" (*Collected Essays* 289). DuPlessis belongs to that "little company." Unlike Duncan's intimates though, her feminist project insists upon a different kind of engagement with refusal, a rejection of the metaphysical transcendence Duncan ascribes to such meaning-making by working with everyday debris. Rather than move beyond history, as Poetry with a capital "p" might do, both DuPlessis's poetic politics (i.e., writing as a woman in a heteropatriarchal literary institution) and her political poetics (i.e., gendering writing to deconstruct institutional politics) necessitate she *anchor* her work in history. Those anchors though are deceptively weak. They are like the fragile filaments and threads that trail off the torn and rough edges of materials in many of her visual collages. Some of those collages can be found in three full-color reproductions of her combined poetic and visual art: *The Collage Poems of Drafts* (2011) and two post-*Drafts* projects, the digital chapbook *Churning the Ocean of Milk* (2014) and the limited edition sewn volume *Numbers* (2018). There is also the black-and-white collection *Graphic Novella* (2015).

Andrew R. Mossin, out of his correspondence with DuPlessis, posits that her post-*Drafts* long poem, *Traces, with Days*, marks a new phase of her poetic experimentalism, "one with roots in collage." However, if we consider how her critical scholarship and teaching have examined the bricoleur modernism of Mina Loy, Ezra Pound, and T. S. Eliot, or even H.D.'s palimpsestic mythopoetics, then it is not farfetched to say that collage has implicitly, if not explicitly, informed her poetic genealogy. About her own above-mentioned collage books, DuPlessis comments that "I was trying to attend a mode of visual art to which I had always been deeply attracted, despite having no particular visual or technical training" (quoted in Mossin). These projects open the possibility of explicitly tying together her visual collages' rootedness in a politics of refuse, refusal, and the refused and her feminist poetic politics, a means of framing the political, antiliterary significance of her "Singing Smudge" (*LW* 87).

DuPlessis's practice of visual collage predates her aforementioned recent collage-poem volumes by almost a half-century. She dates her first collage, *Rage*, as from 1964. This is a mixed-media assemblage of torn pieces of paper, including postal items from the United Kingdom and a beer label whose brand name is cut down to the titular word, all mounted on a piece of plain brown cardboard, ripped from a typical packing carton. Her earliest works continue in this mode, literally salvaging and manipulating trash and waste, mostly paper products, and juxtaposing the fragments in abstract, nonfigurative geometric forms with letters, sometimes words, and other graphic markings popping out.[7] DuPlessis identifies the earliest collage she has shared publicly, titled *Wood-Machine* (circa 1966–1967), as her fourth (E-mail to the author, 16 Aug. 2022). The construction is a 6 in. by 7.5 in. assemblage of text scraps and twine, laced over a cog-shaped Ackermann's Titan thread wheel bought in Strasbourg, France, during her second trip to Europe (E-mail to the author, 16 Aug. 2022). Unlike most of her more recent collages, *Wood-Machine* is more of a sculptural assemblage than a collage proper, insofar as its materials are mounted on a wooden board, in the style of German Dadaist Kurt Schwitters's Merz sculptures (DuPlessis, "Collage-Homage" slide 7).

These early constructions predate DuPlessis's activism, as her own feminist consciousness and sense of solidarity with various New Left movements emerged concurrently with the spring 1968 student strike at Columbia University, where she was studying and working as a teaching assistant (DuPlessis, *BS* 21–22). By her own account, she was an "inscribed female," constructed and contained by Cold War America's heteronormative patriarchal codes before she began her undergraduate career at Barnard College, almost a decade earlier (16). DuPlessis's early "pre-political" visual work evinces an aesthetic sensibility of trying to break her way out of such ideological inscription. These works of her youth exhibit a sophisticated, modernist aesthetic—the creation of new texts and, as Robert Duncan might put it, new contexts out of the relocation and juxtaposition of everyday detritus from the waste bin of history.

Over the decades, that aesthetic would come to inflect DuPlessis's later self-consciously political poetics. Moving between text poems—most of the prose poem variety—and visual collaged poems and images, often on facing pages, *Graphic Novella* (2015), which DuPlessis has referred to as "an unintentional 'preface' to *Traces, with Days*," exemplifies her mode of self-consciously putting collage into the service of a politicized poetics of singing smudge (E-mail to the author, 24 Feb 2022). One of these images consists of numbers in black boxes, randomly arranged, nonsequentially, in a black line frame open on the right-hand side of the page. Over this field, and often overrunning the frame, are images of strips of paper, most bearing small messages—or maybe micropoems—typed upon them, each written below a number sign (#). One of these micropoems-within-the-visual-poem reads:

#
Before there can be "system"
there must be assemblage.
Or maybe bricolage.
Or something else that ends in -age.
(*GN* 65)

Here DuPlessis takes a twenty-first-century medium—tweets from the social media platform Twitter (when it was known as such), designated by a hashtag (which, ironically, makes the message its own referent, a self-referential loop)—and forces them into an anachronistic form, the typewritten or word-processed poem. Once written, the tweet (or the performative simulacrum of a tweet, if it were never tweeted) is printed, cut out, adhered to the page. So much invisible labor—the *work* of writing and art-making—is captured in that fragment that not only *narrates* the need for "assemblage" or "bricolage"—and the missing term "collage"—to make (and undo) a "'system'" but also *performs* and *embodies* such work. All systems begin in some form of assemblage and making, even the heteropatriarchal one we wish to refashion, and all deconstructions and resistances end up creating new systems in their place. Both lessons are important, but this collage's enactment of the performance and visibilizing of the making is where DuPlessis's concepts and narratives get sweaty, as Sara Ahmed would say. That's where the work is—where we realize someone, some *body* is working.

Even Kurt Schwitters did not fully admit that making art of waste can be political. He, like Robert Duncan, instead believed assemblage and collage result in transcendence, an apolitical overcoming of the state. "The function of art can never be the promotion of a social agenda. . . . It is precisely in its engagement with things that are not immediately necessary for life's most important requirements that humanity is freed from everyday trivialities and elevated above itself and its passions," he writes in "Art and the Times" (1926) (231). Collage, for him, is an intellectual endeavor, a means "to exercise and fortify the mind," not the body (231). Or as he wrote in "The Origin of Merz" (1941), sculptures like his, made of "trash because they [i.e., their constituent objects] had been thrown away," produce "a convincing, utterly general expression" (473). The German lesbian Dadaist feminist and collagist Hannah Höch, a close friend of Schwitters, offers insight into why formal, aesthetic transcendence— no matter how it torques its constitutive stuff into abstraction—never fully detaches from the social materials from which they originated or from their manipulator's body. In her early Dada photomontages from the 1910s and 1920s, Höch famously "critique[s] Weimar bourgeois culture and traditional gender roles and celebrate[s] the pleasures of modernity and the New Woman" (Lavin, *Cut* 35). Recycling and distorting images from glossy magazines, she deconstructed and reconstructed the German mass media's sensationalized figure of the New Woman, as well as imperialist and primitivist representations of African and European Black subjects, as in her *The Ethnographic Museum* series, "one of her messiest" feminist projects (Lavin, "Mess" 89). DuPlessis cites these early works as direct inspirations, though she also sees them as rife with problems, still reproducing and not fully succeeding in their critiques of both chauvinist and racist ideologies ("Collage-Homage"). These works' political shortcomings owe to the degree to which the waste materials repurposed by Höch remain too closely tied to their original media contexts. Despite their fragmentary and juxtaposed compositions, they are still representational, and thus they reproduce, if not exactly narratively, then in terms of semes and visual themes, the very ideologies Höch sets out to trouble.[8]

Lesser known are Höch's lace and embroidery collages from the same period, in which she made abstract and geometric images out of patterns she had created for popular women's magazines while employed by the publisher Ullstein Verlag (Herrmann 11). Created by the only woman among the Berlin Dadaists, Höch's abstract visual constructions made with sewing and embroidery templates or wallpaper and fabric border designs—as in *White Form* (1919) and *Reed Pen Collage* (1922)— extend, through their materials, a culturally constructed feminine domestic sphere into a masculine aesthetic space (Höch 52, 53). She chastened her admirers through her essay "On Embroidery" (1918): "But you, craftswomen, modern women, who feel that your spirit is in your work, who are determined to lay claim to your rights (economic and moral), who believe your feet are firmly planted in reality, at least y-o-u should know that your embroidery work is a documentation of your own era!" (72). Her collagist reinvention of such handwork patterns documents not her own actual moment but instead a future time, an imagined time with greater feminist potential. The refused material of women's lives is reenchanted, creating a fantastic aesthetic space that "take[s] up a position between the world of ideas and the real world," as Höch writes in her postwar essay "Fantastic Art" (1946). "It reflects the tension between the two, the degree and the nature of their non-congruence.... Today fantastic art is no longer illustrative—as it once used to be—[instead] it transports the fantastic back into things" (233). As she argues in "On Collage" (1917), poets understood that potential before avant-garde visual artists: "The process of remounting, cutting up, sticking down, activating—that is to say, alienating—... has always been done" in literature, in challenging syntax and even phonemes and morphemes as might be demanded for a particular text, and it "has been perfected in poetry" (16).

Though DuPlessis might not know Höch's embroidery and domestic pattern collages nor cite them as direct influences, her visual objects and collage-poems are the products of a similar reenchanting disfiguration performed through the manipulation—literally, the handling—of objects that move through domestic spaces, often fated to become mere waste. Having passed through her hands, selected and caressed and torn and cut and glued by her fingers, these bits of garbage are imbued with new meaning and possibility. Reassembled, they are conduits of the poet and artist's person, forming her personal intervention into a world that is implicitly refashioned simply because these bits have been pulled from it and put into new relation with each other, with their original contexts, with her, with us. They tell us little about Rachel Blau DuPlessis, the person. Yet they are deeply personal, intimate. The art made of life's leavings.

Sometimes what's left are invaluable gifts, like her friend Mary Oppen's hand-dyed tissue paper, "left ... at her death," which are incorporated into the collage-poems of *Churning the Ocean of Milk* (DuPlessis, foreword to *Churning*). But even there, something so personal is combined with the waste originating at public sites, such as a torn ticket stub for the Cho Eung Ek Genocidal Center, the Cambodian "museum of crim / es against humanity" (DuPlessis, "And if the baby cries ...," *Churning*). More than just a personal souvenir of the poet's own travels, that remnant of a ticket also signals how the collagist lyric functions as a site of both private and collective mourning. All is broken and torn: the ticket missing a bit of its upper left corner, fixed askew upon deceased Mary Oppen's torn and rough-edged sheets and set near DuPlessis's oddly right-justified poem, reminiscent of a Hebraic text. Though we must read left to right to understand its English, the right justification suggests we *could* or *ought to* read right to left, perhaps singing it like kaddish, a prayer for the dead, perhaps for the millions dead of another genocide, the Shoah. The physicality of the verbal text's presentation reinforces this sense, for the right-hand field of the poem's laser-printed text is cut out with a thin border of white space. That space causes the line to break into the field of Oppen's paper, thus creating sightlines that guide us from the margin where the verbal text begins into the center of the frame, predominated by a visual field of torn, collaged objects.

And if there were not enough breakage and tearing with the materials laid upon the page, the verbal text is fractured further, linguistically and from within, as line breaks, set upon the furthest margin, cut through individual words—"th / us," "crim / es," "no / tice" ("And if the baby cries ...," *Churning*). Two out of three times, those breaks do not even make poetic sense, for they slice through monosyllabic words, integral units of meaning. If new syllables are produced here, at the cuts along the edge where the entire visual poem is marked and framed, and thus where the boundaries of what we can see and hear are exposed, they are nonce syllables, creating stutters obfuscating the semantic sense of small words. Only in one instance of such a cut are already-distinct syllables phonemically marked, and that cut merely highlights negation at the line's end and the poem's edge: "no." There is no room for mere individual grief here, in this aesthetic context pointing us to intersections of the personal and geopolitical, private loss and historical catastrophes. "Don't take a selfie / in front of photos / of the murdered prisoners," DuPlessis warns in the preceding poem, probably cribbing found language from a placard in the Cambodian museum of Khmer Rouge atrocities ("Everything its own manifest," *Churning*). Though she claims she is working through the "volatility of the cosmological" with these pieces, the final word—like the final phrase of her brief foreword to the collection—is about "the pain of the historical," particularly as such pain is felt by those who have been shunted aside, even exterminated, as they and what they have created and experienced are discounted as nonhuman waste (foreword to *Churning*)

Like her predecessors, DuPlessis understands that collage presents the socially marginalized the means of creating alternative spaces and histories, rooted in our experiences of alterity, silencing, oppression, even genocide. How her visual work in the collage arts always harkens back to the materials and the material world out of which it emerges, as well as to her body's manipulation of both, should sharpen our awareness that this, too, is how her exclusively verbal texts' "smatter smatter smatter" also work in a feminist and materially bounded way informed by collagist sensibilities (DuPlessis, "Mackle, Shard, and Trace," *LW* 87). They, too, are the embodiments of her weak resistance and sweaty concepts. But all working bodies are easily forgotten in this age of digital media and connectivity, where dataflows erase the bodies behind the devices. Returning to the micropoem-in-the-visual-poem from *Graphic Novella*, we should focus not only on "something else that ends in -age" (65), but we should focus on the suffix "-age" itself. Think of how it appears in action words and words of creation (to assemble, or the French *bricoler*, to tinker or to cobble together), rather than use the noun as an epochal designator preceding and metaphysically flattening history and the labor of making history (as in, "age of social media"). Yes, such a sign or signage reifies the action and activity of making. Even poetry is ineluctably attached to and dependent on consumer capitalism. But that reification, so out of place and time, is visible as such.

In *Graphic Novella*'s collage-poem of tweets, we can see what it means for DuPlessis to have taken the time not only to type a tweet, but to *re*type it, then print it, and *then* paste it! Memes and tweets and DMs, this is the weird shit of our lives, dominated as we are not only by consumer capitalism but also by semiocapitalism. This poem embodies DuPlessis's resistance to such systems by pitting one form of system-making assemblage and coding with her own. "The collapse of the political class—and not simply in one place—is now patent," she writes elsewhere in *Graphic Novella*. "Public good twists to private gain. They are selling the state to high rollers. And molding citizens into clumps of waste and confusion" (28). (Incidentally, she wrote that before Donald Trump, the most infamous of Atlantic City casino and New York City real estate moguls, announced his presidential bid, way before he fanned the flames of neofascism and hijacked the American political system.) How do we break this mold? We must mark what we are or have become in a different way—by making the waste of our lives into some other action word, undoing ourselves as consumers to do us, to recreate ourselves and the polis and its systems, differently. . . . #Wastage

Acknowledgment

I am deeply grateful to Rachel Blau DuPlessis, as always, for answering my queries and sharing her unpublished and in-process materials with me.

Notes

1. Although Jodi Dean exclusively addresses comradeship as a socialist enterprise, both in terms of ideology and established forms of activism, her ideas are extensible to collectivities constructed out of feminist weak resistance if we qualify her anti-identitarian premise. Social identity markers are challenged and transformed through the comradeship emerging out of microsocial and micropolitical experience, rather than organized activism. They are not, as Dean maintains, thoroughly erased.

2. DuPlessis challenges the supposed distinction between lyric and language-based or material forms. She self-consciously takes up these questions and, in the process, politicizes the issue. Such politicization anchors her later work closer to the moments and contexts sourcing her materials and their assemblage than what Jonathan Culler theorizes happens in most lyric. "One of the things that lyrics may do is project a distinction between the immediate, historical, communicative situation and the level at which the work operates in its generality of address and its openness to being articulated by readers who will be differently situated (situated in part by the history of these works themselves)" (Culler 301). In contrast, what I call DuPlessis's collagist lyric strains such "distinction" and calls into question the "generality"—or universality and transhistoricism—assumed as the basis of lyric and, indeed, any aesthetic form.

3. In "Reader, I Married Me: Becoming a Feminist Critic," DuPlessis narrates her and others' self-identification as feminist academics in the late 1960s as entailing locating themselves "at one and the same time inside and outside an institution, in a contradictory position. . . . We seemed to be constructing a mixture of radical and liberal feminism," seeking access to an institution to transform it from within, rather than just reform or overthrow it (*BS* 22).

4. The other poem from *Late Work* that DuPlessis has described in this way is "Angelus Novus" (88–98), not discussed here (E-mail to the author, 24 Feb. 2022).

5. Such caring and touching is as much imaginative as it is sensorial and haptic. As theorist María Puig de la Bellacasa writes, "A politics of care goes beyond the bifurcation of consciousness that would keep our knowledge untouched by anxiety and inaccurateness. Involved knowledge is about being touched rather than observing from a distance. . . . While touch is maybe the sense that best embodies the involved intensities of caring doings and obligations, speculative thought on the possibility of care troubles longings of immanent immediacy" (93; original emphasis).

6. For the first recovery of "Many Keys," as well as an account of its bibliographic history, see Keenaghan, "There Is No Glass Woman." The republished version is cited here.

7. In several e-mails from August 16, 2022, DuPlessis sent the author images of *Rage* and other unpublished early collages, and described their compositions and contexts of production.

8. In "Interview between Edouard Roditi and Hannah Höch" (1959), Höch indicates how the origins of avant-garde visual collage are inherently political. She and her fellow Dadaists in 1910s Berlin had developed their photomontage techniques by appropriating the Prussian army's practice of juxtaposing actual troops' faces into prepared images of regiments in fields or barracks, with those soldiers' heads cut out (Höch 186–87). That Dadaist technique for creating nonrealistic, distortive, and alienating images was implicitly anarchist, a critique of the modern European state's use of realist illusions of the military and other entities to prop up its power.

Works Cited

Ahmed, Sara. *Living a Feminist Life*. Durham: Duke University Press, 2017.
Bookchin, Murray. *Social Anarchism or Lifestyle Anarchism*. Chico, CA: AK Press, 1995.
Bourriaud, Nicolas. *The Exform*. Translated by Erik Butler. New York: Verso, 2016.
Butler, Judith. *Excitable Speech: A Politics of the Performative*. New York: Routledge, 1997.
Culler, Jonathan. *Theory of the Lyric*. Cambridge, MA: Harvard University Press, 2015.
Dean, Jodi. *Comrade: An Essay on Political Belonging*. New York: Verso, 2019.
Deleuze, Gilles. "Literature and Life." *Essays Critical and Clinical*, translated by Daniel W. Smith and Michael A. Greco. Minneapolis: University of Minnesota Press, 1997, 1–6.
———. *Expressionism in Philosophy: Spinoza*. Translated by Martin Joughin. New York: Zone, 1990.
Deleuze, Gilles, and Félix Guattari. *Kafka: Toward a Minor Literature*. Translated by Dana Polan. Minneapolis: University of Minnesota Press, 1986.

Duncan, Robert. *Collected Essays and Other Prose*. Edited by James Maynard. Berkeley: University of California Press, 2014.

———. *The H.D. Book*. Edited by Michael Boughn and Victor Coleman. Berkeley: University of California Press, 2012.

DuPlessis, Rachel Blau. E-mails to the author, 16 Aug. 2022.

———. "Collage-Homage: Invitation au voyage." Slideshow and notes. Presentation at Thirteen Million Pillars of Grass: A Gathering, Gathering, The Flow Chart Foundation, Hudson, NY, 31 July 2022. Unpublished.

———. E-mail to the author, 24 Feb. 2022.

———. *Late Work*. New York: Black Square Editions, 2020.

———. *Around the Day in 80 Worlds*. Buffalo: BlazeVOX, 2018.

———. *Numbers*. Cincinnati: Materialist Press, 2018.

———. *Days and Works*. Boise: Ahsahta Press, 2017.

———. *Graphic Novella*. West Lima, WI: Xexoxial Editions, 2015.

———. *Churning the Ocean of Milk*. Alligatorzine, 2014, http://www.alligatorzine.be/pages/151/zine160.html.

———. "Polymorphous Poetics: Robert Duncan's *H.D. Book*." *Contemporary Literature*, vol. 55, no. 4, 2014, 635–64.

———. *The Collage Poems of Drafts*. Sheffield, UK: Salt, 2011.

———. *Blue Studios: Poetry and Its Cultural Work*. Tuscaloosa: University of Alabama Press, 2006.

———. "The Critique of Consciousness and Myth in Levertov, Rich, and Rukeyser." *Feminist Studies*, vol. 3, nos. 1–2, 1975, 199–221.

Franks, Benjamin. "Prefiguration." *Anarchism: A Conceptual Approach*. Edited by Benjamin Franks, Nathan Jun, and Leonard Williams. Routledge, 2018, 28–43.

Fraser, Nancy. *Unruly Practices: Power, Discourse, and Gender in Contemporary Social Theory*. Minneapolis: University of Minnesota Press, 1989.

Golding, Alan. "Macro, Micro, Material: Rachel Blau DuPlessis' *Drafts* and the Post-Objectivist Serial Poem." *Poetics and Praxis "After" Objectivism*, edited by W. Scott Howard and Broc Rossell. Iowa City: University of Iowa Press, 2018, 69–81.

Herrmann, Daniel F. "The Rebellious Collages of Hannah Höch." *Hannah Höch*, Hanna Höch. London: Prestel and The Whitechapel Gallery, 2014, 8–15.

Higgins, Scarlett. *Collage and Literature: The Persistence of Vision*. Routledge, 2019.

Höch, Hannah. *Hannah Höch*. London: Prestel and The Whitechapel Gallery, 2014.

Jaussen, Paul. *Writing in Real Time: Emergent Poetics from Whitman to the Digital*. Cambridge: Cambridge University Press, 2017.

Keenaghan, Eric. "There Is No Glass Woman: Muriel Rukeyser's Lost Feminist Essay 'Many Keys.'" *Feminist Modernist Studies*, vol. 1, nos. 1–2, 2018, 186–204.

———. "Openings: Some Notes on the Political in 'Drafts.'" *Jacket2*, 14 Dec. 2011, https://jacket2.org/article/openings-some-notes-political-drafts.

Kennedy-Epstein, Rowena. *Unfinished Spirit: Muriel Rukeyser's Twentieth Century*. Ithaca: Cornell University Press, 2022.
Laporte, Dominique. *History of Shit*. Translated by Nadia Benabid and Rodolphe El-Khoury. Cambridge, MA: MIT Press, 2002.
Lavin, Maud. "The Mess of History, or the Unclean Hannah Höch." *Hannah Höch*, Hannah Höch. London: Prestel and The Whitechapel Gallery, 2014, 88–95.
———. *Cut with the Kitchen Knife: The Weimar Photomontages of Hannah Höch*. New Haven: Yale University Press, 1993.
Majewska, Ewa. *Feminist Antifascism: Counterpublics of the Common*. New York: Verso, 2021.
Mossin, Andrew R. "Collage and Poetry as Social Document." *Hyperallergic*, Oct. 2020, https://hyperallergic.com/576635/rachel-blau-duplessis-poetry-collage/.
Pound, Ezra. *Guide to Kulchur*. New York: New Directions, 1970.
Puig de la Bellacasa, María. *Matters of Care: Speculative Ethics in More than Human Worlds*. Minneapolis: University of Minnesota Press, 2017.
Rukeyser, Muriel. "Many Keys." *The Muriel Rukeyser Era: Selected Essays*, edited by Eric Keenaghan and Rowena Kennedy-Epstein. Ithaca: Cornell University Press, 2023, 232–41.
Schwitters, Kurt. *Myself and My Aims: Writings on Art and Criticism*. Edited by Megan R. Luke. Translated by Timothy Grundy. Chicago: University of Chicago Press, 2021.
Stein, Gertrude. *Writings, 1903–1932*. Edited by Catherine Stimpson. New York: Library of America, 1998.
Vaneigem, Raoul. *The Revolution of Everyday Life*. 1967. Translated by Donald Nicholson-Smith. London: Rebel Press, 2006.

CHAPTER SIX

En Dehors Garde Collage Homage

SUZANNE W. CHURCHILL, LINDA A. KINNAHAN, AND SUSAN ROSENBAUM

> For writing is a practice—a practice in which the author disappears into a process, into a community, into discontinuities, into a desire for discovery.
>
> —Rachel Blau DuPlessis, *The Pink Guitar*
>
> Even reckless, but determined (or stubborn), I was willing to play and fail.
>
> —Rachel Blau DuPlessis, *Blue Studios*

Modus Operandi

Inspired by Rachel Blau DuPlessis's scholarly innovations and forays into the essay form and especially her use of collage in relation to an evolving feminist poetics, our collaborative essay adopts the feminist strategies she has modeled, piecing together, as collage and bricolage, personal reflections on how her work has influenced and energized our own scholarship and teaching. We consider the groundbreaking influence of her scholarship in early venues like *HOW(ever)*, experimental scholarly essays in *The Pink Guitar*, and poetic compositions that foreground collage and visual dimensions. Our three different voices are set apart by < > yet combined in the overall collage. Passages from Du Plessis's writings are indented and italicized, except where they appear as epigraphs to individual sections.[1]

I. Instigations

2017. A group of feminist scholars are collaborating with a team of students, librarians, and IT professionals to create a website dedicated to Mina Loy. We want to develop a feminist theory of the en dehors garde—a term we coined to account for women, people of color, and others who, like Loy, have been excluded or marginalized in histories and theories of the avant-garde. Whereas "avant" means "before," implying that artists are in front of culture and ahead of their time, "en dehors" means "toward the outside" or "turning outward." Rather than assuming a militant position at the forefront of culture, en dehors garde artists often came from the outside and circulated on the margins, working strategically to transform gendered, racialized, and ablest visual cultures and literary traditions that excluded, objectified, or belittled them.

We don't want to authorize a new theory: we want to generate theory in a new collaborative way. So we orchestrate a digital flash mob, inviting scholars, students, artists, and writers to submit digital post(card)s to our website, expressing their ideas about the en dehors garde. Contributors may sign their names, adopt pseudonyms, or remain anonymous. No prerequisites or terminal degrees required.

We receive dozens of post(card)s, including a set of seven handmade collages, signed "RBD."

II. Crisis in Consciousness[2]

RBD's *Crisis in Consciousness* combines diverse genre fragments, circulating around a cropped comic-book image of Wonder Woman and slicing off her head and lower legs—more drawn tools (including drills and screws), a sketch of a woman's hand kneading bread, rows of books, a photo of a woman gazing at boats, part of a map. A quote from Loy's "Aphorisms on Futurism" diagonally slashes the back side, recalling Loy's vexed association with that movement and her erasure from narratives of its avant-garde masculinities. Drawings of tools hearken to Dada's interest in the female body and machine technologies, suggesting one of many avant-garde strategies for objectifying the female body—often transforming it into a site for mutilation, decapitation, gagging, mechanization, and so on. The avant-garde fragment as a mode for disabling female bodies (think of Hans Bellmer's dolls, reassembling fragments) is repurposed through the relational elements of this collage to critique impulses crossing avant-garde and popular cultures, intent on decapitating the (Wonder) women who promote the "NOW-ness" of Loy's aphorisms.

1987. First encountering *HOW(ever)* at a grad-student conference at Rutgers, presenting on Elizabeth Bishop. A group of young feminist scholars/poets has set up a table, selling (or giving away?) issues of *HOW(ever)*, a journal of innovative writing by women founded by Kathleen Fraser. This was, for me, a small but critical shift beginning in my then-new thinking about feminism, feminist poetry, and more. I thought my Bishop paper was on feminist poetics, but these slender, stapled issues, with their innovative mix of writing and criticism, changed my whole thinking about what "feminist ideas," "feminist practice," and "feminist poetics" could be. RBD is contributing editor for the journal's duration, 1983–1992. Her pieces lead me to read her more extensively as I am drawn to the conjunctions of feminism and innovative experimental writing she (and others) articulate so lucidly in these buff-colored pages.

2022. For this essay on RBD, I reread these issues of *HOW(ever)*, taking notes as I go. Taking note.

< >

1989. A junior in college, I enroll in Professor Carla Kaplan's class "Feminist Perspectives on Literature." For the first time I am given the tools to begin to understand not only the history of English literature but women's place in that history, including the gaps, omissions, biases, and prejudices that had shaped the "canon" and my literary education thus far. I am inspired by how modernist women writers responded with such creative spirit to the challenges of writing as women; Virginia Woolf's *A Room of One's Own* becomes my handbook.

> In London, 1964, I tore a label (beef: Courage and Barclay) until the word that was thereby isolated in a broken circle is the rip of "RAGE." Make that a collage! (*PG* 162)

< >

1987. I'm an English major at a small liberal arts college. I've lost my faith in god but found the modernists—Forster, Lawrence, Woolf, Joyce, Eliot, Williams, and Stevens. "Poetry // exceeding music must take the place / Of empty heaven and its hymns," Stevens reassures me ("The Man with the Blue Guitar" 135). Imagination, the "ghostlier demarcations" of art, and the "keener sounds" of language will suffice my "rage for order" ("The Idea of Order at Key West" 98–99). I can be the maker of the meaning I crave:

> She was the single artificer of the world
> In which she sang. And when she sang, the sea,
> Whatever self it had, became the self
> That was her song, for she was the maker.
> (Stevens, "The Idea of Order at Key West" 98)

I do not question why Stevens imagines the singer as a "she"—why he feels compelled to feminize the work of the poet and position her on a distant horizon, even as he enters and inhabits her mind. I place myself by the sea and sing "her" song, which is Stevens's song. I embrace his idea that "poetry is the supreme fiction," though I wince at the words "wince most when widows wink" ("A High-Toned Christian Woman" 77–78). I'm ready to "Let be be finale of seem" but am repulsed by the "cold" and "dumb" dead woman's "horny feet" protruding from under the sheet ("The Emperor of Ice-Cream" 79–80). We don't critique such eruptions of misogyny in class. I recoil from them reflexively. Something is stirring.

< >

1985. *HOW(ever)*, volume 2, number 4, postcards—excerpt from RBD's talk "Other/how," given at St. Mark's Poetry Project, June 1985, as part of "The Tradition of Marginality"; to be published in its entirety in *Sulfur* (and later to appear in *PG*). I notice:

- In just one paragraph, posing major critical questions about "avant-garde" and gender.
- Attraction to avant-garde practice—"suspicion of the center, the desire to 'displace the distinction between margin and center'" (11); "drawing on avant-garde practice seems more fruitful for me-the-woman" (12).
- Articulates cautions: Suspect "secretly, lovingly" maintaining the "idea of poet as priest," "poem as icon"; "turn yr. back on it" (12).
- "Is its [avant-garde practice's] idea of language social?"—rejecting notions of language transcendence, or any avoidance of the social in writing practices ("Dialogic reading means dialogic writing") (12).
- WOMEN and avant-garde: ASK "Where is/are its women: where in the poems, serving what function? Where in the social matrices, with what functions? Where in its ideologies? How does it create itself by positioning its women and its women writers?" (12).

< >

1991. I've made my way into graduate school and am seeking women poets in the underground stacks of the library. A squat, fat, cream-colored volume with the word "OTHERS" printed in gold catches my eye. It is a bound volume of the little magazine *Others*, which ran from 1915 to 1919, publishing poets I recognize—Stevens, Eliot, Pound, Williams, and Moore—alongside a host of other unfamiliar names: Mary Carolyn Davies, Jeanne D'Orge, Mina Loy, Alfred Kreymborg, Skipwith Cannell. It occurs to me, with great astonishment, that T. S. Eliot was once an unknown poet! Modernism suddenly, magically opens as a vast, complex, contested terrain of "others."

< >

1989. But I am irked by a contradiction in Woolf's logic: she argues for the need to write as a woman, to record "those unrecorded gestures, those unsaid or half said words, which form themselves, no more palpably than the shadows of moths on the ceiling, when women are alone, unlit by the capricious and colored light of the other sex" (88), to locate creative power in one's gender "differences" (91), but at the same time she insists on the need for women's writing to transcend any gendered expression of anger or pain (what Lauren Berlant calls in a great essay "the female complaint"), so as to achieve the ideal of an "androgynous" mind, a mind "resonant and porous . . . [that] transmits emotion without impediment; that it is naturally creative, incandescent and undivided" (102). Woolf emphasizes, "It is fatal for anyone who writes to think of their sex . . . for a woman to lay the least stress on any grievance; to plead even with justice any cause; in any way to speak consciously as a woman. And fatal is no figure of speech; for anything written with that conscious bias is doomed to death. It ceases to be fertilised" (108).

> *They often distill an almost intransigent emotional knowledge, and sometimes a deep, proud pain.* ("A Letter on Loy" 501)

III. Domesticity Is Back[3]

> These are suspect places.
>
> —Mina Loy, "Songs to Joannes"

RBD's *Domesticity is BACK* plays with surrealism's appropriation of the domestic, famously articulated as "the chance encounter of a sewing machine and an umbrella on an operating table" (Isodore Ducasse, or the Comte de Lautréamont) and replayed in images by Man Ray, Dali, Magritte, Cornell, and others that invest the objects with sexual associations (umbrella, male; sewing machine, female). The collaged image of sewing machine, umbrella (the kind used in a fancy drink), and cup is backed by the phrase "Domesticity is just TOTALLY SURREAL." The objects allude to a male line of surrealism held in tension with the "domestic" as a denigrated realm, delegated to women but appropriated at will by male artists to serve their creative identities. This "avant-garde" dynamic renders women's spaces and experiences truly "surreal" in male-defined circuits of art and imagination.

2001. I am revising my dissertation on *Others* into a book. Our twin sons have started kindergarten, and I am breastfeeding our new baby. I don't have enough milk, so I'm pumping after I feed him, the TV on to distract from the throbbing of the breast pump. I watch the planes fly into the towers, the towers tumble. Again and again. And again.

I am trying to understand how poetry structures and reflects our worlds, our thoughts, habits, beliefs, and inhabitations. These are the questions modernist poets asked, seeking to strip away conventions deemed superficial, to get at the core, essence, or truth. What they reveal in their processes of dislodging and renovation are constructions of gender, sexuality, race, religion, and class—some new, many age-old, lodged in the stanzas, the rooms of the lyric tradition. Reading their poetry might help us understand modern processes of constructing selfhood and otherness, help us dislodge ourselves from habits of thoughts and inhabitations we inherit through language. I am trying to devise a method of close reading that I call "cultural formalism"—close reading that is not closed off, objective, or scientific, but self-interested, contextualized, socially embedded, and politically active. But how to do this?

RBD publishes *Genders, Races and Religious Cultures in Modern American Poetry*, unfolding a new method of "social philology": a reactivation of close reading to examine in poetry the textual traces and discursive manifestations of a variety of ideological assumptions, subject positions, and social concepts concerning gender, race, and religious culture (*GRRC* 1).

She's done it again, said what I wanted to say, before me, for me:

> *One wants any study of poetry to engage with poetry as such—its conventions and textual mechanisms, its surfaces and layers—and not simply to regard the poetic text as an odd delivery system for ideas and themes.* (*GRRC* 7)

Yet one also wants:

> *the techniques of close reading to reveal social discourses, subjectivities negotiated, and ideological debates in a poetic text.* (*GRRC* 12)

< >

1999. The first MSA Conference, Penn State University, Seminar on Modern and Contemporary Women Poets. The interest in this topic is so great that the seminar is divided into two sessions; the first session, led by Linda Kinnahan, features invited participants Rachel Blau DuPlessis and Linda Wagner-Martin; the second, led by Lynn Keller, features the poet Kathleen Fraser. I am a recent PhD in the first year of a new job. Seminar participants are invited to submit essays reflecting on the connections (not necessarily ones of influence) between a modernist and contemporary woman poet. I sit in awe in a room with poets, scholars, and poet-scholars whom I have long admired and whose work I have turned to for essential guidance. The generosity of LK, LWM, and RBD toward this group (mainly grad students and young scholars and poets), and the energy and excitement that the seminar generates, stays with me. There is a palpable determination to conjoin feminism and modernism, and these seminars help realize that goal, connecting not only modernist and contemporary women poets but feminist scholars of different generations.

< >

Sew, a needle pulling thread.

IV. Mona Lisa Corrected[4]

> Rhetorically "For the Etruscans" mingles manifesto, analysis, intercuts of material from that workshop, letters to friends, the fluid form of talking, and a sense of audience—the enormously excited and participatory group of women for whom, to whom, from whom I was speaking.
>
> —Rachel Blau DuPlessis, "Reader, I Married Me"

RBD addresses *Mona Lisa Corrected* to "The Art Museum of Patriarchy." The post(card) visually combines media genres (a photo of a rose, an ink-drawn visual instruction for using a tool placed to bore into the Mona Lisa's forehead) with the iconic image of womanhood and of Western art, asking how "woman" is retooled and acted upon through foundational art traditions.

1988. *HOW(ever)*, volume 4, number 3, alerts. Several authors' pieces focus on Moore; this section includes an excerpt from RBD's tour de force essay "No Moore of the Same." I've been subscribing for a year to the journal now. I'm alerted to ever-new lexicons regarding form, language, gender, power.

- A language of textuality brought to Moore's "complex relations to poetry as an institution": "text as a concept"; "textual problems"; "textual issues" (11). BOOM—locating a feminist politics in textuality: self-erasure, self-revision, collaboration, citation: "textual strategies" that delegitimize "authority" (12).
- What was this way of talking about form???? Moore's denial of work as "poetry": her oeuvre a "test of poetry," and her "shrug of a genre category . . . a radical gesture of rejection" (11). Feminist resistance as textual maneuver, shifting the ground. Disrupting "binary gender-gestures. Something very radical, very undermining" (12). Form as a minefield.
- Authority of textual institutions, canons, notion of "author"—EX-PLODED. RBD's Moore is a secret agent, allowed "in" behind a "facade" of following expected orders, inscribing a "mimicry" of what we expect in poetry that stealthily allows her to "substitute her own," re: stanza and line form, language use, rhythms, etc. (12).

I read Moore anew. Agog.

< >

I discover Mina Loy, whose writing dismantles me, disrupting my habits of reading, knowing, inhabiting:

> FORGET that you live in houses that you might live in yourself.
> ("Aphorisms on Futurism" 149)

> Houses hold virgins
> The door's on the chain
> ("Virgins Plus Curtains Minus Dots" 21)

> The door was an absurd thing
> Yet it was passable
> ("The Effectual Marriage" 36)

I am trying to understand Loy's disjunctive writing, to write about "The Effectual Marriage," both her long, sprawling, narrative poem and the tight, imagistic box Ezra Pound reduced it to in his anthology. He makes the poem as solid as a brick house. Intellectual. Logopoeic. But Loy's not only that. She's brilliant and messy and urgent and emotional and sexual and pleasurable and tormented. Tormenting. How do I make sense of this?

Before I can make sense, write sense, RBD publishes "Seismic Orgasm: Sexual Intercourse and Narrative Meaning in Mina Loy." She forges the path, she opens the way, writing of orgasms, breaking taboos, dislodging assumptions.

> *Loy's satiric, ironic, wickedly learned and passionate voice goes far to destabilize lyric assumptions about the romance plot, female silence, and objectification.* (*GRRC* 52)

RBD's satiric, ironic, wickedly learned and passionate voice goes far to destabilize scholarly assumptions about argument, evidence, logic, and cultural meaning and value.

< >

1984. *HOW(ever)*, volume 1, number 4, alerts—reading RBD's "The Work of Susan Howe": a two-page double-columned essay, meeting the call for a different form of critical commentary, "not complete in the scholarly sense." This section of the journal is dedicated to "informal commentary and information on new or neglected books by relevant women poets, in brief letter, journal or notation form . . . with the hope of removing prohibitions linked with thinking/writing critically" (11). This piece alerted me to RBD's early embrace of reforming, with flexibility, the critical essay, and undercutting some of the (gendered) assumptions associated with "critical" thinking, "completeness," "rigor," and so on. I would discover her experiments with the essay in journals, ferreting them out, often needing the help of interlibrary loan services for small and avant-garde venues not held at Notre Dame (*Hambone, Sulfur, Poetics Journal*), as I furthered my graduate research (1980s). It was a big hallelujah moment when so many of these essays were collected in *The Pink Guitar* (1990), so different from the more traditional (but mind-blowing) essays in *Writing Beyond the Ending: Narrative Strategies of Twentieth-Century Women* (1985), which is forthcoming when this *HOW(ever)* piece appears.

V. WOW Are You Ever[5]

> I did not want hierarchy or claims of controlling authority over a set of materials; thus, I chose "collage" and "the field" as modes or methods of thought, quite aware of using modernist "devices" for feminist purposes.
>
> —Rachel Blau DuPlessis, "Reader, I Married Me"

In *WOW Are You Ever* RBD collocates images of fragmented body parts from the media into a collage blazon, capturing the ideological processes of normalizing the "white woman-ity" that absorbs the unaware consumer.

A room where clippings paper the walls.
("For the Etruscans," *PG* 10)

2022. What kind of "room" is formed or deformed through collage?

< >

1989. In the seminar that begins with Woolf, we later read RBD's "For the Etruscans." This essay opens a way forward, a different kind of feminist modernist response to the challenges that women writers face, an essay that makes room for the varied complexity of voice, thought, and lived experience, including women's anger and suffering. RBD's use of collage strikes me as a method of modernist experimentation that does not preclude the personal or autobiographical but also opens that voice to many others, without limiting the kinds of gendered experience or range of emotions that may be included. Essay in the French sense of *essayer*, to try, to experiment. Collage permits the movement between, the contradictions of, the personal and the social, the I and the we, I and its others, writing and discourse/history/power, the essay and other genres and media, a method I find inspiring, experimental, and essential to RBD's feminist en dehors garde aims.

< >

Encountering "Pater-daughter" when starting to think about a dissertation (which ended up being on the problem RDP sets up: how to be a woman poet in relation to a poet like William Carlos Williams, navigating radical and sadly regressive gender politics at once); how collagelike form offered a strategy.

> *A both/and vision born of shifts, contraries, negations, contradictions, linked to personal vulnerability and need. Essay and sermon. A both/and vision that embraces movement, situational.* ("For the Etruscans," PG 6)

< >

1985. *HOW(ever)*, volume 2, number 3, "Writing, an Excerpt"—RBD's poetry, writing notes, language collage.

- Cover visual is a collage page from *Writing* and "Working Notes."
- Page-space and word collage, marks on page, physicality of language (fonts, ink hues, pasted materials from different textual materials).
- Working notes: stress on marginality.
- "Writing from the center of, the centers of, otherness . . . Understanding formal marginality. Marginalization. Setting the poem so there is a bringing of marginalization into writing" (1).
- Motherhood: "As to the subject: a first or really second month of a baby who comes as otherness, as difference"; "Poetry too pretty: creating 'beauty'? Creating chora. Beginning-middle-end, ha" (1).
- Pages 2–5, excerpt: visual page, spacing, handwriting in margins, double or triple columns (variable reading); blank spaces; parentheticals; regular syntax collides with fragmented, associative, sound-imaged and -generated language.
- "Marginalia without a center?" (5): language meaning embodied in forms through which it is conveyed, arranged, spoken, etc.
- Dancing with "theory" in experiencing, relaying baby talk, "creating chora" (1). ("Pre-oedipal plot? The mother, hidden . . . A text to speak now, writing, writing the sung-half song") (5).
- This is RBD "on the cusp": *Writing Beyond the Ending* is just out; all of "Writing" is forthcoming from the first issue of *Ottotole* ("a new publication of prose and 'writing about writing'"); the landmark essay (in form and feminist substance) "For the Etruscans" is about to appear in Elaine Showalter's *New Feminist Criticism*.

(Reader could be writer, writer reader. Listener could be teacher.) ("For the Etruscans," *PG* 6)

< >

1989/2022. I wrote my seminar paper on "For the Etruscans"; I unfortunately lost it, but I have my penciled notes for the essay that still resonate as I write today:

- How does RBD seek to transform the forms of writing, and how does her essay embody her theoretical ideals?
- Form of essay is a thesis. A collage v. allusive breaks rules but sets up new ones.
- Form should be subversive.
- Expression of struggle, not authority... an endeavor, not an accomplishment, is her goal.
- Criteria could be the work the essay does socially. The doing is the value. The act of how we examine something. "importance of contradiction and nonlinear movement"

< >

RBD's close reading of Countee Cullen's "Incident" astounds me (*GRRC* 17–19). "I am no whit bigger," yet my understanding of the roots of whiteness, its poisonous impact, has been enlarged. This small detail—a word meaning particle or iota —reveals

> that words and their "social evaluations" are no small matter (*GRRC* 19).

< >

2022. I'm interested in Rachel's early and ongoing commitment to the fragment, the small thing, the piece, and the collocation of such as a way of feminist theorizing and poetics. I want to look at "small" forms arising out of the format of *HOW(ever)* (postcards, alerts, short essays) and the postcards more recently displayed on the Mina Loy: Navigating the Avant-Garde website.

> Tactics which deny or subvert the authoritative text have haunted me. I wanted polyphony; I wanted excess. I wanted to achieve uncontrollable elements. I wanted to layer and propose discontinuities until there was almost no "poem"—no "art object." ("Darkest Gush" 8)

VI. Wrenches[6]

> But from the very beginning I knew I was making principles of art integrate with principles of analysis in ways that aroused readers to feeling, understanding, and response. These essays are sensuous theorizing.
>
> —Rachel Blau DuPlessis, "Reader, I Married Me"

RBD's "Wrenches" retools the postcard, using found objects—wrenches—to literalize Mina Loy's demand for a feminist reconstruction of consciousness. Whether turning mass-produced objects into collage, poems into essays, or theory into post(card)s, RBD blurs the lines between "poetry," "criticism," and "theory."

1987. *HOW(ever)*, volume 4, number 2, postcards—from "Language Acquisition" (1986 in *Iowa Review*) on Kristeva—enacting a process of critical inquiry that presses on the role of the "question," the energy of "questioning."

- Selected excerpt is a cascade of questions, enacting the "question" as both critical process and as feminist tool.
- Language theory/modernism/gender.
- Poses a question Kristeva asks about "why... does Virginia Woolf 'not dissect language as Joyce does?'" RBD unpacks the assumptions of this question with about ten other questions, showing how this question "can be translated into a series of other questions that makes this language a question" (14).

> *I want a feminist marbling of the paper, with its own curiosity and gall. Time to refigure work within the "work" of art.... For when work is taken up, the monologue of "lyric" cracks open, revealing occluded dialogues.* ("Marble Paper" *BS* 96)

< >

1999. The first MSA conference, in a seminar on gender and women poets, in which RBD talked about strategic approaches to scholarship as a feminist—the need to follow critical expectations to meet demands of tenure, review, while also pursuing a revisionary approach to the essay, in pieces such as those appearing in *PG*, that brought feminist practice into collision with standard critical practice. The women in that room are among the most interesting feminist scholars in modernist/contemporary poetry now, but then, most were just starting careers. We were hungry to hear her feminist thoughts on navigating the system of the (nonfeminist) institutions we had so recently entered.

> *The essay form permitted me to say what I wanted, and how, to link and to leap. Reader, I married me.* ("Reader, I Married Me," *BS* 26–27)

< >

1991. *HOW(ever)*, volume 6, number 3, postcards, "Thinking about Annie Finch: On Female Power and the Sonnet"—one of three responses to Finch's "The Sonnet Transfigured" (which appeared in volume 6, number 2).

- Invited in by RBD's casual tone of musing: "I experience intellectual curiosity about Finch's idea that the sonnet concerns love for the repressed female power" (16).
- Calm, paced interaction with Finch's argument. So unlike so much lit crit that is self-proclaiming and denigrating. But clear in its own stake and position. I am intrigued, asking what form of critical discourse is modeled here? Can our critical essay-ing be feminist and generative in its form, voice, approach? At the time, in my first year as an assistant professor, I start to think about these questions as I design the university's first course in feminist theory and literary criticism. RBD is by my side.
- Poetic forms and gender ideologies. Lyric ideology. Sonnet historicized. The work of form and genre (disguised as transcendent) carrying ideologies of sexualized power and objectification. These ideas (also in *The Pink Guitar*) seed a book I later write on feminist experimentalism and the lyric. RBD stays by my side.

> *In my essays' psychic and speculative search for contradictions, for wholeness, linear and constellated forms coexist.* ("For the Etruscans," *PG* 13)

< >

In a graduate seminar on modern poetry, we read RBD's *The Pink Guitar*. I know from Wallace Stevens's "The Man with the Blue Guitar" that "Things as they are / Are changed upon the blue guitar" (133). But Things as they are / Are transformed, radicalized by this Pink Guitar. Here, now, a new way of writing, a new way of engaging with these male modernists, these male teachers, who have excited my imagination yet left me unsatisfied, frustrated, wanting something more, something different. In "Pater-Daughter: Male Modernists and Female Readers," I encounter a Mater-Daughter relationship, a mentor on the page who feels my excitement and expresses my rage:

> *Reading the radical literature of our time, reading* Spring and All. *See at the end how the final flower to bloom is a black-eyed-Susan "rich / in savagery— / Arab / Indian / dark woman." This, the final statement of an amazing document of change, of challenge, of difference, of the new (and Williams so excited and effervescent) returns to the "savagery" of sameness. Oldness. . . . I am roused by the work's saucy claims; I tumble back the same hill again, a boulder heaved and lost by some repetitive hero.* (PG 41–42)

Jack fell down and broke his crown, and Jill came tumbling after. But this time Jill stands up, brushes off the mud and finds she's not alone, because another Jill, a Rachel, is speaking a new language, writing a new rhyme, and opening new doors, pathways to a criticism that is personal, inventive, imaginative—as saucy and effervescent as Williams, full of feminist vim, vigor, and venom of the most restorative kind.

> *Proposition 5: Modernist agendas concealed highly conventional metaphors and narratives of gender, views of women as static, immobile, eternal, goddess-like. Until the problematic of women is solved, no writer is truly modern. Modernist agendas conceal highly conventional views of race—African-Americans as primitive, "colorful," picturesque people. Until the problematic of race is solved, no writer is truly modern.* (PG 44)

And so I follow her up the hill, lugging my toolbox, to begin the work, the practice of dislodging. I am always following her, two steps behind. (More than two. But I can see her, and she beckons me to join her.)

> *These poetic objects are filled with stored human labor, stored human thought, habituations. It is a work, a practice to begin the long social process of dislodging.* (PG 44)

VII. What the Actual[7]

Non lineage, nonlinear narratives, achronological. Contemporary writing. Writing among our contemporaries. Rethink nature of influence, not just for poets and artists but for ourselves as scholars.

RBD's "What the Actual" performs an "aesthetics of dissonance" that expresses dissidence, particularly feminist dissent. Techniques of parataxis and juxtaposition flatten hierarchies of meaning and value. Thus collage offers not only a mode of feminist artistic expression but also a model for "feminist historiography," one that calls attention to the constructedness of histories of the avant-garde (Harding 25) and, by extension, allows for reconstructed feminist lineages. These strategies unsettle and reconsider lineages to stitch together feminist historiographies.

1990s. RBD at a conference on contemporary poetry; panel on feminism, packed with women and maybe two men; in audience, during discussion, saying that for her generation of poets, it was a "shock of recognition" to read then-ignored modernist women, reading them as though they were contemporaries (how we think about lineage) (early 1990s).

> *One might argue for Loy's proleptic influence upon me.* ("A Letter on Loy" 500)

< >

2022. On my rediscovering RBD's early essays, thinking about what we have termed the en dehors garde: I am struck by a passage she wrote about discovering Loy, a writer from the past, who for RBD was really more a "contemporary of the present."

> *One might argue for my (i.e. a critic or a poet-critic's) influence on Loy: by virtue of the poems highlighted in contemporary readings a certain Loy is created and sustained. One might argue for a community of interest between us—the intensities of our feminisms, both filled with skepticism about pieties, inflect the nature of our poetries.* ("A Letter on Loy" 500)

< >

1992. *HOW(ever)*, volume 6, number 4, postcards—a reflective farewell in *HOW(ever)*'s final volume, titled "The Unwritten."

- The journal as "bridge between underknown modernist women and ourselves" and a "space for sisterhood of exploration" (14, 15).
- "I see the fruits of its exploration in many places now" (15). Understatement of the year. Wow. So true to this day, in this moment, in this essay.

VIII. Time's Up[8]

> The multiple pressures of living out feminist thinking led me again and again to this non-objective, polyvocal prose, whose writing I experienced as the most pleasure when it became most speculative and most uncontainable, most meditative and most passionate.
>
> —Rachel Blau DuPlessis, *The Pink Guitar*

In "Time's Up," RBD invites us to rethink our relationship to time and the "new." Is a work "new" when it is created or when it is encountered for the first time? What is contemporary art or literature, and who are our contemporaries?

2022. We are coauthoring an essay about Rachel Blau DuPlessis and the influence her scholarship has had on ours. We pick up *The Pink Guitar*. Pluck a few pages. The notes sing out again, slightly discordant and still resonant.

> *So, it has seemed most crucial for feminist writing to reexamine and claim the innovative writing strategies for which our century is noted, turning collage, heteroglossia, intergenres, and self-reflexivity (to name just some) to our uses.* (*PG* viii)

It occurs to us, with great delight, that RBD has been practicing en dehors garde techniques all along. Her work has been leading us around to where she started, circling, spiraling, around a center that need not be occupied but must be dismantled, undone. We thought we were following her on a linear path, always two steps behind, but her work enacts an ongoing, nonlinear, creative and critical exploration—the work of unearthing, prodding, provoking, rehabilitating. She has always been inviting us to take up the practice, to join in the dance, to participate in the en dehors garde experiment.

> *Exploration not in service of reconciling self to world, but creating a new world for a new self.* ("For the Etruscans," *PG* 19)

Notes

1. DuPlessis's collage post(card)s are referenced throughout, providing many of the section subtitles. Web links to the postcards are provided below.

2. "Fans of Mina know this as a now-time rousing NOW-citation of absolute NOW-ness typical of the manifesto mode," (post[card] submission form). DuPlessis, *Crisis in Consciousness*, 2017, https://mina-loy.com/endehorsgarde/crisis-in-consciousness/.

3. DuPlessis, *Domesticity Is BACK*, 2017, https://mina-loy.com/endehorsgarde/domesticity-is-back/.

4. DuPlessis, *Mona Lisa Corrected*, 2017, https://mina-loy.com/endehorsgarde/mona-lisa-corrected/.

5. DuPlessis, *WOW Are You Ever*, 2017, https://mina-loy.com/endehorsgarde/wow-are-you-ever/.

6. DuPlessis, *Wrenches*, 2017, https://mina-loy.com/endehorsgarde/wrenches/.

7. DuPlessis, *What the Actual*, 2017, https://mina-loy.com/endehorsgarde/what-the-actual/.

8. DuPlessis, *Time's Up*, 2017, https://mina-loy.com/endehorsgarde/times-up/.

Works Cited

Berlant, Lauren. "The Female Complaint." *Social Text*, vol. 19/20, 1998, 237–59.

Churchill, Suzanne W., Linda A. Kinnahan, and Susan Rosenbaum, editors. *Mina Loy: Navigating the Avant-Garde*. Athens, GA: University of Georgia Press, 2020.

DuPlessis, Rachel Blau. *Blue Studios: Poetry & Its Cultural Work*. Tuscaloosa: University of Alabama Press, 2006.

———. *Genders, Races and Religious Cultures in Modern American Poetry, 1908–1934*. Cambridge: Cambridge University Press, 2001.

———. "The Darkest Gush: Emily Dickinson and the Textual Mark." *Titanic Operas: A Poets' Corner of Responses to Dickinson's Legacy*, edited by Martha Nell Smith and Laura Elyn Lauth, 1999, http://archive.emilydickinson.org/titanic/duplessis8.html.

———. "A Letter on Loy." *Mina Loy: Woman and Poet*, edited by Maeera Shreiber and Keith Tuma. Orono, ME: National Poetry Foundation, 1998, 499–502.

———. Untitled postcard. *HOW(ever)*, vol. 6, no. 4, 1992, 14–15.

———. "Thinking about Annie Finch: On Female Power and the Sonnet." *HOW(ever)*, vol. 6, no. 3, 1991, 16.

———. *The Pink Guitar: Writing as Feminist Practice*. New York: Routledge, 1990.

———. "No Moore of the Same," excerpt. *HOW(ever)*, vol. 4, no. 3, 1988, 14–15.

———. "Language Acquisition," excerpt. *HOW(ever)*, vol. 4, no. 2, 1987, 14.

———. "Other/how," excerpt. *HOW(ever)*, vol. 2, no. 4, 1985, 11–12.

———. "Writing, an Excerpt." *HOW(ever)*, vol. 2, no. 3, 1985, 1–5.

———. "The Work of Susan Howe." *HOW(ever)*, vol. 1, no. 4, 1984, 11–12.

Harding, James. *Cutting Performances: Collage Events, Feminist Artists, and the American Avant-Garde*. Ann Arbor: University of Michigan Press, 2012.

Kreymborg, Alfred, et al., editors. *Others: A Magazine of the New Verse*, vol. 1, no. 1–vol. 6, no. 5, July 1915–July 1919.

Loy, Mina. *The Lost Lunar Baedeker*. Edited by Roger Conover. New York: Farrar, Straus and Giroux, 1996.

Stevens, Wallace. *The Palm at the End of the Mind: Selected Poems and a Play*. Edited by Holly Stevens. New York: Vintage Books, 1972.

Woolf, Virginia. *A Room of One's Own*. New York and London: Harcourt Brace and Co., 1981.

CHAPTER SEVEN

An Extra Horizon Can Be Spun

On Publishing Rachel Blau DuPlessis's Numbers and Life in Handkerchiefs

ARIEL RESNIKOFF

> Babel striates the poet herself
>
> —Rachel Blau DuPlessis, *The Collage Poems of Drafts*

> The needle's eye
> Of the horizon in the noise
>
> —George Oppen, *Collected Poems*

I. En Route to *Numbers*

> The turn of the line
> the turn of the age
> the knife-edge of nowhere
> as a one-dimensional flat
> on a two-dimensional page
>
> —Rachel Blau DuPlessis, *Numbers*

In 2016, I coedited with Orchid Tierney and Julia Warner the first volume of a two-part text and print material archive and book called *Supplement*, which was published as a collaboration between the Materialist Press, the Kelly Writers House, and the Creative Writing Program and Center for Programs in Contemporary Writing at the University of Pennsylvania. The idea for *Supplement* was to document the various activities, events, and praxes of writing in the expanded field in and around Philadelphia over a two-year period. We solicited work and put out an open call for submissions from writers and artists living in Philly, as well as those who had passed through Philadelphia in the past year or so to read, perform, or otherwise present their work.[1]

The result was a unique hand-bound volume that included a radically diverse spectrum of contributors, with sixty-plus years between the youngest writer, Kaitlin Moore, and the eldest elder, Jerome Rothenberg. The other contributors to *Supplement v.1*, just to give a sense of the remarkable range, include: erica kaufman, Kevin Killian, Rae Armantrout, Rob Halpern, Cynthia Arrieu-King, Susan Bee, Levi Bentley, William J. Harris, Kyoo Lee, Rachel Levitsky, Jason Mitchell, C. A. Conrad, Tracie Morris, Jena Osman, Gabriel Ojeda-Sagué, Jennifer Scappettone, Christopher Soto, John Yau, Rachel Zolf, Laynie Browne, and DuPlessis, among many others. For the cover of the book, we used a photograph of a stained-glass seahorse in a window that once sat on the far wall of the Rose Room at Snockey's Oyster and Crab House in South Philadelphia. There, the poet Jason Mitchell hosted his iconic Philadelphia reading series, "Frank O'Hara's Last Lover," for many years, until the closure and subsequent demolition of Snockey's.

The volume contains a great number of hybrid textual-visual works including an excerpt from an ongoing collaboration between the painter Susan Bee and the poet Rachel Levitsky, as well as collage-poetry from Laynie Browne and Jennifer Scappettone. All the visual works are done in the most full and careful color, since quality of visuality is one of the founding principles and core values of the Materialist Press. On the back of *Supplement v.1* we included lines from the great Philadelphian modernist, H.D. (1886–1961):

> We are voyagers, discoverers
> of the not-known,
>
> the unrecorded;
> we have no map;
>
> possibly we will reach haven,
> heaven.
> (59)

On November 16, 2016, another great Philadelphian poet, Rachel Blau DuPlessis (b. 1941), who had recently become a friend, e-mailed me warmly and excitedly in response to *Supplement*:

> dear Ariel—oh my—this is a beautiful gorgeous experience, this Supplement. I hope you do it again. The color plates had me swooning, mainly because (as you know) I have work in color (collage poems) and have never had such a gorgeous presentation. (And I didn't know Laynie did collage also.) I began a racing fantasy that you a) began a press and published my book of collage poems called Numbers b) began a press and published work

by lots of contemporary poets who do collage work—JUICY—would really be fascinating to see.

I was stunned by DuPlessis's e-mail, since indeed, five years earlier, I had cofounded the Materialist Press with Julia Warner and Livingston Miller, in the spirit of Charles Reznikoff's (1894–1976) Objectivist Press, with a special emphasis on care for visuality and the print object. The idea there was to follow in a rich tradition of DIY avant-garde bookmaking—intersecting with Reznikoff's Objectivist Press as an inheritance—toward publishing radical contemporary experimental and especially hybrid work. The press was, and is, a micro- and quite intermittent press; so it was no surprise that DuPlessis had not known of it previously. But her "racing fantasy" was already a half-reality, I realized, and I immediately felt that I needed to see her *Numbers*. I responded to her message enthusiastically:

> Re: yr racing fantasy: Julia Warner (the design editor and co-publisher of Supplement) & I began a small fine-arts press on the west coast called The Materialist about 5 years ago; we publish intermittently, since we are on opposite coasts & both in school, but all of the books we publish are hand-bound artist books like Supplement . . . so, just to say that I LOVE this idea, & wd be very keen to begin thinking about ways to put it into action.

We scheduled a meeting at DuPlessis's house for the following week, and over coffee she brought out the box containing her loose-leaf manuscript of *Numbers*, a numero-poetic, almost gematric, a book of collage-poetry that looked when she first cracked it open like some sort of found illuminated assemblage.

Although I had been following DuPlessis's work for a number of years—especially in relation to the objectivists, since I had written my MA thesis on Zukofsky's Yiddish—I had not previously known of her collage praxis, or if I had, I hadn't given it much notice yet, and I had certainly never before seen anything quite like the work of *Numbers* she was laying out in front of me. Almost immediately, I began taking photos of the pages on my phone and texting them to Julia Warner in Cincinnati; and by the end of the meeting, I checked my phone and found this text from Julia: "YES!!!!"[2]

What so draws me to DuPlessis's *Numbers* and her collage-poetry more generally? I asked myself in my notes for this essay. There are many directions I might take such a question—I replied to myself—many essays I might write on this topic from various points of intersecting interest. I commented to DuPlessis, on the day she first showed me *Numbers*, how moved I thought Rezzy and George would be to see us sitting together over this wild numerological-poetic work she had created, interconnected poetic kith and kin—kindred practitioners in a Jewish experimental tradition spanning generations, numerous as the stars. My particular commitment to and passion for DuPlessis's work then—as an editor and publisher of two of her books, and the point of interest I've chosen to write this essay from—comes directly from this poetic-familial orientation (for how could it not?); and my fascination with her collage-poetry, in particular, stems from my sense for this work within the context of a post-objectivist contemporary poetic landscape and living legacy. DuPlessis for me is one of the key inheritors, innovators, and experimenters within a contemporary nexus of secular diasporic Jewish poetics, what I call here and elsewhere "expanded-Yiddish"—a conscious or unconscious afterlife of radical Yiddish modernism, born in the wake of an imposed eclipse; and her collage work I believe is the furthest iteration of this affiliation in her "poetry of a life," as we say, and in the long biography of her prolific writing. How could our Materialist Press—a press founded in tribute to the Objectivist Press and in memory of Reznikoff and Oppen—not publish this forceful and strange post-objectivist expanded-Yiddish book? The following week, it was decided: Julia Warner and I would edit and publish *Numbers*, and DuPlessis's "racing fantasy" about the future of this hybrid work would come to be.

II. Learning to Read the Desert

> Non-mastery of this digest of emptiness,
> it's unstoppable non-narrative
> fragments any alphabet
>
> —Rachel Blau DuPlessis, *Numbers*
>
> But an extra horizon can be spun
> a "floating weft line" run
> randomly thru the weaving
>
> —Rachel Blau DuPlessis, *Numbers*

My first reading of *Numbers* was more of a first viewing as I witnessed the collages from the noon-lit comfort of DuPlessis's living room without approaching the written texts themselves to start—reading words and lines here and there but not focusing on them, rather broadening my optic reach to the wider visual frame of each page. In retrospect, my eyes had been primed for DuPlessis's collage style by my longtime engagement with the work of the second-generation New York–school artist George Schneeman (1934–2009). Schneeman's collages—and especially his collage collaborations with poets like Ted Berrigan (1934–1983), Harold Schimmel (b. 1935), and Anne Waldman (b. 1945), among others—inhabit a visual-poetic hyperspace very much adjacent to DuPlessis's collage-poetics/aesthetics. The space I am describing—this "extra horizon," as DuPlessis writes—is somewhere between the book sitting on the shelf and the artwork hanging on the wall: it is the book and the artwork both—in the most physical and object sense—and indeed Schneeman's collages are very often used as cover art for books of poetry.

DuPlessis has never been a visual artist primarily, however—as Schneeman was, though he had dreamed of being a poet when he was young—but she comes to collage from the side of being a contemporary poet and critic, drawn to the openness and challenge of an intermedia approach and in particular, I think, to the object-ness of it. Although I had not really known DuPlessis as a collage artist until she showed me *Numbers*, after witnessing the manuscript and later witnessing her *Life in Handkerchiefs*—both wholly visually at first—I understood that her work, especially her later and latest work, fully necessitates intervention into collage. And out of necessity, thinking of Reznikoff's "first there is a need," DuPlessis has developed a singular and highly compelling visual-textual praxis that lives beside, inside, and on all sides of her writing.[3]

When I began to read the texts of the poems in *Numbers* within the larger collage-poetry forum, I quickly noticed a fascination, almost obsession, with the scrap, residual, and most of all: *debris*. As DuPlessis writes early on in *Numbers*:

> Whatever. For failure is a definite part
> of the endless debris
> and practices of art.
>
> (8)

And a little later: "collage is a deictic practice of debris." I recognized this "deictic practice" from the first moment I encountered it, in relation to and in conversation with Charles Reznikoff's poetics of "refuse"—a subject I've written on at length elsewhere—as framing of refuse and things refused in perpetual act of aesthetic/poetic refusal. During a reading introduced by George Oppen (1908–1984) at the San Francisco State Poetry Center in 1974, Reznikoff reads what I believe to be an ars poetica for such "deictic practice of debris," prefacing a scrap of verse by saying, "This is one that George likes—I'm glad I have it": "Among the heaps of brick and plaster lies / a girder, still itself among the rubbish" (107). Although Reznikoff is not explicitly engaging in a collage practice in this poem in any sense, the conceptual undertow of the work is quite clear: a poetics/aesthetics of framing in those things generally left and kept outside of frame, "heaps of brick and plaster . . . a girder," or as DuPlessis writes in *Numbers*: "random debris / sometimes almost garbage" (107).

There is something deeply Jewish at play within this shared poetics between DuPlessis and Reznikoff, not to mention Oppen and me. In the Bible, Numbers is called *Bamidbar* in Hebrew, meaning "in the desert." DuPlessis's book comes to us from this state, I think: from a state of wandering between states—wondering, gleaning, and reassembling these in-betweens, as she writes "construct a between zone" (*N*

24)—where "wandering creates the desert." I read DuPlessis's *Numbers*, in this sense, as a hybrid numerological exploration in poetry of the maskilic (Jewish Enlightenment) *talush*—the writer, artist, or intellectual who leaves the world of thick Jewish language and culture for the secular world of Enlightenment, yet never fully arrives in the new world and is always marked by that other Jewish world and language they left behind, even as they are unable to ever return to it. I had long thought of the work of Reznikoff and Oppen, and also Louis Zukofsky (1904–1978), in relation to this Jewish Enlightenment archetype, but it was only in discovering *Numbers* that I began to register DuPlessis's work as a part of this conceptual sphere. Something about the explicit Jewish wandering in the title of the book, and the poet's marvelous mishearing of Moses in the wilderness, via Alexander Pope: "I lisped in numbers, for the numbers came" (*N* 46), made me begin to think of this collage-poetry as a *talush*-work—as opposed and against the masterwork—which traces another path athwart: "irregular counts of unusual links" (82).

If *Numbers* is a book of wandering through desert in perpetual *talushkeyt* (wholly embodying the always wondering *talush*), the illuminated assemblages in the book might be mini tabernacles the poet builds as sites of poetic devotion on the paths ahead—from trash, scrap, almost anything lost or forgotten: "it was a key," she writes, inflecting a Yiddish idiom, "that no one knew from nothing" (18).

Later in *Numbers*, we find the following: "And 'yod' is a letter. But also a number. For the number 10 is shown by the letter 'yod'" (20). Here DuPlessis engages playfully with a Jewish numerological pun that unfurls in several directions at once. Yod is indeed the tenth letter in the Hebrew alphabet, therefore containing the numerological value of ten—the ten men it takes to make a Jewish prayer quorum, for example—and the yod is the first letter of the word "Yehudi" in Hebrew, meaning "Jew," and it is the first letter of the word "Yiddish," meaning "Jewish." In his iconic poem "1919," the Yiddish American modernist Jacob Glatshteyn plays on the same pun as DuPlessis.

> Lately, no trace remains
> of Yankl son of Yitzhak
> except a tiny red point
> rolling crazy thru streets
> with hooked-on awkward limbs ...
> (209)

Glatshteyn's "tiny round point" (*kleyntshik pintele a keykheldiks*) refers to the Hebrew orthographical sign of the *hirik*—a lone dot that sits below a Hebrew or Yiddish letter indicating the phoneme /i/ (in Hebrew), as in "ee," or else /I/ (in Yiddish), as in "if," which is often accompanied by the Hebrew letter yod.[4]

In Glatshteyn the pun is stretched even further, since he uses the Yiddish word *keykheldiks* to describe the point as specifically "round," connoting the antisemitic

American slur invented at Ellis Island. The yod in Glatshteyn, as in his Yiddish name "Yankl son of Yitzhak," has gone missing, and only the tiniest dot of Jewish recognition persists at the site of the Jewish tongue (his Yiddish).

In DuPlessis, we find the yod constructed from a bright pink luggage label cut-out, layered on a small bag one might mistake for a paper pocket. She titles the piece "Yod—Its Little Eye" in unconscious homage to Glatshteyn's *pintele yid*, running a string through the "tiny round dot" of the letter, the orthographic mouth of the collage, questioning herself later in the book in the voice of the *talush*:

> why do collages
> often incorporate
> canceled stamps & used
> bus tickets, domesticated
> tokens of state power?—
> to say someone or something
> has gotten somewhere?

(94)

Her answer comes in the facing collage: "This is something called / a whirlwind book," she writes:

> the papers are
> bound together
> but all the pages
> are of different sizes.
>
> Speaking from the spot of dust

(95)

In the Biblical Numbers, God directs Moses to number all the wandering Israelites who made it through the exodus from Egypt. In DuPlessis's *Numbers*, numbering as such becomes a bridge between the linguistic and physical worlds—a sort of mystical poetic realism—that takes numerological collage-poetry as a system of "microscopic cellular / movement far beyond our senses" (*N* 16). Writes DuPlessis:

> In a system
>   where numbers are not
> anything but
>   letters in another guise
>
> translations
>   of simple words or sums

> will multiply
> implications.
> (72)

And a little later:

> It traces another path athwart:
> irregular counts of unusual links.
> (82)

Then, finally:

> And often the systems speak
> double-coded, over-layered languages
> to make sure that every cell-ly entity
> has enough to go on.
>
> This seems to me
> Exactly like poetry.
> (88)[5]

III. Midrashic Interlude // In Memory of Kevin Killian

> The Gestalt is patterned oddity.
>
> —Rachel Blau DuPlessis, *Numbers*
>
> If there was no poetry there would be no
> toy, face, torment, healing, gladiola, prix fixe, heaven
>
> —Kevin Killian, "The Flowering Face"

Once we decided we would publish *Numbers*, the question became how to pay for the publication. This is often the case with the Materialist Press, as we fundraise project by project. *Numbers*, however, would need to be printed primarily in color, which would cost a great deal more than something like *Supplement*, for example, in which we printed in color only for certain specific contributions and printed everything else in black-and-white. *Numbers* is a full-color hand-bound book, so the production estimates came out much higher than our usual projections. We knew we would need to fundraise, therefore, beyond our usual means, and so we decided to host a gala, including a dinner, small art auction, and poetry reading, in the San Francisco Bay Area. As we were brainstorming who might read at the gala, DuPlessis suggested the great Kevin Killian (1952–2019), a legend and eminence of the San Francisco New Narrative scene, and a dear friend of DuPlessis.

I wrote to Killian on the evening of November 8, 2017, to invite him to read at the fundraiser without yet knowing him almost at all—though we had published him in *Supplement*—at DuPlessis's suggestion. Killian replied the following morning: "I would like to say yes to your event. Please tell me how I can help . . . [Dodie] and I are both tremendously indebted to Rachel Blau DuPlessis." DuPlessis it turns out had been one of the first publishers of Dodie Belamy's (b. 1951) work in a national (non-DIY) context; and Killian had been invited some years back to Philadelphia as the Rachel Blau DuPlessis Lecturer at Temple University: "one of the happiest weeks of my life," he wrote me.

The guest of honor at the event was another old friend of DuPlessis, George and Mary Oppen's daughter, Linda, who commented to me almost exactly the same thing I had commented to DuPlessis as we sat for the first time over *Numbers*: how happy George and Rezzy would have been to know that we were working together to bring this work into the world. When Killian arrived, he approached Linda Oppen and me, hugged us both tightly, and without skipping a beat, he laughed: "Resnikoff and Oppen at a fundraiser for DuPlessis! The perfect occasion to have you sign my autograph book." Killian presented us with a notebook full of signatures, and he flipped to Charles Reznikoff's and George Oppen's facing autographs. "Sign below your kin." Killian gestured to the page, and Linda and I both signed excitedly, if haphazardly—neither of us had expected such a thing to happen that night.

Killian gave a brilliant reading in support of DuPlessis's *Numbers*, and his presence and performance at the gala helped us raise the necessary funds to publish the book. Almost exactly two years later, we reached out to Killian again to see if he might like to host a launch event for *Numbers* as part of reading his series at Alley Cat Books in San Francisco: DuPlessis would read with Beverly Dahlen (b. 1934). Killian was elated by the idea, and he and I began planning an event for early September 2019. The last time I saw Killian on this earth he said to me, "It will be so good to have Rachel in San Francisco again!" On June 15, 2019, Killian passed away suddenly. That August, DuPlessis and I decided that we would host the final reading of Killian's series as a *Numbers* West Coast launch—a reading Killian had helped plan—in his memory. Introducing DuPlessis and *Numbers*, I remarked *this book would not exist without Kevin*.

IV. From Publishing *Numbers* to Publishing *Life in Handkerchiefs*

> Words vibrate also, and can also be
> unrepeating fractions
> of themselves.
>
> —Rachel Blau DuPlessis, *Numbers*

> Words are only like the shards you might fit together
> (if that), reconstruction
> with only half the aura—barely.
> Words are pulverized dust, endlessly scattered.
>
> —Rachel Blau DuPlessis, *Life in Handkerchiefs*[6]

In early 2022, DuPlessis sent me another collage-poetry manuscript, this time as a digital pdf: a book called *Life in Handkerchiefs*. I had seen pieces of this book on other occasions and was already interested in it, especially in its use of text in relation to textile. DuPlessis pitched the manuscript as a sort of sister volume to *Numbers*, and as I began to glance at the pdf she had sent I could easily see what she meant: writes DuPlessis in *Life in Handkerchiefs*, quoting Adorno's *Minima Moralia*:

> those things . . . that fell by the wayside—
> what might be called the waste products
> and blind spots that have escaped the dialectic.

(19)

And a little later in the same poem:

> Thus poetry might better submerge
> into a theory of debris, or of hankies.
> Or perhaps simply become the debris,
> as a hanky

(19)

The collage-poet's "deictic practice of debris" is fully at work in *Life in Handkerchiefs*—as is the expanded-Yiddish dialect(ical) inflection of her *talush*, as she writes:

But what did I know from dread? "Vos veys ikh fun" all that?

> Nothing.
> I knew from nothing
(31)

A kith cousin of Jerome Rothenberg's (b. 1931) "Cok Boy—'vat em i doink here?'" (139), DuPlessis's Yiddish-inflecting hanky-gleaner builds textile altars as texts ("polylingual 'polymorphous perversity,' / and the flush of lubricious transitions / into multiple desires" [*Life* 57]), investing everything in the specificity and object-ness of the task at hand: "The dividing line among scarves, shawls, foulards, dishcloths," writes DuPlessis,

> dish towels, washcloths, cleaning rags, napkins, kerchiefs, collars (and perhaps cuffs), headwraps, mufflers, mantillas, even shrouds, diapers, rags as menstrual napkins, and hankies are not blurred, exactly but when you think of it—all are simply squares or rectangles or other shapes of textile, for use. (102)

The intense emphasis on the materiality of the text in *Life in Handkerchiefs* is a further and ever-fiercer articulation of DuPlessis's dream for her collage-poetry: to seek and find that extra horizon where the textual becomes tactile, and poetry is renewed on the page as a lost object reassembled in a found collage. "The tidal wave / of time," writes DuPlessis, "Language / struggles if it can to high ground"

> so it can make a story
> embroidered with details,
> or a song about annealed
> singularities
> to warn (or encourage)
> the next set
> of strangers arriving at
> "the border."
(95)

Life in Handkerchiefs (2023) is one example of the kind of work that Julia Warner and I are both committed to publishing: hybrid works by our contemporaries and elders, works that might not work for more text-only-oriented sorts of presses. In a small publishing climate where many of our greatest eminences in contemporary writing must query and search out a publisher for their work book by book, without much publishing stability at all, and especially within the context of hybrid or multimedia writing, our Materialist Press aims to cultivate a "haven"—thinking again of H.D.—where innovative visual-textual works like DuPlessis's *Numbers* and *Life in Handkerchiefs* can harbor at the fertile threshold of poetry and book art.[7]

Notes

1. Throughout this essay, I refer to collages that appear in the two volumes of poetry that DuPlessis has published with Materialist Press to date, *Numbers* and *Life in Handkerchiefs*. In each case, the volume in which the image appears and the page numbers, where available, are cited in the following notes.
2. "Deux mille dix," *Numbers*, unpaginated.
3. "Collage Is a Deictic Practice of Debris," *Numbers*, unpaginated.
4. "Yod—Its Little Eye," *Numbers*, unpaginated.
5. "This Is Something Called," *Numbers*, unpaginated.
6. "Introductory Remarks," *Life in Handkerchiefs*, 5.
7. From *Life in Handkerchiefs*, 25.

Works Cited

Doolittle, Hilda. *Trilogy*. New York: New Directions Books, 1998.
DuPlessis, Rachel Blau. *Life in Handkerchiefs*. Cincinnati, OH: Materialist Press, 2023.
———. *Numbers*. Cincinnati: Materialist Press, 2018.
———. *The Collage Poems of Drafts*. Sheffield, UK: Salt Publishing, 2011.
Glatshteyn, Jacob. "1919." *American Yiddish Poetry: A Bilingual Edition*, edited by Benjamin Harshav and Barbara Harshav. Stanford, CA: Stanford University Press, 2007.
Killian, Kevin. "The Flowering Face." *Argento Series*. Krupskaya Books, 2001.
Oppen, George. *Collected Poems*. New York: New Directions Books, 1975.
Reznikoff, Charles. *The Poems of Charles Reznikoff: 1918–1975*. Santa Barbara, CA: Black Sparrow Press, 2005.
Rosten, Leo. *Joys of Yiddish*. New York: McGraw-Hill, 1968.
Rothenberg, Jerome. *Poland/1931*. New York: New Directions, 1974.

PART III

Across Traditions

Romanticism, Objectivist and Projectivist Poetics, Secular Judaism, and the Witness of History

CHAPTER EIGHT

Between Objectivist and Projectivist Poetics

Rachel Blau DuPlessis and the "Force Moving"

JEANNE HEUVING

> Not to propose, but to have the work propose through her.
>
> —Rachel Blau DuPlessis, *The Pink Guitar*

> The problem of writing for me is how to get an ethical literature without any didacticism or political forcing. How to address human issues without being trapped by the ego-, ethno-, phallo-, logo-centrism of humanism.
>
> —Rachel Blau DuPlessis, "'Uncannily in the Open'"

IN 1985 RACHEL BLAU DuPlessis initiated a large shift in her poetry with the creation of her "portal" poem "Writing," leading her from the comparatively more circumscribed and iconic poetry of her earliest work to the sustained long poem project of *Drafts*.[1] As an early scholar, theorist, and activist of an emerging feminism, DuPlessis initially engaged feminist critique in her poetry through addressing the misrepresentation of women, especially as these occur in myth and poetry. Yet this direct approach to misogyny left her with a narrowed set of subjects and a first-person poetic speaker who experiences herself through a set of either-or conundrums: "Me goes leaping full and empty" and "whether I speak / about Her / or whether being her, I can speak" (*TR* 6, 14). In her portal poem "Writing" and in *Drafts*, DuPlessis moves beyond a first-person poetic speaker for the third-person speaker of "Writing," in response to an array of theories and practices brought about by the historical "turn to language." For DuPlessis this change was no simple paradigm shift. With her dual commitments to feminist critique and poetry writing, she needed to remake the grounds of her writing and therefore herself.[2] DuPlessis accomplishes this through her poem "Writing" and the essays collected in *The Pink Guitar: Writing as Feminist Practice*, written and revised in the same period as her poem. A highly porous writing in which feminist polemics combine with poetic evocations, *The Pink Guitar* evinces characteristics of feminine *écriture* and projective prose. This collection of essays moves between expansive sets of feminist issues and specific meditations on how to write. Crucial to this endeavor is her essay "'While These Letters Were A-Reading': an Essay on Beverly Dahlen's *A Reading*," in which she locates a practice that enables her own "force moving" (*PG* 110). It is through this interventionist writing that DuPlessis finds her way to her long poem, *Drafts*.

In her early poetry and throughout her career, DuPlessis has found much instruction in George Oppen and his objectivist poetics, namely his stress on experiential sincerity and political ethics, which for her necessitates feminist critique.[3] Indeed the stress on objects and objectivity in objectivist poetics enters this work as an early engagement with the history of poetry. In her initial poetry, DuPlessis locates her experience in carefully crafted poems with clear beginnings and endings, focusing on diverse objective realities that constitute her existence, including poetry as a set of formal possibilities. While objectivist values and practices are important throughout her career, they do not readily lead to the shift that DuPlessis needed to make in order to realize her eventual claim "that feminist revision would necessitate the multiple, forceful, and polyvocal invention of a completely new culture and the critical destabilizing, indeed the replacement, of the old" (*BS* 31). In her essay "Otherhow" in *The Pink Guitar*, she first begins creating what she later develops as a critique of the "foundational cluster of poetry": "Poetry gendered in a different way than fiction is? Sometimes it is possible to think so. Love, Beauty, Nature, Seasonal Change, Beauty Raked by Time, Mediating Vision or Muse, the pastoral, the carpe diem motif, the satire—all these prime themes and genres from the history of poetry seem to have swirls of gender ideas and gender narrative blended like the marbleized end papers of old books. It's so beautiful, so oily with color, who could want to pick it apart?" (140).

A few years later DuPlessis develops her fully analyzed critique of the "foundational cluster of poetry," combining her own discoveries as a poet and feminist theorist:

> To talk about lyric, one must say something about beauty, something about love and sex, something about Woman and Man and their positionings, something about active agency versus malleability. This is a cluster of foundational materials with a gender cast built into the heart of the lyric. The foundational cluster concerns voice (and silencing), power (appropriation and transcendence), nature (as opposed to formation and culture), gaze (framing, specularity, fragmentation), and the sources of poetic matter—narratives of romance, of the sublime, scenes of inspiration, the muse as conduit (Vickers 1981). There is often a triangulated situation in the lyric: an overtly male "I," speaking as if overheard in front of an unseen but postulated, loosely male "us" about a (Beloved) "she" (Grossman 1992, 227). To change any of these pronouns ("I" speaking directly to a "you," for example, an "I" who is a "she"; readers claiming to be female) is to jostle if only

> slightly the homosocial triangle of the lyric (Sedgwick 1985). The history of poetry shows that these—the foundational cluster, the tropes that Homans describes, the general gender narrative or pattern book of moves—are materials, to echo Annabel Patterson (1987), in which a large cultural investment has been made. ("Corpses" 71–72)[4]

I replicate DuPlessis's scholarly rendition of this "foundational cluster" in all its specificity because it manifests how entrenched asymmetrical gender relations are in poetry and what she is up against.

Poets' critiques of the perceived limitations of poetry do not always lend themselves to more poetry writing—witness the rejection of poetry by Laura Riding and the decades of poetic silence by George Oppen. Yet DuPlessis, intent to write poetry that engages critique, finds her way through the changed writing of her essays in *The Pink Guitar* and her poem "Writing." Throughout her career, DuPlessis's scholarship and poetic writing have informed each other. Prior to her essays in *The Pink Guitar*, DuPlessis published two impressive scholarly works: *Writing Beyond the Ending: Narrative Strategies of Twentieth Century Women Writers* and *H.D.: The Career of That Struggle*. This work, along with her initial poetry published in *Wells*, and the first section in *Tabula Rosa*, "from *The 'History of Poetry*,'" retain fairly strict disciplinary and genre expectations. In *The Pink Guitar*, DuPlessis opens the floodgates writing a highly porous set of essays that move between scholarly research and poetic evocation. The associational aspects of this writing, one perception, one observation, one question, leading directly to the next, reminds one of projective verse—and the transformative writing it enables.

Insufficient inquiry has been given to how, by midcentury in America, two poetics from seemingly opposing camps create poetic options in which both work against the interference of the poet as ego and a prefabricated, calculative language.[5] But while objectivist poets find correction in a close connection between the poetic speaker and the others, objects, and words of their writing, projectivist poets engage the resources of the subject in process as the writing moves from one perception, one language phrase, one word to another.[6] Projective poetics are particularly crucial for writers who elect fundamental change in the restrictive nomenclatures by which they are socially identified, whether by gender, race, ethnicity, or sexuality. Indeed, projective poetics enable writers to engage—without professing—received ideas, forms, and representations through a writing whose value resides in the movements and transformations of the writing. This is an immanent writing that acts on prior formations through the action the writing performs. If objective poetics are anchored to reality by values of sincerity and materiality, projective poetics depend on the poetic speaker's authenticity, her combined bodily, emotional, and cognitive responses as these evolve through the language she writes. Importantly, projectivism is different from expressionism in that it presumes a gap between the writer and her writing and between the propositions that she forms. "Gap," in fact, is the title for DuPlessis's "Drafts 5, 24, 43, 62, 81" and "100."

While it is impossible in any poet's work to declare this is an objectivist practice and this is a projectivist practice, all the more so as the influence of both poetics are consciously and unconsciously engaged by contemporary poets, projective and objective poetics do offer rather different orientations. DuPlessis's foray into projective poetics in *The Pink Guitar* and in "Writing" enable her to realize a manifold presencing that exceeds the limited, analytic critique of her prior writing.[7] This changed orientation is necessary for her to create her long poem, *Drafts*, as she takes this process-based writing into more objectivist directions. As such she moves her own work closer to her claim that feminism must lead to "the multiple forceful and polyvocal invention of a completely new culture." *Drafts* is this new culture in that a woman writer takes up aspects of her culture, as conveyed in its words, and fashions her writing as a thinking *with* words in a poetics of *"intricate bottomless tangibility"* ("Statement" 18).[8] *Drafts* is not a "woman's language," as is sometimes called for at this time, but rather a woman's poetry of thinking as broadly and as specifically as possible. While "Writing" focuses itself through the capacious topic of "otherness," *Drafts* elects single word explorations.[9] In doing so, she changes from the "the" writing of "Writing" to the "a" writing of *Drafts*, a fundamental difference between projective and objective poetics.[10]

To call DuPlessis's essays in *The Pink Guitar* projective prose is to stretch the definition of projective verse. However, the difference of this writing from her previous academic and poetry writing cannot be overemphasized. The essays proceed through combined physical, emotional, and cognitive responses, one assertion or question leading to the next. The sense of pressure by which each next occurs resembles projective verse, manifested in its segmented typographies, blocks of print, rather than the continuous, indented paragraphs typical of prose. In "*f*-Words: An Essay on the Essay," DuPlessis has described the possibilities for the feminine or feminist essay (depending on how one reads "*f*-words," there are other possibilities), drawing her examples from her own writing in *The Pink Guitar* as well as other essays in a way that coalesces with Olson's articulations of projective verse. This capacious writing is distinguished by its "response" and "responsiveness," and is less a personal writing (i.e., not an outlay of the egoistic subject) but rather a "positional" or a located writing (17, 28). Moreover, the essays are highly "wrought," their "language" deployed "not as a summary of findings but as the inventor of findings" (19). As such *f*-essays present that which is seen "under the conditions established in the course of writing." They are connected to the need for a revolutionary writing: "It was worth your life to 'get' a specific book or document or event—to ingest it, to digest it, even to detox it—a reading beyond reading, an impelled and compelled reading." DuPlessis further notes the importance of analysis to the essays but also its insufficiency: "The word *analysis* . . . doesn't get the lift and loft of feeling-thinking . . . the notion that cultural acts lay on our fibers" (18).[11] DuPlessis establishes a criteria for what counts as an "*f*-essay": "The question—Does this need to be written?—is an ethical one. Authenticity and sincerity exist in the motives for writing, not the results, which better be contents under pressure" (26). At one point, DuPlessis recognizes how her enthusiasm for the "*f*-essay" shares in Olson's need for animating ideals, for "this excessive, creative feminine ... sounds like Charles Olson's Noble Mayan all over again" (34).

DuPlessis's s mode of writing in *The Pink Guitar* enables her to expand the scope and the precision of her writing, creating both ground and method for her future work. Her initial essay, "For the Etruscans," can be seen as creating her own "company," to deploy a word Robert Creeley frequently used in relationship to his affiliated band of poets and was a calling to arms. Little is known of the mysterious, revered Etruscans, as DuPlessis maintains is the case for women, given their historical misrepresentation and absence. In this essay, DuPlessis notes the denigration of scholarship on women's writing and their exclusions from male literary company. DuPlessis asks, "What holds civilization intact? The presence of apparently voiceless Others, 'thoughtless' Others, powerless Others against which the Law, the Main, the Center, even the Diffusions of power are defined" (3). She concludes her essay: "Exploration not in service of reconciling self to world, but creating a new world for a new self." She signs off from this essay dated 1979/1984, "for the Etruscans," enlisting her readers to join her in this just-created company. Other essays in the volume take up modernist and avant-garde poetics but simultaneously establish how these in the hands of male practitioners depend on gender asymmetry and misogyny. Of these works she succinctly asks, "How does it create itself by positioning its women and women writers?" and notes, "Nothing changes by changing the structures or sequences only.... Nothing changes by changing the content only" (*PG* 141, 153).

If "Writing" is the portal poem for her extended poem *Drafts*, her essay on Beverly Dahlen is the portal essay to this new way of writing. DuPlessis begins her essay on Dahlen by quoting William Carlos Williams and linking this quotation to Olson's "Projective Verse": "'Not to attempt, at that time, to set values on the word being used, according to presupposed measures, but to write down that which happens at that time ...' and 'To practice skill in recording the force moving.' ... Such a statement is reheard, for instance, in parts of Olson's 'Projective Verse'" (*PG* 110).

DuPlessis's linking of Williams and Olson through Dahlen's example is most important for her evolving work. Yet there is an important difference between Williams's statement of the "force moving" and projective poetics, namely Williams's election of the verb "recording." For Olson as well as DuPlessis in *The Pink Guitar* and "Writing," the force moving is the writing itself, as writing leads to more writing. Or as Olson writes, "The distinction here is between language as the act of the instant and language as the act of thought about the instant" ("Human Universe" 4). Williams's emphasis on "recording" manifests the division in his own writing between a writing that evinces projectivist inclinations, "the force moving," and his objectivist commitments "no ideas but in things," both commitments well evidenced in *Spring and All*. To argue, as I do here, that DuPlessis's writing at this time is projective, is to draw attention to how she must write over and through the aporias that her feminist critique uncovers to create her own poetry. To claim her writing in "Writing" and the essays in *The Pink Guitar* are a writing of the "force moving," not a "reporting" of it as Williams inscribes, is inherently difficult since the transitioning and transforming writer and writing exist in a tension with each other, moving between postulations rather than establishing conclusive formulations. However, this is the claim of this essay.

DuPlessis's enthusiasm for Dahlen's *A Reading* enables her discovery of a new way of writing that answers to DuPlessis's needs to be a "desirous reader," scholar, and poet: "The role of Beverly Dahlen's new work cannot be underestimated in entering these questions of poetics and the discourses of (on) writing at a very high and brilliant level, claiming no revision. While this may not be fully true, it makes a commitment to 'the force moving.' . . . Thus in *A Reading*, the irruption of combinations of what we know in words and out, phrases, expression, cullings, not treated with any form of ironic contempt . . . or as a downfall from wholeness, but as part of the (language) materials of the mind at work" (*PG* 111–12). She elaborates: "Dahlen's *A Reading* is an articulation between lyric (the force moving) and documentary (record without judgment). And something else, this palimpsest where language (and thus social registers and discourses) constantly overwrites and whispers the otherness of half-seen, shadowy words. An 'it,' a space half-entered" (111–12).

While DuPlessis does not retain here her initial claim of Dahlen's writing in relationship to Olson's "Projective Verse," substituting the word "lyric" for what might be put as "projective," and "documentary" for what might be put as "objective," she does note the effectiveness of how Dahlen's writing displaces a wrongful writing, in which women are misrepresented and not presented, misspoken or not spoken at all. It is a writing of metonymy not metaphor, "a continuous stream of metonymy, which uncannily, the more it extends outward . . . the more it seems to layer itself over and over, a texture of singing through porous time and porous ego. Elusive. Fast moving. An impressionist surface of reflection and swift change" (*PG* 112). As DuPlessis further elaborates: "To write metonymy is to write all margins, no page. Is to make some critique of the center such that the binary distinctions between text and space disappear, and so that a work bleeds, as is said of a photograph printed to the edge. All is margin, all is center. And the once-compelling binaries like full, empty; frame, presence; absence, mark; become pluralized into voided markings, marked void" (112).

Dahlen's is a writing of in medias res, a writing of the phrase and not the sentence, of "the intense pressure of, pleasure of the gap," and, as DuPlessis quotes from Dahlen, "finished never done" (*PG* 113). DuPlessis concludes: "A person sits still in the middle of her life and writes herself something to read. She calls it *A Reading*. She is who she is, but also she is not" (113). Now the either/ors of identity that mark DuPlessis's early poetry have become both/ands; the split subject, I or she, is doubled. She asks why the work is called *A Reading* and answers, as a reading, "it alone will offer every new mark stroked a plethora of further paths and spoors. Because only metonymy guarantees the exasperating plenitude of signs, tones, registers, margins and pages alike . . . procedures for writing so excessive and marginal that it may begin to say: woman" (114). In her celebration of Dahlen's writing of the "force moving" and the creation of her own projective prose, DuPlessis has made a great leap from the gender binaries of her early poetry. Keller succinctly describes this change from DuPlessis's early poetry to her later work: "The speaking subject is construed as constructed within—or within and beyond—language, not represented through it" (284).

Before turning to "Writing," I wish briefly to consider the achievement and limitations of DuPlessis's preceding poetry. In both her 1980 *Wells* and in Part I of *Tabula Rosa*, "from *The 'History of Poetry*,'" deliberate feminist critique in the ways that women have been portrayed and the gender dynamics underlying these are prominent throughout. *Tabula Rosa* is divided into two parts, "from *The 'History of Poetry*'" and "Drafts," in which "Writing" and her "Draft 1" and "2" appear. DuPlessis initiates the first part with an epigraph presumably written by her since there is no other attribution: "She cannot forget the history of poetry because it is not hers" (1). Although these early poems are insightful and inventive, in comparison to the poetry DuPlessis comes to write, they are limited by the need for situating gendered experience through first-person poetic speakers; binary gender depictions and oppositional strategies; coherent arguments and/or narratives with definite beginnings and ends; the consequent need for closure and solutions to unresolvable gender aporias; and the election of metaphor over metonymy. One of the ways these limitations surface is how the first-person poetic speaker experiences herself as in an "undertow," the title of the first section of *Wells*, split between "I" and "she." This is evident in the short poem "A Poem of Myself," in which the poem begins with a sense of restriction: "I cannot move at all and will not either" (*SP* 13). Because she cannot move, rather than be subjected to a situation out of her control, she enlists her will; she "will not." The speaker directs her attention to the nature around her and meditates: "The trees begin swaying as I watch them / turning inward and outward onto myself." Yet the speaker's deliberate attention to nature is interrupted since she is on a "terrace" and must "come in," into a socially defined space. She extends her meditation into what it means to come in, to enter, specifically in this situation and more generally:

> Standing in entrances. About to come in.
> My shoulders are hunched forward to hide my breasts.
> When am I going to come into the room?
>
> Come in, come in, I say to all the fragments.
> (*SP* 13)

While the poem ends with a possibly light tone, the ending also feels forced. The speaker has been enjoying seemingly unimpeded pleasure in nature, but she cannot continue in this state since she must "come in" from the terrace, feeling a need to hide what marks her as woman. As her life is fragmented, so is her poetry, and it is only through commanding the fragments to "come in" that she can make her life cohere.

"Eurydice," also in *Wells*, creates an alternative version of the Orpheus myth. The title *Wells* of the volume is rich, conveying both the positive and negative aspects of wells—wells as a source of water and welling and wells as dark, enclosed places into which if one falls there may be no return. Both senses of wells pertain in "Eurydice." The poem engages how Eurydice is lost not only because of Orpheus's unwanted action as the myth tells it, of looking back at her, but because

> Songs are his,
> melody like a great linked chain.
> Touch is his,
> outlining the edge of my dance.
>
> I cannot find my center
> I cannot find my path.
> Now he can make me open, shut and open
>
> Now I have lost myself.
> (*SP* 27)

Yet the multi-sectioned poem enacts the continuance of Eurydice who, to move beyond her mythic fate, vows to go "deeper / into the living cave" (*SP* 32). Her life depends on her going deeper into the well and metamorphosing into a force of nature: "a vein of silver in the rock" and "white root threads" that "can make the rock crumble into rich earth" (33). While the poem is largely told in the present tense, and often from a first-person perspective, it concludes in the future, mythicizing this "She" who gives birth to herself:

> She will brood and be born
> girl of her own mother
> mother of the labyrinth
> pushing the child herself outward
>
> > great head, the cave large inside it
> > great limbs of a giant woman
> > great cunt, fragrant, opening
> >
> > seeds of Eurydice
>
> (*SP* 34)

The poems in "*The 'History of Poetry'*" perform interventions into poetic forms themselves in an attempt to locate the actual female person fictionalized through idealized gender types. One of the most adventurous poems in the volume, "Crowbar," establishes itself as a crowbar of the poetic tradition of *trobar clus*. The first-person poetic speaker enters the poem, questioning who is speaking:

> Is it
>
> Me
>
> As She
> or Her?
>
> Or is me He?
> [...]
>
> whether I speak
> about Her
> or whether, being her, I can speak—
> given the range of "speaking" in the first place—
> at all.
> (*TR* 13–14)

"Crowbar" ultimately questions the means of poetic production, a seeming mimesis created by mirroring relations that leave the poetic speaker with multiple conflicting desires:

> The desire for the one seen in the mirror
> the desire for one who mirrors
> the desire for the mirror
> the desire for being the one who mirrors
> the revolt of the mirror
> the sestina.
> (*TR* 16)

The poetic speaker notes her complicity with the beauty of past poetry but also the difference of her desire: "It is impossible, / love, to love / and impossible to unlove // green shapes of fair women" (*TR* 17). DuPlessis concludes "this ancient targeted song" through a doubled typography that brings out how this weaning from poetic tradition has left her "HU / A / NGRY" (*TR* 25).

    In "Writing," written at approximately the same time as her essay on Dahlen, DuPlessis brings her insight from Dahlen and her ongoing exposition of projective prose in *The Pink Guitar* to her poetry writing. Although DuPlessis was much influenced by Dahlen's example, perhaps in part because of Dahlen's very emphasis on "reading" as DuPlessis herself is in "from *The 'History of Poetry*,'" DuPlessis begins her new work as "Writing." Typographically, "Writing" is unlike her preceding poetry and her later *Drafts* as each segment of this serial poem occupies a separate page, and most pages begin and end with a period. Regular and italic type and DuPlessis's own handwriting intersperse and entangle, sometimes as two columns on the page but other times more variously.

Titling her poem "Writing," DuPlessis signals her poetry's response to the historic turn to language and the diverse practices present at this time, including deconstruction and feminine *écriture*, while noting how a different kind of debate ensues when such writing is "literature" or "poetry."[12] In order to bring her feminist critique to "Writing," she creates an immanent writing infused by her own existence that gives rein to both visual and aural materialities. This is a poetic speaker who wants the privileges of an unmarked male poetic speaker without relinquishing the truth of her existence, without voiding herself. DuPlessis's own handwriting on otherwise typed pages indicates her response to this dilemma, as this writing manifests her self-presencing through material inscription, *her* deliberate marking of the page with her own hand. And it indicates that she newly has arrived at a fuller presentation of herself than that which animates her early poetry—an existence that includes the critique and promise of feminism, and extends it. As she writes in her essay "Otherhow," "I wanted simultaneous presence without authority" (*PG* 148). She elaborates in "Writing" by stating there is "an 'I' who is the hidden / subject and object of each of these verbs"; but also "wanting to have her book virtually nameless . . . so that / we are where // we are (*TR* 71, 81).

She begins "Writing" through an attention to marks and marking devices, including ink and the period, and different pathways:

> Smudge, ballpoint, iridesces
> behind the.
>
> Oily shadow grains an entry
> scrap.
>
> Night
> underpainting
> confident. An a.
> [...]
>
> What paths inside
> other
> territory of utterance
> hear me
>
> smudge and hear me
>
> whiteness
> (*TR* 55)

In the very first section, DuPlessis introduces the articles "the" and "a," each followed by a period, which she will later return to in the poem as she considers its shortcomings. The line "hear me" says a great deal in a poem given over to moving beyond the first-person poetic speaker since through this phrase the speaker opts both for a position of command and refused willful agency. Indeed, beginning with "me" rather than "I" or even "she," DuPlessis elects the pronoun that creates the most "objectness" of the "I" as well as its most intimate designation. The poetic speaker is now at one with the sounding of her poem, what Kathleen Fraser calls DuPlessis's "sound-hungry ear."[13] The forward motion through the poem is often through a kind of listening, a tenuous tonal register that enables the verse to move in multiple directions. Importantly in the poem, narrative, argument, and closure are abandoned for an associational reasoning of a combined bodily, emotional, and cognitive responsiveness. And while DuPlessis begins with "me," the first person soon morphs into an unidentified first-person poetic speaker and sometimes a "she" *and* "I" that rather than existing in the either/or relationships of the preceding poetry are both/and, no longer split but doubled.

DuPlessis comments on the overall focus of "Writing" as "otherness" in a set of notes published at the end of this poem in *Tabula Rosa* and in subsequent publications of it:

> Writing from the center of, the centers of, otherness.
> Making otherness central.
> Taking myself as central, yet in all my otherness.
> (84)

She describes the effect she is after in the poem's unusual typographies:

> Setting the poem so there is a bringing of marginalization into writing. "No center" of a section alternates with small contained sections. Sections contained by other sections, over writing, writing over, or simultaneous with. So that one section does not have hegemony. So the reader does not know which to read first, or how to inter-read . . . So that one does not learn mechanically; the reader is at large, as the poet is. . . . (84)

She also discloses the uniquely biographical time of this piece:

> As to subject: a first or really second month of a baby who comes as otherness, as difference, which cannot necessarily be understood easily, but demands to, needs to be felt, understood. (84)

One of the exceptional graces of this writing is the way it can include specifically female and feminine contents without reifying, sentimentalizing, or abjecting them. The doubled and contingent subjects of "I" and "she" brought together augment each other, as in "Dreaming I'm crying / it's she's crying" (*TR* 62). While women's tears as represented are often in their reception reduced to sentiment or bathos, here the doubled pronouns and the doubled "dreaming" "crying" deepen them. The phrasing reminds one of Marguerite Duras's switching between "I" and "she" in *India Song* as well as in other works. Similarly, the phrase "My mother I will, she said" compounds subjects, echoing the game "Mother may I." (56). Is this a mature poetic speaker speaking back to a mother who may urge passivity and acquiescence as a form of safety, or are these the words of an infant or toddler, whose willfulness is an example of the "otherness" of this poem, challenging her mother, the unidentified writer of this poem. There is the rhythm that the baby creates, "wet baby / dry baby . . . / the end ends up every / where" (68). Avoiding a depressive description in which the demands of motherhood are often cast, DuPlessis gets at the rhythms of a life that can have its own humor, and in fact calls up the very writing of "Writing," with its beginnings and ends everywhere. Without fanfare, the beauty of life is rendered beautiful: "Big finger to the little sleeping mouth // makes sure, / the even silence breathing" (77). And unfairness to those sidelined, "happening on the side," is noted: "The poet's wife, old woman / hushed in the kitchen drying / dishes, the whole / interview" (73). It is a poem that allows "baby wipes" and "tampax" to be mentioned rather than brought explicitly to the reader's attention as in some feminist art of this period (57, 83).

Similarly, nature is brought into the poem as itself, neither scenic as in "A Poem of Myself" nor used as redemptive metaphor as in "Eurydice." The time of "Writing" recalls Williams's *Spring and All*, an early cold spring that promises something more:

.Snaggles, spiggles, stalks
peck out snow.
Fresh, purple, haiku,
heuristic.
(*TR* 64)

The double "gg"s in the first line replicate visually and aurally how they "peck out snow." The next two lines mark this poetic writing through a meta statement about the first two, a "heuristic." The potential purple of poetry is confined to the color purple, perhaps the faint color of the indented snow for one who might examine it. One gets it all, fresh perception, sound, and visual materialities. The disappointments of a single day are simply included, not stretching throughout time as in a lyric of seemingly more robust expressiveness nor excluded from a meditative poem in moderating its affective registers:

This is a day   this waiting cold and no
"work" done   the blankness of receipt
no "papers" marked   a kind
of revulsion to every

thing no

"poem"
(*TR* 76)

Although "Writing" has a unique place in DuPlessis's oeuvre, it is also connected to a fortuitous time in her life. An infant has arrived in DuPlessis's household, adopted by DuPlessis as biological pregnancy had become impossible. The use of periods throughout may signal a joyful end to an anxious time of trying to get pregnant, when women's periods arrive with considerable disappointment and even grief. DuPlessis is putting the period to this previous time, while punctuating her own female existence with a period that precedes and ends each section (Heuving, "Interview" 411). This is a multiply valenced period, real and emblematic: "beet red drops at the bottom / of pee" (*TR* 82). The "green women" who "cannot be loved or unloved" in "Crowbar" have morphed into her daughter, named Kore. The double "gg's" of nature writing in the "haiku" section, the shortest page in "Writing," are now presented as the sounds her daughter is making in learning to speak her name: "kkhkkhggh."

Yet as definitive and celebratory as is DuPlessis's poem in its turn to writing, it introduces a series of questions about how to write:

> Jonquils, ruffled perianth,
> rains beat them down,
> a few
> more
> bulbs split
> their green
> arrowheads. Not a question of
> making images. Making
> what?
>
> Climax? Silence? Poignant?
> Points? The Memorable?
> Fleshy thick the -y suffix
> added means pleasure or cuteness
> (*TR* 78)

DuPlessis meditates on her poem, querying that she is not after making images, but making what. The "split" "bulbs" in their fleshiness interface with the fleshiness of writing that can be thickened or thinned by the addition of a "y." Questions about the intent, means, and meaning of this writing topple over on one another.

DuPlessis includes a critique of what it means to write within the projective aspect of this open writing. While given the multiplicity of relations set in play one might assume the relationships between the objects of the poem are best represented through the indefinite article "a," yet DuPlessis judges them because of the ultimately reified space of "Writing" to be relations of "the":

> Impossible maybe to write
> the techne of dailiness the hand reaching onto the shelf the
> dust
> collected into a particular corner
>   how to discuss to represent
> the pulses of pleasure and heartlessness
>
> all this has been "the"
> just where I thought I began
> beyond.
> (*TR* 65)

Drafts will correct for the "the" of the, as its title implies, not "Writing," but merely provisional and contingent *Drafts*. If there is a concern with how "Writing" reifies, there is a concern with how it debases: "Too many subplots / bleating / chaotic lambs" (*TR* 63). I am reminded of Ezra Pound's Ur-Canto, "Canto One," in which he despairs how to write his *Cantos* so that they will not be just "a rag-bag to stuff all its thoughts in." "Writing" in all its artful inclusions is hardly a "rag-bag," yet it does not answer fully to DuPlessis's aspirations to write a long poem.

Given the felicity and serial composition of "Writing," one might have expected a rapid succession of similar works. Yet a temporal hiatus occurs between "Writing" and DuPlessis's initial *Drafts*. DuPlessis dates "Writing" 1984–1985, and she dates "Draft 1" May 1986–1987 and "Draft 2" June 1986–January 1987, apparently working on these at the same time. She completes "Draft 3" and "Draft 4" in 1987. DuPlessis is working out how to create a long poem and is changing her writing to move away from the projectivist propensities of "Writing" and toward the objectivist values she has garnered from Oppen. In both sets of poems, projectivist and objectivist practices are present, but the balance shifts.[14] "Writing" is significantly motivated by the question how to write and proceeds through associational reasoning that encourages combined bodily, emotional, and cognitive responses. In *Drafts*, process-based writing persists, but thinking becomes more prominent.[15] In order to write her long poem of continuance, DuPlessis seeks both ballast and a line through. Her election of a particular kind of thinking corresponds with her description of Oppen's writing, whose "serial works are based on thinking rather than knowledge (don't misunderstand this): a motivated, apparently non-tendentious, even random cast into and among materials, which is open-ended and changing" ("'Uncannily'" 213). And it is through the thinking in *Drafts* that that "the" of "Writing" that troubled DuPlessis becomes relationships of "a."[16]

While the wide-ranging topic of "otherness" provides grist for "Writing," along with its meditation on how to write, individual entries in *Drafts* create their focus through singular words. Dahlen's preference for psychoanalytic writing and psychological interpretation enables her to write her serial poem. DuPlessis is far less interested in psychology than in ontology, especially an ontology that foregrounds linguistic signs.[17] The seriality of this work is not created through the "leaps" made between separate pages and diverse typographies of "Writing," but rather through larger units in which segmentation enables writer and reader alike to contemplate affirmation and negation, openness and contradiction. As DuPlessis writes of Oppen: "One is often straining for meaning as it shifts, via line break, right under your eyes. Indeed, any given line may have two centers—a completed thought and an incompleted thought (in the swing to the next line)" ("'Uncannily'" 222). DuPlessis's claim for what makes Oppen's works political resonates with *Drafts*: "Oppen exposes and explores the riven and fraught nature of subjectivity in a state of political and existential arousal that cannot (yet) be satisfied" ("'Uncannily'" 204).

Yet as much as DuPlessis might share with Oppen his "Not only to say, but to be IN IT," being "in it" is different for her than for Oppen because of the differences of their engendered existences.[18] It is not entirely surprising, then, that "Drafts 1–4" are based on singular word topics in this order: "It," "She," "Of," "In." Prepositions in many languages are the most difficult parts of speech to get right perhaps because of how they locate persons with respect to complex social designations. If verbs create action, prepositions orient and direct this action. DuPlessis is putting her incisive and comprehensive feminist insights into a practice in which all language deployed is potentially engendered because engaged by her as she wishes to think. Only some words convey specific gender contents, but all words communicate differently given who utters them and in what context. To be "in it" for Rachel Blau DuPlessis is different than to be "in it" for George Oppen.

In many ways "Writing" is a writing of "yes," insofar as one written page leads directly to the next, the no "no" that Freud finds characteristic of dreams and that DuPlessis finds defining for Dahlen (*PG* 117). In "Draft 1," DuPlessis structures her poem around two large handwritten symbols, "N" and "Y," for "no" and "yes."[19] DuPlessis's critical oppositions in her earliest poetry to the ways that gender and women historically have been cast yielded a wide-ranging repertoire of negations. The "yes" of "Writing" as a portal poem enables *Drafts*, in which affirmation and negativity are brought into new relations. "Draft 1" arrives at a double assessment: "there is a yes and no" "walled" and/or "welled" up (*TR* 95). The "walled" and "welled" are written above and beneath each other, asking the reader to conjure how each yes and no may both wall and well. "Draft 1" meditates directly on the "I" as one entity within *Drafts*:

To reinvent "attention" is narrow tho tempting.
Doesn't get the folding.   I
is it.
(*TR* 89)

DuPlessis may be criticizing "Writing," in part, as a writing of mere attention and for the ways it does not get at complications of the "folding," of the "I," the textual palimpsest of any one writer's writing and life. The spaces before and within the "I / is it" enhances both the power and it-ness of "I." Earlier in "Draft 1" she proffers: "It is the / 'it' characteristic of everything." Yet later in this "Draft," "in" and "it" are stopped by periods.

> Let silence
>   in the form of words
>   in.   IT.
> (*T* 11)

"Draft 2: She" turns the pink of *The Pink Guitar* to red, a color DuPlessis associates with otherness, as brought out in the "Notes" to "Writing" (*TR* 85):

> "I be a good girl with my magic
> markers."
>
> (marks hands up red
> makes henna dark touch)
> (*T* 11)

In "Draft 3: Of," she notes, "Hard to get home; but this is, this travelling / of / is / home" (*T* 21). In "Draft 4: In": "So one is finally of it, and the 'parts' and configurations are / no longer accessible." This leads her to a recognition of how outside the poetic speaker is the world and leads her to these boldfaced assertions: "**Implacable** // the world," so then, "I am getting the force of it, **in**" (*T* 26, 27).

There is certainly thinking in "Writing," but the piece moves more as do projectivist works through an associative composition. In "Drafts 1–4," the projective aspects of this writing are chastened by focusing on specific words and thinking through and with them. In *Drafts* DuPlessis is newly enabled to think as she will, as her thinking ever extends itself into diverse registers and materialities. However, all of herself got there by way of "Writing" and the projective prose in *The Pink Guitar*, the creation of a new grounds and subjectivity for her writing. Projective practices are particularly useful in transformations of selves and subjectivities because of the very leaps and non sequiturs they encourage, thereby creating in DuPlessis the very possibility of her own force moving.

Notes

1. Ron Silliman called "Writing" a "portal poem." DuPlessis remarks how this poem "tipped [her] into *Drafts*" (Heuving, "Interview" 401–11). As in the case of ports, "portal" indicates a place of entry.

2. For a strong sense of how for DuPlessis feminist critique and poetry writing vie with each other, see Martindale, "Interview."

3. There are multiple accounts of how DuPlessis's poetry and poetics intersect with objectivist poetics, including several by DuPlessis herself. See especially DuPlessis and Peter Quartermain's "Introduction" to *The Objectivist Nexus*, and DuPlessis's "'Uncannily'" and "Objectivist Poetics." For an excellent overview of DuPlessis's *Drafts* in relationship to objectivist poetics, see Alan Golding's "Macro, Micro."

4. DuPlessis is referencing these works: Nancy J. Vickers, "Diana Described: Scattered Woman and Scattered Rhyme," *Critical Inquiry*, vol. 8, 1981, 265–79; Allen Grossman, "Summa Lyrica: A Primer of the Commonplaces in Speculative Poetics," *The Sighted Singer: Two Works on Poetry for Readers and Writers*, Baltimore: Johns Hopkins University Press, 1992; Eve Kosofsky Sedgwick, *Between Men: English Literature and Male Homosocial Desire*, New York: Columbia Press, 1985; Annabel Patterson, *Pastoral and Ideology: Virgil to Valery*, Berkeley and Los Angeles: University of California Press, 1987.

5. I am suggesting the commonalities in objectivist and projectivist poetics through my word choices. While these poetics are often contrasted with each other, they share important aspects. They should be seen as involved in the same set of issues that Pound and Hulme flagged in their refusal of the use of language as a set of "counters" or language poets' refusal of prefabricated reference. In the twentieth and twenty-first century, political, economic, and language franchises go hand in hand. George Orwell identifies these propensities as a "debasement" of language, albeit his solutions to this debasement are rather different than posed by the poetics examined here. Mark Scroggins in "From the Late Modernism of the 'Objectivists' to the Protopostmodernism of 'Projective Verse,'" while differentiating between objectivist and projectivist poetics, explores how Olson's "Projective Verse" engages with Zukofsky's statements on the objectivists.

6. I am drawing from my discussion of projective verse in *The Transmutation of Love*, 27–29, and from my discussions of projective and objective poetics, in my "The Material and Medium of Language" (65–68) and in "Coda" (171–72). In *The Transmutation of Love*, I use and modify Olson's useful descriptions of projective verse and stress that his "ONE PERCEPTION MUST IMMEDIATELY AND DIRECTLY LEAD TO A FURTHER PERCEPTION" also implies one language phrase must lead to another language phrase, one word to another word. I also suggest that his emphasis on "IMMEDIATELY" and "INSTANTER" limits an understanding of a more pervasive projective practice. Rather, what is important in projective verse is not the speed with which the writer writes but that one perception/language phrase must stimulate the next perception/language phrase, in a concatenating composition, whether the poet writes fast or slow. In *The Transmutation of Love*, I argue that projective verse begins with Ezra Pound and H.D., continuing into the twenty-first century. Marjorie Perloff maintains that Olson took his projective poetics from Pound ("Charles Olson and the 'Inferior Predecessors'").

7. One can only remark on the prescience of DuPlessis, Dahlen, and other experimental and avant-garde writers who by the 1980s are finding a way to move beyond the limits of analytic critique, without abandoning its insights. In 2015, more than thirty years later, Rita Felski published her *The Limits of Critique*, a useful account of how the "heuristics of suspicion" have come to dominate cultural and literary scholarship. Yet, while experimental and avant-garde writers found a way to register and move beyond critique, Felski is stopped by an additive set of values: "Critique proves to be a remarkably efficient and smooth-running machine for registering the limits and insufficiencies of texts.... It is conspicuously silent, however, on the many other reasons why we are drawn to works of art: aesthetic pleasure, increased self-understanding, moral reflection, perceptual reinvigoration, ecstatic self-loss, emotional consolation, or heightened sensation—to name just a few. Its conception of the uses and values of literature is simply too thin" (188). For too long, critics have ignored the careful and inventive work of many of the most insightful writers of our time, failing to see how these writers have conjoined critical analysis with a wide-ranging responsiveness—new ways of being—as in the case of DuPlessis.

8. DuPlessis notes that she takes these words from Zukofsky although she amalgamates them.

9. For DuPlessis's chart of how the single words of her first nineteen "Drafts" lead chronologically to the next nineteen "Drafts" and so forth through related words up to "Draft 114," see her *Selected Poems* 98–99.

10. I do not mean to make the absurd claim that these articles are particular to either objectivist or projectivist poems but rather to suggest how these words provide different orientations, orientations that sync with objectivist and projectivist poetics, respectively. Moreover, while poetics encourage certain practices, the practices of any one poet or in any one poem simply are too diverse to be labeled in this way. Zukofsky's most famous poem may be *A*, but he also wrote the poem "Poem Beginning 'The'" and noted how important are both little words "a" and "the." DuPlessis is trying to locate a way of writing a long poem by responding to how her poetry can be characterized by "a" or "the," how these "micro" words become "macro" orientations, to borrow from Golding's vocabulary and essay title for discussing DuPlessis, "Macro, Micro, Material: Rachel Blau DuPlessis's *Drafts* and the Post-Objectivist Serial Poem."

11. See note 7.

12. In her "notes" to "Writing," DuPlessis remarks how "Writing" is "part of the debate, or a contribution to the debate, between literature and writing (Silliman said poetry I think)" (*TR* 84).

13. Fraser's comment is on the back cover of *Tabula Rosa*.

14. DuPlessis comments, "Thinking the poem, thinking the poem writing—the goal of both objectivist and projectivist positions, and where they fuse—can emphatically include thinking about some things some of those writers didn't particularly think about" (Mossin 39).

15. In delivering a version of this paper at the 2023 Louisville Conference on

Literature and Culture, I received commentary from Alan Golding that DuPlessis's projectivist poetics may well continue into *Drafts* in her ongoing ambitions for her long poem.

16. See note 11.

17. For a close comparison between Dahlen's *A Reading* and DuPlessis's *Drafts*, see Keller, *Forms of Expansion*, 239–307.

18. DuPlessis quotes from Oppen's working papers in "Objectivist Poetics," 27.

19. DuPlessis clarifies that the handwritten, broadly inscribed "N" and "Y" are "no" and "yes" (Heuving, "Interview" 406).

Works Cited

DuPlessis, Rachel Blau. *Selected Poems 1980–2020*. Tucson: Chax Press, 2022.

———. "Statement on Poetics." *Inciting Poetics: Thinking and Writing Poetry*, edited by Jeanne Heuving and Tyrone Williams. Albuquerque: University of New Mexico Press, 2019, 13–37.

———. "Objectivist Poetics, 'Influence,' and Some Contemporary Long Poems." *Poetics and Praxis "After" Feminism*, edited by W. Scott Howard and Broc Rossell. Iowa City: University of Iowa, 2018.

———. "'Uncannily in the Open': In Light of Oppen." *Thinking Poetics: Essays on George Oppen*, edited by Steve Shoemaker. Tuscaloosa: University of Alabama Press, 2009, 203–27.

———. *Blue Studios: Poetry and Its Cultural Work*. Tuscaloosa: University of Alabama Press, 2006.

———. *Drafts 1–38, Toll*. Middletown, CT: Wesleyan University Press, 2001.

———. "*f*-Words: An Essay on the Essay." *American Literature*, vol. 68, no. 1, 1996, 15–45.

———. "'Corpses of Poesy': Some Modern Poets and Some Gender Ideologies of Lyric." *Feminist Measures*, edited by Lynn Keller and Cristanne Miller. Ann Arbor: University of Michigan Press, 1994, 69–95.

———. *The Pink Guitar: Writing as Feminist Practice*. New York: Routledge, 1990.

———. *Tabula Rosa*. Elmwood, CT: Potes & Poets Press, 1987.

———, and Peter Quartermain, editors. "Introduction." *The Objectivist Nexus: Essays in Cultural Poetics*. Tuscaloosa: University of Alabama Press, 1999, 1–22.

Felski, Rita. *The Limits of Critique*. Chicago: University of Chicago Press, 2015.

Golding, Alan. "Macro, Micro, Material: Rachel Blau DuPlessis's *Drafts* and the Post-Objectivist Serial Poem." *Writing Into the Future: New American Poetries from "The Dial" to the Digital*. Tuscaloosa: University of Alabama Press, 2022.

Heuving, Jeanne. "The Material and Medium of Language." *Inciting Poetics: Thinking and Writing Poetry*, edited by Jeanne Heuving and Tyrone Williams. Albuquerque: University of New Mexico Press, 2019, 63–80.

———. "Coda." *Poetics and Praxis "After" Objectivism*, edited by W. Scott Howard and Broc Rossell. Iowa City: University of Iowa, 2018.

———. *The Transmutation of Love and Avant-Garde Poetics*. Tuscaloosa: University of Alabama Press, 2016.

———. "An Interview with Rachel Blau DuPlessis." *Contemporary Literature*, vol. 45, no. 3, 2004, 397–420.

Keller, Lynn. *Forms of Expansion: Recent Long Poems by Women*. Chicago: University of Chicago Press, 1997.

Martindale, Kathleen. "Interview with Rachel Blau DuPlessis on Ethics, Rhetoric and Discourse." *Feminist Ethics*, vol. 3, no. 1, 1988–1989, 44–66.

Mossin, Andrew R. "'Thinking the Poem; Thinking the Poem Writing': An Interview with Rachel Blau DuPlessis." Conducted by Andrew R. Mossin. *Golden Handcuffs Review*, no. 30, 2021, 37–60.

Olson, Charles. *Human Universe and Other Essays*. New York: Grove Press, 1967.

———. "Projective Verse." *Selected Writings of Charles Olson*, edited by Robert Creeley. New York: New Directions, 1966, 15–30.

Perloff, Marjorie. "Charles Olson and the 'Inferior Predecessors': 'Projective Verse' Revisited." *English Language History*, vol. 40, no. 2, 1973, 285–306.

Scroggins, Mark. "From the Late Modernism of the 'Objectivists' to the Protopostmodernism of 'Projective Verse.'" *The Cambridge Companion to American Poetry since 1945*, edited by Jennifer Ashton. New York: Cambridge University Press, 2013.

CHAPTER NINE

"Immerginated Raptures"

Rachel Blau DuPlessis's Drafts 1–38, Toll

JOSEPH DONAHUE

a draft, a stroke, a kind of fear . . .

—Rachel Blau DuPlessis, "Draft 4: In"

I. Forlorn

A contemporary epic opens; an ancient bell tolls.

Struck first in the 1820s, in the 1980s the bell gets struck again. Vibrations of earlier poetic eras pass into and through the author of the epic, Rachel, whose very name will, within the poem, tremble and dissipate into its own eroding phonemes (Rachel, recall, ache el). What bell is this? The answer is hidden in an ellipsis in the epigram from Keats: ". . . the very word is like a bell" (*T*). An old now-suppressed word passes into the contemporary moment. An elided word, conjured yet concealed: in page after page of Rachel Blau DuPlessis's *Toll*, it is the word *forlorn* that, uttered but once, chimes, reverberates, diminishes, returns. It passes beyond the timekeeping of any church, temple, town steeple, or meditation room, echoing out of sacred time and into the secular present.

"Forlorn" is a word not much said aloud anymore, at least by poets; they fear their interiority, so described, would sound antique. Forlorn, as a state of being, however, is pervasive in our time, in poetry and in life, appearing in disguise as depression, abjection, despair, or grief. Forlornness intrudes upon our attention when reading *Toll*, then fades on the wind of the poem's ostensible materials. By eliding "forlorn" in its opening moment, *Toll* provokes a question as vital to the poetic past as to the now, a question inseparable from the history of lyric poetry: how far away are any words, however eloquent, from our most dire states, our truest moods? Pointedly, almost mystically, *Toll* wonders: amid such dark nights what words are with us? Sub-acoustically sounded, the *forlorn* we don't see ripples into all lexicons, all discourses, an all-consuming non-sound between the tolling of the known. Should readers be content to find in "forlorn" simply an intuition of death, *Toll* will indulge them. After all, in this life-poem, loss runs riot. Words are at once fructifying and memorial, are "teeming and bereft." No matter that "forlorn" is withheld; it's already everywhere. DuPlessis's contemporary epic calls into being a world where all writing can seem, at times, a continuation of the tolling, the taking toll that the tolling announces, the sound that lingers, the poet will tell us, "between the unspoken / and the disappearance" (222).

II. Wells

This ever-resonating toll was struck long before *Drafts*, even before the poet's first book saw print. A particularly forlorn tolling or perhaps just the fading echo of a cry for help, it might be said, pulled the initiate DuPlessis into the objectivist nexus. A letter from her found its way into the work of George Oppen. In "Speech at Soli" he quotes the Rachel not yet DuPlessis (Blau up to 1968, thereafter Blau DuPlessis):

> Adolescent young girls fall into wells
> Says a letter
> (*New Collected Poems* 238)

Far from bell or tower, lost in the distance from others, the call of community, religious or secular, amplified by the stone and water, maybe, these incidents could be a country newspaper mishap, a fairy tale, a sex crime, a suicide, a Vermont honor killing. Perhaps these forlorn girls were merely admiring their own beauty reflected in the water and slipped and were happily rescued. People do get rescued. (That's a story worth telling as well.) But the heat with which Oppen responds to the letter implies the tawdriest of fates. Readers of the work he was yet to write might see beyond his response to the gift of an image from his protégé. They might see into Oppen's own deepest terror, death by water, the shipwreck of the singular, a catastrophe one does not survive. In return for Rachel's dismaying prophecy, Oppen has advertised what will be a foundational trope of her yet-to-be-written poetic work, in fact the very title of her first collection, *Wells*, wherein DuPlessis reveals herself to be equally obsessed with helplessness, death, uncertain depths, and distance from the daylight world. The recurrence of the figure of the well throughout *Toll* makes explicit certain continuities between her earlier and later work. (Both *Wells* and *Toll* offer instances where "To write is to drown.") The very first poem in *Wells* expands the scope of the titular trope, from death, darkness, and confinement to the downward pull of invisible forces. "Undertow" declines the triumphalism of, by contrast, Adrienne Rich's dive into the wreck. DuPlessis's diver does not return to light and air. The poet imagines, rather, complete surrender to the aquatic realm, a moment that will find countless analogs in *Drafts*.

> Snapped off trees
> Infertile mud
> The uprooted

My place.
I am the grief.

The undertow
Sucks me down
My breath rock hard
Under the quick water
(*W*)

III. Among the "Actives"

The subaquatic fantasia played out in *Wells* verges on the mythological. The dreamlike terror of endless depth is associated in modernist poetic tradition with Orpheus, his body sunk, his head adrift, and with Eurydice, who, via Rilke, stands at some absolute limit for knowledge of the interrelation of realms. Voyaging into, inhabiting, and returning from such a state of nonbeing being is the obsessive concern of *Toll*. Of even more pressing concern is the telling of the states' own coming into being. This telling shapes both the methods and the content of *Toll*, given as it is to the relentless imagination of psychic and cultural liminality. An earlier borrowing by Oppen from a letter of DuPlessis's catches student activist Rachel comprehending the dilemma of what might be considered a second negative state or possibility of being. This second negative state is a version of the first, depth. It is depth cut loose from verticality. Depth (falling into a well) is an obliterative rendition of the second state, distance, a less immediately lethal condition and one DuPlessis finds both dangerous and desirable. Distance is associated not, here, with death but with the social world. In a letter to William Bronk in May 1968 Oppen relates that DuPlessis called him from the early moments of the Columbia sit-in. The sit-in (which would receive national attention and be dramatized in the film *The Strawberry Statement*) responded to a variety of immediate goals: the discovery of Columbia's research contracts with the military, the presence of military recruiters on campus, and the expansion of the university into the surrounding community. Amid the unrest, DuPlessis talked with Oppen for half an hour. She wanted to be among the "actives," Oppen tells Bronk, "and felt that she somehow was not and could not wholly be so" (*Selected Letters* 176). Oppen then quotes the DuPlessis lines that had appeared earlier in "Of Being Numerous": "'Whether as the intensity of seeing increases, one's distance from Them, the People, does not also increase'" (176).

    This phone call is a rather extraordinary intergenerational literary historical moment. Two distinct points in the trajectory of the Left in American culture, that of Oppen and that of DuPlessis. Oppen's letters record a real-time exchange between two major poets of the presiding generation (though Bronk, here, is more like a silent off-stage auditor in a Beckett play) and a major poet of the future. (Would a filmmaker had been there to hear, if only inside Oppen's head, with what tone of voice he pronounced the word "dramatic" in response to his quotation of the above line. It seems by turns suspicious and admiring.) The conundrum the quoted line sets out about the rupture between perception and participation would certainly be heard with sympathy by Bronk, who himself was a master of both the distant and the dramatic. There was lots of drama to go around. The revolutionary upsurge at Columbia, the tension between various leftist critics of American life, the human concern of Oppen for a young woman he had known since her days as a recent college graduate in 1965 who finds herself in a possibly dangerous situation, all this was already enough (or too much, as Blake might say). Then there were the "dramatic" aspects of the aesthetic dilemma the young DuPlessis rose up as a ghost from a well to utter within "Of Being Numerous." Her lines, quoted within Oppen's poem, reopen the abyss that had famously silenced Oppen for years, the abyss between seeing intensely and feeling solidarity with the masses. The younger poet on the phone is reprising the older poet's seemingly resolved poetic crisis, the resolution that the poem "Of Being Numerous" itself embodies. Speaking presumably about a more abstracted, theorized sociality, "Them, the People," DuPlessis had anticipated her own response to the events of the early phase of the takeover, an intuition not lost on the prophetically minded Oppen: "She had somehow foreseen it." A later letter of Oppen's (both letters are written in May, the takeover having escalated to riots and arrests) compares student protestors to poets. Oppen exclaims to Bronk: "The Kids, the rioting kids. Amazing!" Much might be conjectured about the effect of the Columbia uprising on Oppen's own late poetics. Here, however, the concern is simply to locate DuPlessis in this politico-aesthetic real-life exchange. Yes, she is the ground-level informant to the new Left action, but she is also an avatar of the future author of *Drafts*. (Could it be Oppen saw the epic of his spiritual daughter unroll before him?) Then, as if secretly sending poetic guidance to the future editor of the letters, to assist her as she herself undergoes a long poem, Oppen says to Bronk, "These kids are furthering the experiment of life or of consciousness." Of these furthering kids DuPlessis would think hard about experiment, life, and consciousness in the years to come, and how to put them all in a single poem, once the revolutionary moment of May 1968 gave way, much later in the 1980s, to the repressive regimen of Reagan. But Oppen's not done. He gets eerie: "Strangely," he writes, "they are zealots of catastrophe Resembling, in this way, the poets." Oppen pinpoints, in a volatile and historical moment, an emerging alignment of poetic attributes: uncanniness ("Strangely"), religious fervor ("zealots"), the genre of the apocalyptic ("catastrophe") that contributes to an elite collective identity ("poets"). It's as if he is taking a moment on behalf of literary history to delineate the tensions that underlie DuPlessis's *Drafts*. While Oppen's sympathies are with the kids, he is caught between two moments. The older poet is sharply aware of the psychology and history of fascism. He's seen the unleashing of repressive forces before. Perhaps Reznikoff is at his ear, whispering warnings. But the Oppen still coming to be, the Oppen of an apocalyptic sublime who will follow the lead of Robert Duncan, is sizing up 1968 as well, and who's to say he's not feeling set free, ready now to move to California?[1]

Among the poets Oppen calls "zealots of catastrophe," in what way is DuPlessis there, along with David Shapiro, Hugh Seidman, Ed Foster, Hilton Obenzinger, Lou Rowan, no doubt others, in her protest, expressing, as she does, both her presence and her apartness? Among, but not of, the "zealots of catastrophe." Placing DuPlessis at the Columbia uprising brings a particularly charged critical concern back to the word "distance," the second negative state that will order the perceptions of the world in *Drafts*. This initiate into poetic mysteries is drawn, in both the original letter and in the phone call to Oppen, to a seemingly tragic divide between perceptual particularity, "the intensity of seeing," and the communion of the participatory, seen by her to be a desirable but perhaps inaccessible experience. To see intensely confirms the poet's forlorn apartness from collective identity. The "rioting kids" are first, potentially revolutionary masses, and second, immediate and elite revolutionary *actives*. The lines of DuPlessis that appear in Oppen explore in political, aesthetic, and psychological terms a cosmogonic dynamism that exists for the younger poet between intensity and distance. This forlorn severance is her *Bereshit*. The lines tucked away in the work of a precursor are her first iteration of what might be called her objectivist sublime.

For DuPlessis, in evoking such a sublime, wouldn't it be best to be devastated across a spectrum of situations and experiences, dispossessed in the culture, bereft in the self, and lonely in the act of writing? This is quite possibly true. Yet the power of DuPlessis's poetry arises from her abhorrence in finding herself anywhere near such conditions. She is temperamentally a poet of Emersonean self-confidence who finds herself at times brought low, placed by fate in painful conundrums. From this dialectically charged condition come moments of what the poet will call "Immerginated rapture," moments as determinative to the shaping of *Drafts* as any compositional procedure. The cultivation and fear of intense seeing (and the vexed question of belonging) extends to the eye of the mind as well—that is, to memory, the power of which troubles the poet. If by the logic of her early poems adolescence is to drop down, be thrown down, the well of the past, and writing itself are forms of drowning, it is hardly a surprise to find the Lord of the Drowned, Hart Crane, appearing in *Toll*, deftly and pointedly revised, his line from "Passage," "My memory I left in a ravine" (*Complete Poems* 21), becoming in "Draft 33" "my memory was left in a ravine" (*T* 228)—a revision that suggests both kinship with and distance from Crane. In DuPlessis's rendering the "I" has disappeared and with it the heroic selfhood that emerges from Crane's Orphic initiation. However, the narrative of mythic transformation, of such salience to late Oppen as to Spicer, Duncan, and Blaser, plays an ever more elaborate part in the writing of *Drafts*. (The open wells that girls are thrown into, or throw themselves into, or find themselves trapped within, may be a stern message from the patriarchy to errant daughters, but it may also be the call of Orphic waters.)

Toll dramatizes the opening of a chthonic realm and provides an account of the origins of poetic song and its transformative power, as do other modern and contemporary works with Orphic ambitions. Something of DuPlessis's revisionary relation to the Orphic tradition is revealed in how she qualifies rapture. Consider her coinage "immerginated." It is a matter, as Stevens might say, of the commodious adjective, though this adjective is less welcoming than it is intransigent. It stands before the word "rapture" like the guard before the gate in Kafka's parable of the law. It's as if DuPlessis wants us to see the word "rapture" but be kept from experiencing it. The opening syllable, is it a prefix? "Imm" suggests a state of being within, immersed. The first two syllables almost lead us back to DuPlessis's figuration of the well and so to the early equivalence of writing and drowning. But with the arrival of the "g" what the sounds suggest changes. Immerse gives way to emerge. The rapture DuPlessis is both proposing and withholding keeps contrary tendencies in balance. We are within yet are at least partially without. As if rapture here, which itself signifies being seized, being taken away, being consumed within a higher force, is so precisely modified that it becomes nothing we could ever really feel. However, in its provocation of contrary meanings, the coinage also mimics the phenomenon of rapture. "Immerginated" could be an invention by a feminist historian of mystical tradition who seeks to both analyze and classify the experience of rapture while respecting the capacity of the experience to exceed analysis and classification. Such a historian might well ask: do you see a figuration of sexual trauma within these syllables? Does "immerginated" suggest womb-like properties, an ongoing parturition? Has the well now become a womb? Does "emergency" hover around the "g" and the "n"? And the ultimate question regarding the nature of rapture cannot desist from insistence: is a rapture that can be modified in fact rapture? This hard-to-parse process is a hermeneutical initiation to an experience often understood to be transcendent. We are not in the world of the rapturous immergination but the world of immerginated rapture. And rapture, whatever the adjective that finds itself called to a mystic marriage with this noun, retains its uncanny properties, at once affirming identity while offering a possible otherness to any aspiring rhapsode.

IV. What Did Your Parents Name You Rachel For

Reading *Toll*, the reader is allowed only once to say the elided word, "forlorn." A related word arises as a more forthright if extratextual guide to the abject depths that the poet by turns accepts and evades. The word is "fated." The two words are not equivalent; we can be forlorn and free; we can be fated yet find ourselves euphoric. "Fated," in fact, may well be the word that makes us forlorn. Our fatedness, and our resistance to it, appears in Oppen, forthrightly, as *amor fati*, the love of fate. This is as well the essential turmoil of *Toll*. *Amor fati* stirs the younger poet's passion for the provisional, the contingent, the by chance, and then the consciously chosen. Much in *Toll* demonstrates that our rationality, our wit, and our diligence operate in a world that allows us, through them, only a degree of self-reliance and freedom. In the world of *Toll*, the ludic, the willfully arranged, the learned, the witty, and the securely secular Jewish are justly celebrated. But this last adjective invites further word, not simply because key elements of Jewish literary and religious culture are crucial to the workings of *Toll* but because "Jewish" can guide our understanding of these elements. "Jewish" marks the deep interplay of fatedness and freedom that govern the structure and meaning of the poem. It is in regard to Jewishness, both as the world understands it and as the poet understands it, that DuPlessis advances an identity that disallows much of what seems to me a deep impetus in her work toward the forlorn. DuPlessis wants no Jewishness that is fated, no Jewishness that derives merely from a biological cult of the matrilineal. The galling remark, quoted above, appears in DuPlessis's far ranging essay "Midrashic Sensibilities: Secular Judaism and Radical Poetics." A "fully affiliated Jew" cuts to the quick of it: "What did your parents name you Rachel for, if you're not going to be Jewish?" (206). There is a complexity in the remark of the fully affiliated Jew regarding fatedness. Being Jewish in his or her view requires more than what birth to a Jewish mother confers. There is also Jewish education and ritual participation. One must be, presumably, "affiliated." You are a Jew, but you must then "be" a Jew, enact Jewishness. Or else you are this Rachel, a Jew who is not a Jew, who bears the name of what she is not. DuPlessis counterpoises this guilt-trip gift of the fully affiliated with an Enlightenment vision of rational religion, hers by way of her childhood experience in Ethical Culture. "Distance," in this instance, is not the outcome of a forlorn logic that finds the poet in exile within herself from the self imposed on her by fate. It is the given of a modern secular identity. As in her ghostly lines in "Of Being Numerous," distance, as it touches on Jewishness, is understood as that of the self's apartness from a collective, not from The People, here, but from the cultic and the ritual universe of traditional religion that has scant place in her esteem.

As a critic, DuPlessis turns being of the chosen into being as choosing. She is relentless in allying Jewish identity with choice, and she carefully frames her imagination of such a choice. What she presents as choice she explicitly calls "elective affinities." In doing so, she makes a myth of the matter of choosing to be of the chosen, a choosing it need be added that is endlessly complicated by both the culture of Judaism and the culture within which Jewishness is recognized. Regarding both cultures, it can be asked: can a Jew ever stop being a Jew, regardless of what he or she chooses? The nature of modern Jewish identity under the sign of the secular is an immense topic, but a grasp of some small part of it is essential for reading *Toll*.

With the phrase "elective affinities" DuPlessis nods to Goethe, to Romantic ideals of social empathy and affection, friends over family, we might say, and art over religion. In the modern secular world, we are led to believe we choose our fate rather than endure its givenness. This is in keeping with the Romantic theologizing that underlies the tradition of the modern long poem to which *Toll* announces its own affinities, practitioners of which include Whitman, Pound, H.D., Loy, Duncan, Blaser, Oppen, Howe, Mackey, and others. DuPlessis's essay tells us (though DuPlessis the critic and DuPlessis the poet should not be assumed *not* to be at odds now and then) she is a designated female offspring of the Enlightenment. The Jewish past, what was once fated to be, becomes, in modernity, for DuPlessis as for so many others, what a Jew can choose how to have. Such choosing, the avowal of what is commonly called an identity, leads quickly, in a paradox of increasing interest to historians of religion, from the realm of reasoned consideration to the beginnings of an enchantment: "For me religion is a rich cultural resource a little like a museum or a library, to say this very coolly, on which I draw, and in which I wander, one that evokes some feelings for me from puzzlement to joy to fascination" (DuPlessis, "Midrashic" 208). Agnostic curiosity about antique religion ends up sounding, here, less like philosophical skepticism than it does a wonder tale. As with her fellow contemporary, Susan Howe, DuPlessis finds within the cathedral of reason, the museum or library, a space of puzzlement, joy, and fascination. And how distinctly DuPlessian to draw attention to the coolness of how she speaks ("to say this very coolly") about the opening up of poetic space within the heart of rationalist inquiry and secular, civic space (the museum, the library). For her to say she is saying this "coolly" calls to mind antithetical ways of saying it, to say it warmly, for example, either with anger or passion or awe. For readers of DuPlessis the critic, this disposition aligns with her ambivalence, her conflicted feelings about religion. But readers of *Toll* are alerted to the range of further postures, reticence, avowal, skepticism, and even the zeal of Blakean imaginative possibilities regarding the matter of religion's own fate in the secular world, possibilities that cannot be confined to libraries and museums but bears witness to the unfolding of its truth within the prophetic capacities of the serial form.

V. The Ecstasy of Oppen

For DuPlessis the critic, Jewishness arises within one from a cultivation of "elective affinities." It is freely chosen and nothing like *forlorn*. (The banishment of that word if not that category of feeling being the inaugural ritual gesture of *Toll*). Fate, for the critic, resides in the biologism she is at pains to deflect. The critic confides her Jewishness comes to her from her original family "by osmosis." One is not born Jewish, despite what Judaism says. For DuPlessis the critic, having been fated to be Jewish, one then choses to be Jewish. But the critic cannot rest in her Enlightenment vision of reason's right relation to religion. Perhaps because, right there, in the ranks of Ethical culture, the ghost of Emerson appears to her, and with him the call of sublimity, a psychological experience, a rapture, which requires both exaltation and terror, feelings that verify a selfhood beyond that which social identity determines. In *Toll*, the fear of fatedness stirs poetic intensities of the highest order. By contrast to herself as critic, DuPlessis the poet loves moments when reason succumbs to a reality that exceeds reason's means. DuPlessis the poet periodically sets aside the ideal of rational autonomy, finding she cannot turn from a vision of the self as stricken, abject, bedazzled, entranced, abandoned, and elusively forlorn. At times DuPlessis as critic advocates for ways of making poems where reason is the sun shining over the compositional procedures. (What is the grid of nineteen that appears in *Toll* but a display of a mathematically grounded exaltation?) What unfolds in the lines of *Toll*, again and again, is an agon over fatedness, not simply as to Judaic concerns or materials but as to the materials and methods of the poem itself. Warring contraries of freedom and fatedness shape the song, guide its procedures.

Recalling how Hebrew melodies of joy and terror effected both the prosody and the content of English poetry (think Milton, Smart, Blake, various translations of the Psalms), we can see how in the poetry of both Oppen and DuPlessis this agon over fatedness takes on aspects of the sublime. Troubled by fatedness, especially as rendered in the Torah, Oppen will open the book of Job. DuPlessis will open with the sacrifice of Isaac. And both will open with the Holocaust. Notable for their faith in the capacity of the mind to know and comprehend, to discriminate and judge, to confirm reason as the sign of selfhood, both poets find themselves amid intensities of helplessness and terror that are by turns mythic, political, and psychological. Such dreadful ecstasy that so marks the sublime might well trouble two such modern secular Jews. To enter *Toll*'s sublimity, dreadful or not, the word must be cleansed of its association with the God of Abrahamic tradition, of association with politically retrograde religious communities, whether Hasidim or Christian evangelical, or other. It must be cleansed of other suspect conventions, such as the more extreme modalities of women's spirituality. And it must be cleansed of the benign but persistent presence of Oppen. In her quest to position her poem in relation to the objectivist sublime, which I take to be a Hebraic, modernist, post-secular sublimity that draws upon the innately theological speculations encoded with objectivist poetics, and to the ecstatic and terrifying transports associated with it, DuPlessis opens as a satirist. Nervously, but immediately, in the first "Draft," the poet writes out the word so profoundly linked to the Zohar, to the fundamental condition by which one experiences the divine, and linked most immediately to the work of Oppen, "awe."

The first "Draft" is uneasy with a major concern of its, yes, heroic song:

> To what purpose reveal details of fleshy registers one
> CAN have, blah blah   their charm? It's not
> Irony (really) it's awe
> (*T* 2)

DuPlessis seems not yet sure to what degree the poetics of her life-poem is committed to fear and trembling (those fleshy registers) before the sign of the transcendent, or to other ecstatic states within which the transcendent is perceived, and by means of which our relation to some understanding of the beyond is established. The mystical play of letters already at work in the poem's opening, the elided "forlorn," would seem to be denigrated here, yet the nineteenth-century lexicon of high style, forlorn, awe, those states of mind which made Emily Dickinson possible, trouble *Drafts*' invocation. But the great strength of *Drafts* is its refusal to concede the sublime to the skepticism of its literary-historical moment. The poet will not forsake the grandeur of poetry's past however much it must be tested on the pulse of the post-Vietnam world.

The entirety of *Toll* exists, one could say, to find a rational relation to the uncanny monosyllable, to that word: "awe." Ambivalently evoked at the start, awe will eventually take its place in the poem. But how complex is the mix of feelings that surround the annunciation of awe! Look at the tonal work done by the word "really" above. Our immediate sense of these lines is solidified by the invocation of irony, as if the insertion of "(really)" were saying, yes, it is irony. But parentheses are not commas. The "(really)" does not retrospectively modify or comment upon the Irony as it would if it were set off by commas. Nor, were there a comma after Irony, does "(really)" weakly affirm the awe that the line claims exists. The parenthesis serves to insert the comment of a presiding consciousness, which corrects or doubles down on the sentiment the line expresses. "(Really)" signals a division in the speaker of the poem and announces, albeit obliquely, a declamatory impulse that will make itself felt as *Toll* proceeds.

The concatenation of attitudes out of which the utterance of *awe* arises reflects DuPlessis's struggle to come to terms with her own version of *amor fati* in *Toll*, and so with her place in the largely patriarchal tradition of the objectivist sublime. In the category of sublime experience as it emerges from the theological discourses of earlier ages, freedom and fatedness are often rapturously resolved of their differences in mystical union. As the lines above affirm, in *Toll* ambivalence and awe are deeply entwined. The poet is on the defensive. She wants to know what the rationale is. Nonetheless, ambivalence introduces awe, which introduces ecstasy, which is of intense interest to the poet. Ecstasy can lead to awe, reside with awe, or be the consequence of awe, but it too must be retrieved and reimagined, for DuPlessis, from its historical associations with pre-secular discourses such as that of mysticism and with suspect or discredited expressive modalities of modern poetry before it can enter the poem. (In fact, ecstasy will eventually be made over into the poet's own authorized subset of anomalous experience, a rapture as we have already seen she will term "immerginated.") Ecstasy must cop to the theological and masculinist part of its past, even as it proposes, and traditions of women's spirituality confirm, a category of experience that is beyond gender. To accomplish this purification of the past, DuPlessis devises a trial of negativity, a ritual for ecstasy's transformation into a mental state that can live within the laws of the emerging poem. This trial draws the poem close to the void, but a void imbued with immense transformative power, one that permits a severe and carefully curtailed ecstasy, and purges away vatic pretention:

> Engulfed, each night,
> with tsunami from the vibrant void
> of sky and space,
> from the implacable emptiness, or unfillable fatedness
> of all spires, cycles, works, words, worlds, and wires:
>
> Thus. To be so. In is.
> (*T*, "Draft 23: Findings" 156)

"Thus. To be so. In is." A visionary ideal unveiled, in six syllables. A conjectured state of being is rendered in the language of mystical paradox: "the vibrant void." This figuration links a range of religious and literary discourses within *Toll*. The poet's commitment to dark and chastened ecstasies is integral to the book's imaginative logic, to its material, myth, and to its poetic method, which is, ultimately, magic. DuPlessis's improvisational unfolding doctrine of the void provides the poem with a metaphysics, a law of the beyond. For the reader familiar with the poet's earlier work, this doctrine, if that may be allowed, seems both a discovery of *Toll* in the act of its unfolding but also the ever-surprising fulfillment of a belief embraced before the poem's opening. It is there already in the figure of the well. It is there in the young objectivist initiate's fear that writing is drowning. It recurs here, now abstracted, theologized. This reconfiguring of the ecstatic, this "vibrant void," replays a paradox familiar from mystical literature: religious ecstasy is an affirmation of a presence of a divine so alien that it can only be approached by carefully discarding what is not the divine. A similar richly imagined paradox leads DuPlessis to an irony she no doubt appreciates. (Oppen himself, in this instance, the father of objectivist ecstasy, knew his negative theology, deriving his own ecstasy from the negation of a previous mode of the ecstatic: "The self is no mystery / The mystery is that there is something for us to stand on" [*New Collected Poems* 159].)

Even historians of mysticism can find the logic of negation daunting. Thankfully, the simplest rendition of it, the use of the word "no," can advance the understanding of how negation contributes to the speculative power and existential drama of metaphysically minded secular-age poetics. Consider Oppen's annunciation above. This is one of the great moments in Oppen. In a few lines he rectifies the relation between the individual and the cosmos. In following his lead, DuPlessis rebukes Oppen for what she considers his naïve rendering of the experience of awe. For DuPlessis, writing a generation later, the cultural hour for such sentiment has passed. As Oppen rectifies contemporaries and predecessors for their preoccupation with a mundane vision of selfhood, he in turn must be corrected. (As an astute reader of Blake, he might have accepted the correction). With ties both personal and poetic, the younger poet hardly wants to banish the older, but the objectivist patriarch cannot enter her song unharrowed. His aesthetic doctrines are unviable, unbelievable, quite possibly oppressive (the place of the ecstatic in feminist theo-critical discourse being a point of contention, as DuPlessis has made clear in her study of H.D.). The DuPlessis of *Toll* keeps faith with her own earlier self, the objectivist initiate who wrote *Wells*. In the light of a later historical period, where textual self-consciousness would seem to have rendered the stylistics of a naïve phenomenology obsolete, she revises the above quoted line that is the consummate articulation of Oppen's stance toward reality. Here is, again, the full quotation:

The self is no mystery
The mystery is that there is something for us to stand on
(*New Collected Poems* 159)

These lines by Oppen, to be clear, are not quoted within *Toll*. However, within a "Draft" that takes up that matter of Oppen in ecstasy, DuPlessis offers a riposte:

> Where is the place to stand to say this,
> got any syntax to make it clearer
> (*T*, "Draft 29: Intellectual Autobiography" 181)

Again, as with the presentation of the word "awe," DuPlessis satirizes Oppen. It is, however, the first step in a process of preserving the essence of Oppen's lines and making a place for such an essence in her poem. Oppen lays out the logic of negation and affirmation his protégé will follow in her critique of him. "The self is no mystery" is a statement meant to belittle and dismiss a range of other poet's preoccupations. His negation then claims a higher reality for these nouns. The mystery becomes, in his second line, the phenomenal world. The self becomes numerous (and I would say, trending toward numinous). "Mystery" is reborn, not as self-preoccupation but as a summit of contemplation. It is a participatory mystery that quietly exalts the humble perceiver, and most importantly, for both Oppen and DuPlessis, permits a secularized but prayerful speech. DuPlessis's riposte distances herself from the poet with whom she once sought council for the dilemma of distance, while salvaging his poetics of intimate authenticity. The satire has a desperate cast (oracular utterance being a long-standing subject of satire in poetry). The poet presents herself as bewildered and accusatory. She makes of "place" a phantasm. Is Oppen just naïvely phenomenological and incoherent? But vexed ironies are a part of how *Toll* comes to announce its values. The negation of one set of beliefs is the experience that confirms the presence of related but more durable beliefs. Oppen himself, in the lines quoted, has critiqued one version of the self and offered another, a phenomenal self to supersede the psychological self of earlier and other poetics. DuPlessis, within the context of the "Draft" in which her lines occur, will decenter that second vision of selfhood offered by Oppen and establish, by way of a clearly valued method of sense making and world building ("syntax," a synecdoche for linguistics), the terms for a third rendition of the self, which, as will become clear, should be considered as the place where the science of language becomes the practice of magic.

The distance kept by DuPlessis from an association with magical thought and practice is threefold: temperamental, feminist, and stylistic. As for the first, there's the poet's innate skepticism. Even in early work, DuPlessis is too philosophically minded to pass as a hierophant. However, she is also too intrigued by myth, ritual, and incantation, those hallmarks of magical materials at work within secular poetry, to ignore them, to not delve into their relation to both ancient and modern poetry. As for the second, DuPlessis resists the fantasies of primordial matriarchal orders and New Age goddess cults found within some feminist discourses of the seventies and eighties. (Consider, by way of contrast, Notley, Waldman, Vicuña.) As for the third iteration of distance, there's the poet's association with avant-garde poetics of the post-Vietnam era, which to some degree took issue with the mythopoetic imagination associated with the New American Poetry. And yet throughout *Toll*, that distance from the magical diminishes. Admittedly, magic, as either a poetics or a personal practice, can include a bewildering assortment of understandings and uses. Many of these are not pertinent to *Toll*. In *Toll*, magic is highly focused, purified of shamanistic gestures, is circumscribed by, and rooted in, an unflagging faith in Oppen's own chosen method in the quoted lines: negation. Negation in *Toll* brings close an overwhelming absence, one that renders the reader forever forlorn. (There is always an ache in Rachel for what is not there.) But the figuration of that absence is the font of DuPlessis's mythopoeic imaginings, her powerfully theologically inflected poetry.

As we have seen, the poet bases her dissolution of Oppen's pronouncement of awe on a linguistic turn. Linguistics is the law of her disenchanting magic. Critique puts a curse on older models of standing outside oneself. It shows them to be mere tricks by which words create the illusion of presence. But what replaces the earlier or critically suspect presence itself becomes more than a product of verbal prestidigitation. It becomes the "vibrant void." This DuPlessian seizure of perception arises out of critique and sustains itself in the face of philosophical skepticism. DuPlessis will rename this state, this projective *via negativa*, will call it rapture, "immerginated" rapture, as we have seen. Her coinage, as has been noted, holds several related suggestions, immersed, emerged, and these both subjected to a process—"inated," which given the trope of the well suggests inundated. One does not step beyond the self, in an enhancement of perception; one is seized from beyond. This rapture offers an affectively diminished but far more secure affirmation of both what is not "there" and what is most truly "there." Here, as elsewhere in *Toll*, negation acts like the revelation of a divine truth, a truth not made known through any other way of knowing. A mystery "within / The crisis," beyond words, yet powerfully felt:

> Immerginated raptures
>   are unsung (so to speak) because the word
>   doesn't exist
> the word for what we are being led to
> in the way of
> flattened dialectics
> in the articulation of joy despite
> and within
> the crisis . . .
> (*T*, "Draft 29: Intellectual Autobiography" 181)

Joy within the crisis. This passage reprises arguments about the possibility of the sublime as a goal of poetry, and as a bearer of meaning in modernity. The lines are highly compressed and critically cunning. They reclaim from skepticism and from a cultural moment that would curtail the figuration of exalted states one of the loftiest ambitions of poetry. As in the introduction of "awe" to "Drafts," wit leads the way. A particularly unmelodious adjectival coinage distracts the reader's attention from a noun too suspect to be articulated forthrightly. Given that raptures could be said to typify the poetics of a major precursor, H.D., we might see in the coinage the later poet's revisionary wariness in approaching unqualified rapture. The wit continues, in the lines above, with a negation of poetry as either song or speech. Who could ever talk or sing their way past that adjective? And yet, the obstacle is a part of the path: we are being led. There is an initiatory function the apparent disavowal still serves. The raptures do exist, the lines confirm, and they are, as often in mystical literature, wordless. The poet's joke allows the experience into the poem, where it elsewhere will appear not so funny at all.

As the passage goes on, the wit takes a turn. The poet is still talking. The raptures are real. We are led to them by means of (which is what I take "in the way of" to say) "flattened dialectics." Whose dialectics are those? What flattened them? Some force beyond reason? What else might so modify philosophy's oldest method? The rapturous word is beyond articulation, yet dialectics, however flattened, survive, and remain functional. The idiosyncratically qualified rapture exists. The word beyond words can be arrived at through words. But there's that "flattened," a second puzzling adjective that would seem to represent the poet's distinct way of reimagining an otherwise discredited goal of rapture. The flattening may be a musical term, as if philosophical reasoning is slipping into a blues mood. It may be the poet imagining the landscape of negation, briskly noting the stripping away of spatiality, of height, depth, and dimension. Relatedly but far more literally, it may refer to the trope of the page, which, as will be shown, is a privileged, supernaturally invested figure in *Toll*, establishing in its turning a cosmic drama of annihilation and return.

Through the flattening of dialectics to words on a page, DuPlessis paradoxically bestows upon the act of negation something like the *mysterium tremendum* that calls forth the "I am here" in Old Testament narratives ("scared is sacred," *T* 10). These raptures of a word that doesn't exist, a word for the end to which "flattened dialectics" leads, fade into the beyond. In others' hands such raptures might be a Taoist mist of radiant dissolution at the limit of human longing. However, as surely as *Toll* announces the immerginated rapture, the wordless joy that arises within crisis, it asserts with an equally complex conviction the hidden law that unites consciousness and world. Dialectics cannot uncover this but the magic of language can.

VI. The Archangel Deixis

As a sleight of hand or staged illusion can make things appear and disappear, so too does the turning of a page. Beyond that, beyond all the shameless conjuring that our bodies, minds, societies, religions, and artistic works take part in all the time, of making matter appear and disappear, concealing and revealing is with some minor theatrics enough to recover, if only for the duration of astonishment or fright, a religious cosmos. DuPlessis's linguistically grounded critique of Oppen's rhetoric of presence is itself a sleight of hand. With a scattering of syllables, she turns our attention from the speaking persona to syntactic infelicities, and so on to the further distractions of grammar. (Thus, with a flourish, are dialectics flattened.) To what operation of grammar does she lead us? What way of using words furthers the younger poet's spell? Primarily deixis, the pointing moment. Deixis would make disappear another of Oppen's talismanic utterances, in this case, lines that can be said to encapsulate his life's work. Again, the older poet is in awe. Again, the younger critiques what he says while monumentally reasserting the function his words perform. Again, she returns to a moment of ecstasy:

>   Deixis as the pointing
>   Moment of "the the"
>   (trans. that that),
>   puzzle of "What it is is it."
>   ecstasy of "that they are there!"
>   perfection of
>   "Here I/am. There/you are"
>   (*T*, "Draft 33: Deixis" 225)

And here is the Oppen poem "Psalm" from which a crucial line is taken:

Veritas sequitur . . .

In the small beauty of the forest
The wild deer bedding down—
That they are there!

Their eyes
Effortless, the soft lips
Nuzzle and the alien small teeth
Tear at the grass

The roots of it
Dangle from their mouths
Scattering earth in the strange woods.
They who are there.

Their paths
Nibbled thru the fields, the leaves that shade them
Hang in the distances
Of sun

> The small nouns
> Crying faith
> In this in which the wild deer
> Startle, and stare out.
> (*New Collected Poems* 99)

These lines are the poetic credo of midcareer Oppen. They pledge themselves to values, poetic and otherwise, regarding which DuPlessis must think out her relation. To plunge a line so transparently epiphanic into an ordeal of textual references might seem at first a simple defeat of the willfully innocent claim that poetry can recover the world-making force of divine or inspired utterance, creating as it does the world and the people and creatures in it. DuPlessis would seem to decry such illusions. First, because she writes at a later moment when the politics of presence, as performed by Heidegger, a philosopher of significance for Oppen, stood starkly revealed. Second, because she writes from within an avant-garde disposition that at the time took certain styles of authenticity to be exhausted. However, behind Oppen's "That they are there," DuPlessis hears, I would suggest, a long history of inaugural utterances, among them those that lead us back into the world of creation hymns. (Consider the refrain of the Rig Veda: "you are that." Consider the opening of Genesis, where the text points to each act of Creation as it occurs.) Deixis as a linguistic term appears at first glance to demythologize all such flamboyant conjuring. Oracular utterance is now just something words do; divine fiat, a rhetorical effect; the origin of religious authority, a trick of the tongue. But DuPlessis is not done with the mythopoetic uses of cosmogonic utterance. She understands that poetry does well by it, and that lived experience perhaps especially in a secular age takes deep satisfaction in such primordial pointing. With the advent of the angel Deixis, the poet herself points to the small word so crucial to Oppen's ecstasy, "that," the injection by Oppen, which establishes his own essential devotional disposition toward the unfolding subject. Magisterial in its sweep and in the sustenance of its meditation on the nature of language, "Draft 33: Deixis" is DuPlessis's hymn to this suspicious angel. As the canto shows, DuPlessis's ultimate object of critique and of fascination is nothing less than that foundational source of human awe, the ultimate "that," "they are there," the fundamental metaphysical relative pronoun.

As other "Drafts" demonstrate, the angel Deixis revitalizes and universalizes the pointing moment. It is the poet's way of cleansing, of its patriarchal history and of its exhaustion by the previous poetic generation, the core utterance of the mythopoetic. In the quotation above, the poet directly links deixis with both Oppen and Creeley. These two poets are notable for their revisionary stance toward overbearing precursors and for their deixis-friendly oeuvres. As a retort to the grandeur of, for example, Robert Duncan, they offer a self-proclaimed modest minimalism. DuPlessis is not, however, really interested in this minimalist chastening. Or in the aggressively modest stance each of these poets adopts in pursuit of their own version of things unattempted yet in Prose or Rime. Rather, by way of this exaltation of just one of the things words can do, indicate, she recovers for her own concerns one of the most famously world-defining pointing moments in all literature, the origin point of sublime depth and distance and recognition, the famous I-Thou dyad dramatized in Genesis, which will be powerfully performed in "Draft 33." By isolating and uplifting this particular use of language, DuPlessis, with the assistance of her chorus of critical commentators (this poem includes footnotes), creates a version of deixis that stands as the fundamental creational force hidden within all else that language does. The "pointing function" is that which establishes binaries, a this and a that, a him, a her, a here, a there. (As when, in a later moment in the Abrahamic tradition, God points and says, "And lo a voice from heaven saying, this is my Beloved Son, in whom I am well pleased" [Matthew 3:17 KJV].) Or at the zenith, or nadir, of the abject condition, *forlorn*, when Christ himself, on the cross, getting meta-textual, laments he is no longer the subject of God's pointing moment, quotes the book of Psalms: "My God My God why have you forsaken me?" In seeming to destroy the illusion of presence, and therefore the force of cosmogonic utterance, "Draft 33" powerfully revitalizes and redeploys the gesture. It does so in a way that makes a magic of the very knowledge of the working of deixis. Angel Deixis, which hides the genitive singular of Deus within itself, appears by turns powerfully truthful, the supreme thing that language does, rooted in consciousness and human perception, and as a trick, the apocalyptic fort/da.

The pointing gesture itself is the subject of the poet's awe. In this "Draft," deixis becomes her method. Awe, then, for DuPlessis, is not "that they are there," but that they can appear and go away and come back. The prophetic urge to speak on behalf of the numerous and in passing create the effect of the numinous is discretely restored to poetry. As the result of a scholarly hymn to a rudimentary notion in linguistics, the world of ancient Hebraic awe, the antecedent of the objectivist sublime, is placed before the reader. More importantly, and perversely, deixis is welcomed into "Drafts" as the ultimate world-building gesture because it dramatizes the DuPlessian doctrine of the "vibrant void."

To say so returns us to the opening of *Toll*, to the matter of elision. The word "forlorn" was omitted from the epigram from Keats, not simply because of its prominent place in an overthrown regime of poetic diction but because the poet was confident that forlornness would pervade her poem, in spirit because not in letter. Looking at a translation, the poet notices the elision of a phrase from a poem (the "little porch" of "Draft 33"). Elision is our gateway to the vibrant void. "Draft 33" begins with a witty but relentless tour of emptiness. There is, after all, an emptiness at the heart of deixis itself, if not a kind of apocalyptic negation. The pointing moment raises up within consciousness the object of the indication while relegating all else to the background, to the oblivion of the unindicated. While many modern poets pursue apophatic logics—let the ghost of Gustaf Sobin step forth here—DuPlessis fables her vision of the vibrant void without explicit authorization from a tradition of negative theology. The poet finds a critically and scientifically—if linguistics is the science of language—affirmed thing that some words do more emphatically than others: point, or put another way, call before consciousness. The critical chorus that speaks in the poem and from footnotes works hard to distance itself from the ideals and dramatic possibilities of language mysticism. And yet by way of the angel Deixis, DuPlessis has her, as Jon Stewart would say, moment of Zen.

"Drafts 33" begins by pointing to what is not there. The first thing the poem calls into being is not so much absence itself as the understanding that something is missing—in this instance, the word for the balcony of a cuckoo clock (*T* 219). So, within absence, evoked by absence, time comes to mind. This pointing capacity of language is, as DuPlessis makes use of it, implicitly metaphysical. The angel Deixis holds in a single perception presence and absence. The former is subject to the charge of illusion, a frequent imaginative strategy in *Toll*, which signals, as has been suggested, the reaffirmation of presence in a purified idiom. The latter, absence, largely escapes the apparent diminution of status that presence endures. Here we might suspect on the part of the poet a temperamental disposition to negative states, to melancholia, and regarding expression, toward the elegiac. Loss spurs the poet to transform the vibrant void into a myth of the underworld, as occurs elsewhere in *Toll*, when both personal and historical loss lay claim to the content. Here, absence arises as a creedal assertion. Deixis is quietly divinized through the course of this "Draft." Look at what Deixis does: it creates the illusion of distinction. The strategic playfulness of the question "will pointing save us?" introduces the salvific concerns that DuPlessis explores elsewhere when *Toll* reveals itself to be flat-out mythopoetic. Deixis can be the exterminating angel come to visit all articulations of a lived life, all exalted "spots of time," and all personal memory, deciding what will live in our attention and what will not live. But Deixis is also the structuring principle of all otherness. This angel is the fundamental law-giver, or rather a messenger who announces the law, the law of a divinity hidden from all pointing moments.

Again, a particular attribute of language is imagined to be the principal creative power behind the social world. "Draft 33" subsumes the figure of Deixis, the god of distinctions, to the poet's own trope of the toll, which is an acoustic pointing to the state of forlornness. Various things may be diminished or satirized as mere tricks of words, pronouns, places, temporal markers, but for DuPlessis, loss is not illusory. Deixis stands guard at the gateway of death. When the deictic points toward what is not, the poet feels grief.

VII. The Myth of the Little Word

Late in *Toll* comes a Dantesque moment: Robert Duncan and Robin Blaser welcome DuPlessis among them. Perhaps Robert and Robin imagine her redeemed from oblivion owing to her devotion to what Duncan termed the truth and life of myth. But the syncretic ecstasies, ecstasies that coincide with the discovery by a mythyminded poet of points of correspondence between mythological systems, or between mythological systems and the life of love and dream, such ecstasies, so notable in Duncan and Blaser, and that often attend a flight of the spirit to other worlds, afford no real transport in *Toll*. This in some ways reflects the literary historical moment within which *Toll* began. The 1980s saw substantial critiques of the mythopoeic syncretism that much poetic modernism found deeply attractive. Yeats, Pound, and Eliot with their belief systems, rife as they were with reactionary elements and their cosmological visions founded on theosophy, paganism, and an Eastern inflected Christianity, were not hard to read as pollutions of what experimental poetry might yet achieve. Coincident with the ideologically minded reevaluations of modernist poets came a similar assessment of the entire project of comparative religion, founded as it was on the work of Mircea Eliade, whose association with Romanian fascism brought the comparative project under scrutiny. Contemporary poets like DuPlessis, Mackey, Peck, Wolsak, Susan Howe, Fraser, and Taggart, all invested in the long history of poetry's relation to the sacred, wrestled anew with how a mythically informed poetics might contribute to a modernity where the very category of the secular has become increasingly more various and complex and contested, and the role of myth, of religious experience, of the uncanny persistence of the spiritual with art cultures and within the daily life of citizens of the twenty-first century continues to revitalize poetic form as the medium for understanding, critiquing, and participating in a post-secular world.

While there is much that attests to persistence of syncretism in *Toll*, much that places it in the postmodern tradition that evolved from mythopoetic modernism, *Toll* is notably circumspect regarding religious traditions, in relation to which the modern epic poem, from Whitman on, so routinely positions itself in the secular world. For DuPlessis, one myth, grasped deeply, subjected to intense critical scrutiny, will do. One myth makes others imaginatively available. It's a myth we might call the myth of the toll, which is the myth of the space of poetry, which is the reverberating void at the heart of *Toll*. Larger than words or world, this is the DuPlessian void creating the world within which the angel Deixis judges what will live in our attention and what will not. Deixis reveals the historical facts of the poem, most noticeably in evocations of the Holocaust, but also biographical facts, such as the death of the poet's mother. To make sure we don't miss it, DuPlessis reproduces the large black squares in Oppen's FBI file, a state-sponsored interest in creating voids that are not so vibrant, and this in a poem in part concerning her father's death ("Draft 5: Gap"). Seen or unseen, various negations coincide with our own immerginated raptures. Things, people, landscapes, documents, the details of a day appear and disappear, summoned and dismissed by an ambivalent visionary, a fanciful rationalist, a Jew uneasy about religion's appeal to invisible forces, yet who finds a way, in accord with her conscience, to, on occasion, do so herself, through the most materialist of means.

Through, that is, the turning of the page. In the turning of a page, the creating and de-creating of the space of poetry occurs. Surface to depth, depth to shallows. At times the page becomes ocean, as it appears in late Oppen, by turns sustaining and rhapsodic, annihilating and silencing. The reader's hand makes and unmakes the world. In a baroque elaboration of this manual ritual of marking perpetual ending and beginning as we read, the poet turns the larger structure of the poem back onto itself at intervals of nineteen, in the turning of pages recto and verso. Our illusion of a lack of depth is paper thin. We turn the page. The page falls on the previously turned, and we again have depth. Words go down the well. The world goes down the well. In *Toll*, the virginal soul of the world drowns in an inkwell, over and over. This coming and going of depth, of the well of writing, of space, is the monomyth the poet tells again and again with increasing ingenuity and suggestive force, the monomyth whose annunciate is the angel Deixis, selecting what appears and what does not.

Perhaps Duncan and Blaser, there in the afterlife of poetry, have expectations that, having found her own key to all mythologies, DuPlessis might convene her own symposium of the whole. And so, vexing the welcome Duncan and Blaser accord DuPlessis, arising from the depth of a footnote, comes the ghost of Louis Zukofsky. He appears once in the second epigraph and once in "Draft 6: Midrush." His mood is suitably patriarchal for such a summoning. Zukofksy tells a poetic daughter what he told his musical son. From the depths of the footnote, he decries the argument of earliest modernism that the modern poet endures a crisis of myth, that he or she now has no overarching story to tell that binds culture to poetry and to the divine. It is a reprise of the post-Enlightenment lament that reason has stripped the world of enchantment. But Zukofsky, who might be presumed to be suspicious of modernism's mythological syncretist projects, blesses DuPlessis for creating her own myth of the vibrant void. It turns out there is no crisis in his historical hour, not because myth is not needed but because the essence of myth, its world-making power, resides in the very medium of the poet, most especially the objectivist poet, whose devotion is to the little words.

As we have seen, relative articles are discretely cosmogonic. For all the humility in his pondering, the patriarch Zukofsky pushes this further. It is not just deictic words like the definite article "that" but still smaller words, "the" and "a." An entire epic awaits the poet who attends the little words, an epos, which is the very medium of myth. Zukofsky is thus in this moment of critical articulation a refiner of the mythic project, a restorer of the purity of the mythic mode. He's here to tell us we can dispense with rehashing the classics, or hymning a bridge, because all that Pound or Williams or H.D. or Crane or Eliot would accomplish with mythic materials and poetic method lies latent in the least distinguished of syllables. The slightest lettered gasp, the littlest objectivist word, shy as the letter Bet when called before the Lord, calls the world to be.

Throughout the crucial cluster of "Drafts" that appear toward the end of *Toll*, DuPlessis honors the force inherent in little words, contemplation of which is the heart of objectivist piety. From the small words, to the infinitesimal, to the point, DuPlessis works her way through varieties of thinking about the minute linguistic particular. Which is to say, she thinks about scale. Which is to say, the sublime. Once a mythopoeic aesthetic has gone through a ritualized gesture of critique, it can enter the primordial space of poetry. So Zukofsky is welcomed as the fourth among them, providing DuPlessis with an understanding of the implications of the smallest words that both unites her with and distinguishes her from Duncan and Blaser. She extends an arc that begins with the modernist long poem and passes from Duncan to Spicer to Blaser, extends the preoccupation of her precursors as well with belief systems and magical practices from presecular ages. In *Toll* these are subjected to demythologizing, then they are re-enchanted. This re-enchantment is, like rapture itself, carefully qualified. Poetics is the process that makes them acceptable to a secular age, which, thinking again of Zukofsky, would find definite and indefinite articles a most unlikely place to hide a religious universe. Objectivism reveals itself, in DuPlessis's evocation of it, to be the moment of the Creation. Definite and indefinite articles are seeds of light scattered across our language, awaiting only our disciplined attention. It is hardly any wonder that in an extraordinary recent poem, "Psalm 151," published in the online journal *Caesura*, the poet takes up the Kabbalistic notion of the breaking of the vessels.

VIII. Sacrifice

In the ongoing revelation of the objectivist sublime that constitutes *Toll*, the momentous is momentarily asleep in the minute, in the small words as in the play of white and black, of black letters on white paper and white letters on black paper—an established motif within this run of "Drafts," as it is in Kabbalistic speculation. In her spiritualization of the book itself, DuPlessis turns to the most fundamental interaction between the reader and the page, the turning of it, and finds there, rather astonishingly, an essential incident in the Jewish epos, the Binding of Isaac. Could any myth more forcefully dramatize the angelic potential of Deixis, or affirm divine force of little words, and the tragic consequences as well? Read with an objectivist eye, the telling of this averted act of blood sacrifice lives in the indefinite articles. Syllable by syllable, small word by small word, far outside the belief system in which the tale originated, the most forlorn moment in world mythology returns. In *Toll*, the Akedah is one ply in the bind of Judaic themes. But also, the page is a blade. (Look, reader, whose hand is it in?) The knife of the page flashes within the larger ever-repeating metaphysical wounding of recto and verso. The play of such, with its continual raising up of the now from the pile of pages yet to be read and the burial of the read atop the ever-rising heap of previous pages, is the figure that contains all the others. The perpetual creation and destruction of depth, the principal DuPlessian poetic gesture, is her supreme fiction and her foundational myth. Of momentous literary and psychoanalytical concern, the Binding of Isaac formally announces the theme that has run through *Toll* since the elision of the word "forlorn" in the epigram: sacrificial violence. The hand that holds the blade, the hand of death, has shown itself in the Holocaust "Drafts" and in the vast theme of loss that the poem struggles to rise from the waters of the well. The telling of the Akedah is scattered throughout a sequence of "Drafts," evoked in fleeting images that only slowly gather toward the suggestion of the Biblical drama.

The Akedah, whatever else it may be about—the crisis of patriarchal succession, the alliance of the angel Deixis with death, the existential void of fear and trembling, the social function of sacrificial violence—is also about poetics. Most immediately, the Akedah establishes a divine justification for metaphor: a ram caught in a thicket can be like a boy, at least within the schemata of ritual performance. A hapless ram can be switched out for the boy to be slaughtered. Is it reasonable to sense here that all metaphor is forlorn? The perception of likeness and the criteria for the substitution of one death for another haunts DuPlessis's work. These underscore her ever-elaborating self-fashioned doctrine of the void, which continually argues that loss is loss, and no religious or philosophical logic will prove otherwise. Perhaps the boy is saved, if not the ram, but the girl is still down in the well. *Her* agon goes untold. She will not be sung of in Zion. The boldness of DuPlessis's reconfiguration of a central sacrificial drama in the Abrahamic tradition is startling. The sacrifice of Isaac is evoked in the turning of a page, and an angelic hand stops the sacrifice and condones symbolic substitution for literal death, but nothing stops the hand of the reader from turning the page. Are we to imagine that we are Abrahams who proceed toward murder uninterrupted by the divine?

IX. Rachel Drinks from the Cup of Elijah

Toll proceeds to an even more complex act of sacrificial violence, Passover. The poet renders a self-portrait as a nonbelieving Jew at the Passover table. Given that the prophet has not shown up and joined the table, Rachel will not let the wine of Elijah go to waste (*T*, "Draft 34: Recto" 241). The wit of the scene is gently transgressive. The prophetic spirit has passed to a daughter of Israel with strong views on the whole business of prophecy. As she drinks the wine of the prophet, wine shared by all, fulfilling the ritual while critiquing it, we are observing Passover within the "Drafts" titled "Recto" and "Verso." It is difficult not to see in that the larger imaginative structure, again, the monomyth of depth, that folds the ceremony of Passover into its oblivion. The Passover is the hand of the reader passing over the page, turning the page, placing the world of the poem in the void, where memory itself is hardly sufficient to preserve the past. It is the deep paradox for peoples of the book that new pages continually arise. The book finished is then reread, read always again and always for the first time, as a scroll might be unrolled and rerolled. Some survive the reading of the book, and some die during the reading of the book, as all will die until no one is left to read the book, should the Messiah also fail to show up to the feast. In a later work, DuPlessis, in a stunning mythopoeic turn, will again imagine a Passover, this time celebrated on the bottom of the Red Sea. Given DuPlessis's aquatic imaginary, the scene is almost too complex to conjure up. Are these drowned Jews, those unmentioned perhaps in the official record, caught up in the recto turning to verso of the waters? (See *Around the Day in 80 Worlds*, part of the series *Traces, with Days*, page 52.) Is Phoebus the Phoenician among them? Are they the souls of Jews welcoming the souls of their pursuers to the table in a ritual commemoration of an event still in progress? The Dead Sea, the well all fall into, or are thrown into, does it protect a place of remembering, of reconciliation, a life within death where the spirit of Elijah appears as Rachel Blau DuPlessis, who knocks at the door, sits down, sips wine, and begins to tell the epic of all our journeying?

Acknowledgment

A portion of this essay was presented in 2015 at the Louisville Conference on Literature and Culture since 1900.

Note

1. As DuPlessis notes in her "Introduction" to *The Selected Letters of George Oppen*, "In December 1966, the Oppens moved from their Henry Street apartment in Brooklyn Heights to San Francisco. They bought a house at 2811 Polk Street into which they were able to move by the end of 1967" (xix).

Works Cited

Crane, Hart. "Passage." *The Complete Poems of Hart Crane*, edited by Marc Simon. New York and London: Liveright, 2001.

DuPlessis, Rachel Blau. *Around the Day in 80 Worlds*. Kenmore, NY: BlazeVOX, 2018.

———. "Dialogues with Oppen: Appropriation and Gender." *The Oppens Remembered: Poetry, Politics, and Friendship*, edited by Rachel Blau DuPlessis. Albuquerque: University of New Mexico Press, 2015.

———. "Midrashic Sensibilities: Secular Judaism and Radical Poetics. A Personal Essay in Several Chapters." *Radical Poetics and Secular Jewish Culture*, edited by Stephen Paul Miller and Daniel Morris. Tuscaloosa: University of Alabama Press, 2010, 199–224.

———. *Drafts 1–38, Toll*. Wesleyan, CT: Wesleyan University Press, 2001.
———. *Wells*. New York: Montemora Foundation, 1980.
Oppen, George. *New Collected Poems*. Edited by Michael Davidson. New York: New Directions, 2002.
———. *The Selected Letters of George Oppen*. Edited by Rachel Blau DuPlessis. Chapel Hill: Duke University Press, 1990.

CHAPTER TEN

Spark Me Up, or The Light of Shattered Language

The Holy Un[]hole in Rachel Blau DuPlessis's "Psalm 151"

ADEENA KARASICK

> DuPless unknowing. DuPless needing to know.
> DuPless the broken vessels; the edges, cropped and fissured.
> DuPless the word, the clay, parchment, paper. DuPless the holy glue
> of wracked fragments tracing the weight of its mystery.
> —Adeena Karasick

ACCORDING TO THE KABBALISTIC concept of Shevirat ha Kelim, as outlined in several sections of the Zohar (Sifra d'Tzni'uta, Idra Rabba, and Idra Zuta), for creation to occur there needed to be a withdrawal, a constriction of divine light—a state of separation, partition to introduce multiplicity and choice into the world. This partition manifested as ten vessels of light, but because of the intensity of the light, the vessels could not contain it, and they shattered. These shattered fragments fell to earth, became absorbed in all worldly matter, and according to Lurianic tradition, it's our job to elevate the sparks of light still embedded in the broken vessels. Through a diasporic poetics of fierce wordplay, trans/elation, transudations, and homophonic fractures, Rachel Blau DuPlessis's "Psalm 151"[1] in conversation with Mira Schor's 1976 *Book of Pages* and a "kintsugi ethos,"[2] exquisitely luxuriates within this Kabbalistic secret of the shattering of the vessels, simultaneously exposing and syntactically enacting how creation always already arises from destruction and the scattering of light.

I. "And Some Say Alphabet Is Creation"

Composed in twenty-two parts, mirroring the twenty-two letters of the Hebrew alphabet, DuPlessis's alchemical psalmistry begins with a prayer, summoning the breakage—a celebration of all that's fragmented, fissured. And in blessing all that is broken, "Broke. Baruch," it belies not only how translinguistically the word for broke(ness) *is* "blessing"[3] but that inside *baruch* is *ruach* (spirit), highlighting at the outset letters as vessels of spirited discourse.

For, according to Rabbi Dov Ber, the Maggid of Mezritch,[4] in the beginning was את—that is, the letters from Aleph to Tav. In the beginning this primordial light was the alphabet—twenty-two letters to be infinitely remixed, to continually create new meaning and being. As a discourse of light, "the light of light" swelling through "pulses," "probes," "strobes," "waves," waives, DuPlessis highlights how darkness, the "dark-thick IS-ness," is always a form of light, and whether through "Shekhinic cyprine light,"[5] or luminous enormities, or "swelling e-norms / faced clay," letters themselves ignite ever-spiraling creation.

This relationship between language and light is reminiscent of how throughout the Zohar, and in DuPlessis's text, there is a complex exploration of the physical/material properties of the alphabet to contain the uncontainable, how each letter is a vessel of non-containable difference, a system of thirsting signs. And reckoning with the "wreckages of burst starlight," section five illuminates:

> The smooth shape of vessels scooped
> and scraped and scorched
> into incipience for looming light -
> as per this list: a   amphora,   b   dancing bowl
> pert on three wee feet,
> c   d   two vats wide as households,
> e   f   two bottles.   long-necked thirst,
> g   canteen with a baby spout,
> h   rope-patterned vessel, i   water-storage urn,
> j   pinch cub, blessed
> fabrication, blessed
> variety, praise the safe-keeping
> self-keening
> Earthenware Ten. Per se.

This is not unlike how verse fourteen of *Sefer ha-Bahir*[6] explores how the structure of the letter Bet[7] (ב), which is closed on three sides but open in the front, metonymically stands in for the House (Bayit) of the world; and how according to *Book of Letters*, "you can walk into a *Bait*, and you are at home" (Kushner 14). With reference to earthenware, clay pots, bottles, urns, canteens, and kitchen utensils, DuPlessis reminds us how these letters hold us, and through them we are "home." And as this "home" is comprised of letters of light, literal and metaphorical vessels, or in DuPlessis's terms, ten "powers of emanation / with their shardy pointed / emendations, gloss," we attenuate, tend to the "10. Per se," ten vessels of light, ten *sefirot*, ten enunciations that have been "scooped, scraped and scorched" into "resonant vessels," "humped and turned, punched and opened" (almost sadomasochistically, tortured for our pleasure), attending to their untenable containment.

And as these ten letters (a–j), refolded fragments, figures, are ever reconfigured into "bottles" or "bowls," with these bodies of light, DuPlessis highlights how each letter of light is never a "thing in itself." For, as she foregrounds at the outset, to reach its "IS-ness" is "an ineffable task," "a task unspeakable." And, as "some propose shards will change to letters. / And others see sparks capture letters, / others, seeds form letters," "Psalm 151" exposes how the letters themselves are never one but an amalgam of entangled limbs. This is reminiscent of how in Hebrew, no letter is a thing in itself, but the letters themselves are comprised of other letters: meaning, the letter Tsadi (צ) is composed of a Nun[8] (נ) and a Yud[9] (י). The Shin[10] (ש) is composed of three letters: a Vav[11] (ו), a Yud (י), and a Zayin[12] (ז). Not only is each letter foregrounded as an intertextual accumulation but also as a system of relational differences and interdependent signs that contest singularities of difference.

II. "Numbers like Letters"

This sense of relational difference and interdependence is further foregrounded in section thirteen, in which DuPlessis references how in Hebrew letters are also numbers. As a flickered elixir of fractal fractions, lettered sparks are re-arced as algebraic equations, unequal signs to be renavigated for endless investigation and gloss. Section twenty-one further enumerates this by zeroing in on the significance of ten ("one zero," "zero-one"): how "the air counts to one and then makes ten, by adding the zero," underscoring how "the nothingness is always something," and thereby how 1 + 0 points to how all meaning and identity "belong to a double fable," an infinite redoubling, a duplicity, *a DuPlessity*, "a multiple of one as one of / one as all." Further, if, according to thirteenth-century Kabbalistic mystic Avraham Abulafia, language (as lettered numbers) contains a structure that conveys the "true form of identity" (Idel, *Language* 3), and for Edmond Jabès "identity is, but an assemblage of letters," DuPlessis's *ein sofistry*[13] reminds us of the interdependent nature of language and identity.

III. Avowels of Vulval Voyages

And as bodies body forth between the body *corps* and body *text*, a text of "slit flesh," "dislocated bones," "hip sockets," "yearning limbs," and limns, "Psalm 151" embodies "all that was and will be." Specifically invoking the female body, section thirteen praises/raises "the tidal vowels" and their "voyelle volvelle / volute vulval voyages"—a veiled secreting (*s'ecriting*) of how within Kabbalistic hermeneutics the vowels are engendered female. Regularly not committed to writing, vowels remain a spectral presence, a series of unlocatable traces haunting the consonants.

Further, according to the Catalan Kabbalist Rabbi Jacob Ben Sheshet, not only is the scroll of the Torah inscribed without vowels and therefore pregnant with (in)finite vocalizable potential but *should not be vocalized* so that each and every word not be limited but is potentially activated according to every possible significance (Idel, "Infinities"). This vocalization and subsequent activation are echoed and extended by Nahmanides,[14] who points out the vowels are *the form* and *soul* to the consonants and are seen as causing the movement of the combinations of the letters. As the vowels (seen as the spiritual element) are often *excluded* from the graphic score, *the vowels as spectral traces* are in fact always already emanating through the consonants. Present-non-present, the vowels in "Psalm 151," like the Kelipot[15] (clay pots) themselves, "which [consist] of the unassimilable parts of the broken vessels" (Zalman 886), collaborate in an elaborate labor referencing all that is other, that which cannot be assimilated into a system:

> Of shapes, to exist with edges,
> of shapes to contain emptiness,
> made to mimic the withdrawing void,
> sonorous echo ache,
> the resonant vessels sound
> vowels inside their open-ring.

IV. Ever-Avers or Eruverrun

Ending with section twenty-two, metonymically referencing the final letter of the alphabet, Tav—which stands in for *emet* (truth), a truth comprised of Aleph, Mem, and Tav; the beginning, middle, and end of the alphabet—DuPlessis avers (*ouverts*) how truth is inscribed in and through language.[16] Even though Tav is the last letter of the *alefbet*, its left leg is reaching back toward an ever-circulating beginning. Thus the very form of the letter foregrounds how the end is never the end, but a notion of finality or closure must be called into question, reviewed as a series of never-ending traces, echoes, inscribed in spectral dissymmetry. Further, reaching out toward the rest of the letters, Tav enacts how every letter is inscribed in every other letter—that each letter is not proper and unique but an intercombinatory sequence of ever-shifting associations with a range of gematriatic possibilities. In so doing, the language of this section hearkens back to section nineteen, how purity not being the point, but "endless processes, / being as begin." Circulating back in on itself, "Psalm 151" functions in a similar way to how, when concluding an order of Mishna or a tractate of Gemara, it is said, "*Hadran alach*" (We will return to you), giving expression to how we return to the same portion again and again.[17]

As we return again and again, all nomadic vagrant and deeply diasporic, "Psalm 151" becomes "a [v]ast [b]ook of [q]uestions," "where our questions / [] bec[o]me our companions." As the poem's multiple sections ask:

> What is "book"? What is debate? Gloss? What is "vision," dogma?
> who dares say "purity" or "heretic"? Who rides the tidal vowels?
> Doesn't creation demand alphabets as companions?
> When in the world emerged such double forces of making?
> Did time begin before or after letters? How many of them are there?
> Can one speak at all about -site-? And "where"? What time is time
> without itself? And who will say "I know"?

These questions beget further questions, leading to an endless re-questing, "enacting the unanswerable."

Like the very concept of Shevirat ha Kelim, section twenty-two ends on the notion of mending: tikkun, the ways in which we return again and again to restore the light into the world through blessing. And, as DuPlessis uses the word "mend," the poem invokes a weaving metaphor, stitching the relation between all that is intertextilic, textatic with ribbed woven lines, limning illuminate, delineating, nonlinearly outlining the materiality of sentences, entrances, en/trances,[18] s[]owing how all is interwoven as we re-seam semes, seems, streams and re-pair the tattered fragments—rethreading patterns of entangled letters, limbs, cells, atoms, rocks, trees, days, ropes, roots, fibers.

And through rifts refts drifts splits spills spells praising appraising reprising, liaizing matter caressing the chasm between signs sonics and syntax, DuPlessis's lexical synnexes highlight how language is not only a *creative force* that engenders a multiplicity of communicative possibilities but a means to continually reactivate the world. Given that gematria (numerological equivalent) of 151 is also that of the Hebrew words for "a whirlwind or tempest," "to groan or cry out," and both "darkness" *and* "hope," through a textatic scat of shattered matter, 13 pages, 22 sections, 288 sparks, and 10 vessels, the "whirlwind of light" of "Psalm 151" radiates and explodes through an invaginated chiasma of edges, folds, histories, mysteries, veils, valleys, volleys—a *seferotic* prayer of darkness and hope, alight with how an ending is always a mending, an amending, upending; and a finish is always a gloss.

Notes

1. Rachel Blau DuPlessis, "Psalm 151," *CÆSURA*, 15 Nov. 2021, https://caesuramag.org/posts/rachel-blau-duplessis-psalm-151. Throughout this chapter, references to "Psalm 151" are to this online, unpaginated work.

2. As DuPlessis lays out in her notes, "the Japanese technique of golden mending for broken porcelain."

3. In Hebrew, the word *baruch* (sometimes spelled *boruch*) means "blessing."

4. Eighteenth-century Ukrainian Kabbalistic mystic, regarded as the first systematic exponent of Hasidism, the teachings of the Baal Shem Tov.

5. According to Kabbalistic thinking, Shekinah is the divine indwelling female present, and, as per DuPlessis's notes, "cyprine" refers to Susanne de Lotbinière-Harwood's name in French for vaginal transudate (wetness).

6. The *Bahir* (c. 1176) is comprised of twelve thousand words. It gets its name from Job 37:21: "And now they do not see light, it is brilliant [*bahir*] in the skies." Though it has been attributed to Rabbi Nehunia ben haKana, according to Gershom Scholem, it may be based on the *Raza Rabba* (a tenth-century Eastern text).

7. The second letter of the Hebrew alphabet. Kabbalistically it refers to creation and plurality. As a prefix, the letter Bet also means "in." But according to the *Bahir*, this indicates a continuous process of filling. Thus, even if the opening lines in Genesis are translated as "in the beginning," that beginning is filled and keeps filling and therefore resists any notion of a fixed point of origin.

8. The fourteenth letter of the Hebrew alphabet. Kabbalistically it refers to faithfulness and emergence.

9. The tenth letter of the Hebrew alphabet. Kabbalistically it refers to creation. It occupies the place of displacement, the space of the "excluded middle." Graphematically resembling a comma or apostrophe, it signifies an absent present. As in the mark of the pataphysical (the superinducement of the superinducement), the Yud references the elision of the elision that becomes quotation. So, as the doubled mark of an open quotation, it self-reflexively legitimizes and delegitimizes, frames and opens.

10. The twenty-first letter of the Hebrew alphabet. Kabbalistically it refers to power and scription. According to the *Bahir*, "as a prefix Shin indicates the word 'that' and thus is a letter that connects and specifies," see page 103. In form, it can be seen as having three heads on top, thus questioning any notion of irreducible singularity. Further, according to Kushner, "on the right there is a Vav, whose head is bent back a little. In the middle there is a Yud, also leaning back a little. And on the left is a Zayin with three crownlets" (60).

11. The sixth letter of the Hebrew alphabet. Kabbalistically it refers to conjunction and continuity. As a prefix, the letter Vav means "and," and therefore acts as a connective. In Hebrew, the word "Vav" also means hook and thus functions as a sign of accumulation.

12. The seventh letter of the Hebrew alphabet. Kabbalistically it refers to struggle.

13. Ein Sof is the Kabbalistic concept of the infinite—that which is boundless, without end.

14. Moses ben Nachman, also referred to by the acronym Ramban, was a leading medieval Catalan Jewish scholar, philosopher, Kabbalist, and Biblical scholar.

15. The broken husks or shells (in Lurianic Kabbalah) are the spiritual barriers temporarily blocking divine light.

16. This is particularly evident in that the ten commandments start with an Aleph, the Mishna begins with a Mem, and the Gemara begins with a Tet. (Together the initials spell "emet").

17. See Berachos, 166, as cited in Michael Munk's *The Wisdom in the Hebrew Alphabet*, 227.

18. Some of this language is adapted from Adeena Karasick and Maria Damon's Shmata project, "Intertextile: Text in Exile: Shmata Mash-Up A Jewette for Two Voices" in *Habits of Being*.

Works Cited

Derrida, Jacques. *Specters of Marx: The State of the Debt, the Work of Mourning and the New International*. Translated by Peggy Kamuf. New York: Routledge, 1994.

DuPlessis, Rachel Blau. "Psalm 151." *CÆSURA*, 15 Nov. 2021, https://caesuramag.org/posts/rachel-blau-duplessis-psalm-151.

Idel, Moshe. *Language, Torah, and Hermeneutics in Abraham Abulafia*. Translated by Menahem Kallus. New York: State University of New York Press, 1989.

———. "Infinities of Torah in Kabbalah." *Midrash and Literature*, edited by Geoffrey H. Hartmann and Sanford Budick. New Haven: Yale University Press, 1986.

Jabès, E. *From the Book to the Book: An Edmond Jabès Reader*. Translated by R. Waldrop, with P. Joris, A. Rudolf, and Keith Waldrop. Middleton, CT: Wesleyan University Press, 1991.

Kaplan, Aryeh, translator. *Sefer Yetzirah: The Book of Creation in Theory and Practice*. Newburyport, MA: Red Wheel/Weiser, 1997.

———. *Bahir*. Attributed to Rabbi Nehunia ben haKana. Introduction and commentary by Aryeh Kaplan. Newburyport, MA: Red Wheel/Weiser, 1990.

Karasick, Adeena. *Salomé: Donna di Valore/Woman of Valor*. Padua, IT: Padova University Press, 2018.

———. *Of Poetic Thinking: A Pataphysical Investigation of Cixous, Derrida and the Kabbalah*. Spectrum Research Repository, Concordia University, 1997, https://spectrum.library.concordia.ca/id/eprint/280/.

———, and Maria Damon. "Intertextile: Text in Exile: Shmata Mash-Up A Jewette for Two Voices." *Habits of Being*, edited by Paula Rabinowitz. Minneapolis: University of Minnesota Press, 2015.

Kushner, Lawrence. *Book of Letters*. New York: Harper and Row, 1975.

Munk, Michael. *The Wisdom in the Hebrew Alphabet*. New York: Mesorah, 1983.
Scholem, Gershom. *Major Trends in Jewish Mysticism*. New York: Schocken, 1961.
Schor, Mira. *Book of Pages*. Collection of the artist, 1976.
Sperling, H., and M. Simon, translators. Zohar. Vols. 1–5, New York: Paulist Press, 1983.
Zalman, Rabbi Schneur. *Likutei Amarim—Tanya*. Translated by Rabbi Nissan Mindel. Brooklyn: Kehot Publication Society, 1958.

CHAPTER ELEVEN

"Moth: Ode to Psyche" and the Active Romanticism of *Drafts*

JEFFREY C. ROBINSON

THE TITLE OF RACHEL Blau DuPlessis's book *Tabula Rosa* (1987) signifies a feminist intervention in poetry: because there is no "blank slate" of creative "originality" (tabula rasa) for woman poets but only always already masculinist poetry of the tradition looming as a blocking agent (the "I" across the page, as Virginia Woolf put it), they must write through that claustrophobic presence to recover their own vision, language, and voice. Called "from *The 'History of Poetry*,'" the book's first section summons lyric poems from the Western tradition only to rework them by dispersing the (male) lyric subject, rejecting the place of woman as silent muse, and dismantling conventional syntax with its stress on the semantic. This critique of lyric as a masculinist form, fundamental to the work of *Tabula Rosa* and always at play throughout her work, leads in the second part of the book to the serial poetry of her major work *Drafts*, with three long poems: "Writing" and "Draft 1" and "2." No poem in the first section dramatizes the struggle to find a Kristevan "semiotic" language more spectacularly and intricately than "Moth: Ode to Psyche," a feminist rewrite and *détournement* of Keats's Romantic manifesto-ode, "Ode to Psyche." "Moth" rips words and phrases from their home in the "Ode to Psyche" and reseeds them as a sign of at once the inescapability of the poetry of the masculinist tradition but also its availability for feminist disruption and transformation. It flattens the celebratory, vatic, philosophical, and public character of the traditional ode. The goddess Psyche is exchanged for its biological counterpart, a moth (not even the colorful butterfly); and cheerful rituals of masculinist proliferative mythology that appear in Keats become the moth's struggle to give birth to pre- or nonverbal "moth" language, "writing lines of eager slime" (40). The open, enthusiast voice pronouncing through apostrophe, meditating, and awakening in the "Ode to Psyche" is erased in "Moth" for a "tuneless" script (Keats, *Poems* 40). In "Moth," DuPlessis dramatizes a decentering of traditional gender identities toward what she calls a queering—a blurring and expanding—of identity, leading to a more general concern with otherness.[1]

Yet even as she creates a new poem out of a severe critique of an older one, she pulls from Keats's poem radical undercurrents that as we shall see inform her later writing. Serving as the strategic launching point of DuPlessis's postmodernist feminist critique of traditional male, particularly Romantic, lyric expectations, Keats's "Ode to Psyche," as I read it, is itself a radical Romantic reworking of its own poetic history and thus

I shall show provides impetus and even strategies for DuPlessis's strange new poem. Furthermore "Moth: Ode to Psyche," as a singular moment of feminist postmodern refashioning of a canonical lyric, is also pivotal in DuPlessis's poetics. It at once looks back to the history of lyric but in so doing undoes lyric to anticipate the serial poetry she will subsequently write.

At the same time, this disturbing poem develops a thread of Romanticism's radical precepts for postmodernist poetic practice realized in her next careerlong commitment, *Drafts*. As she has said about the place of radical (or "active") Romanticism in her writing:

> In Anglophone culture, the complexity of women's political rage and social desires, their yearning and forceful analyses of their second-class legal and educational status, their powerful goals for female liberation, their libidinous investments in their liberty and in the liberation of other second-class semicitizens are all vital to the Romantic era. The decolonization of women, sexual minorities, other minoritized groups, and enslaved peoples; the establishment and enforcement of civic personhood for all; the ability to value (not just "tolerate") differences and differentials within communities are all indicators of real modernity—a modernism drawing upon the energies of active Romanticism. ("Singing Schools" 47)

Reflecting the multiple strands that, I am arguing, the poem "Moth: Ode to Psyche" generates, my essay begins with a reading of DuPlessis's monumental lyric, interwoven with a reading of "Ode to Psyche" in order to reveal how she critiques its masculinist elements while at the same time drawing on and developing Keats's Romantic experimentalism, what she calls her "complement" of the earlier poem.[2] "Moth" is, I argue, her most intense expression in *Tabula Rosa* of what will be fundamental to and expanded in her later work, *Drafts*. In the second half of my essay, therefore, I look first at her discussion of radical Romantic poetics in her critical writing on Romantic poets William Wordsworth, Mary Robinson, and S. T. Coleridge, and then at moments in *Drafts* where she makes explicit how she draws on the radical Romanticism of William Blake and Coleridge in the formulation of her feminist postmodernism.[3] I conclude by showing how in *Drafts* she developed and reworked for the needs of women poets a form originating in the German Romantic period—the fragment. This quintessential radical Romantic genre practiced and theorized amid the wave of post–French Revolution activism by Friedrich Schlegel (1772–1829) and Novalis (1771–1800) associates absence of "mastery," incompleteness, multiplicity, and the privileging of the part over the whole with poetic manifestations of democratic principles.

Tabula Rosa immediately proclaims a recognition that the poetic act for a woman poet in history is situated amid palpable constraints. Women poets find themselves in a prison, shackled and fettered by rules created by men, including the assumption that in poetry women are most powerfully represented as silent muses that inspire, extend, and shape poetry written by men. At best, it would appear, they can speak with "broken tongue" (Sappho). Yet, choosing pointedly to acknowledge and begin her poetry within these constraints, as Charles Olson said, to "stay in the condition of things" (46), DuPlessis has proposed and devised a counterintuitive liberatory strategy for a contemporary woman poet.

"Moth: Ode to Psyche," taking on Keats's gorgeous, sensuous, and celebratory "Ode to Psyche," is perhaps the most thematically and formally overwrought, the most strenuous, poem in the book, banging at the window of masculinist "lyric" line by line, deconstructing its premises based on the drama of personal visionary enlightenment ("Ode to Psyche" celebrates the light) and deforming its formal orderliness in the process of making room for a new, if "grub"-by and abject, bodily writing. Instead of "sing"-ing ("I see, and sing, by my own eyes inspired" [Keats, *Poems*]), "Moth" liberates a "bareness blaring unarranged" (*TR* 40). An apparent violence driving the poem—a commonplace moth, not the flying beauty of the butterfly, driving out the Apuleian goddess of the soul, the "winged Psyche," and "running Keats' [poem] backward through my poem 'Moth'" ("Darkest Gush"),[4] the darkness of an insect desire pushing out the light—registers the extremity of the woman poet's strategy of revolt. If light, and enlightenment, mark the means and the triumph of the "Ode" ("a bright torch and a casement ope at night / To let the warm Love in" [Keats, *Poems*]), darkness and blindness indicate a major measure of feminist success in poesis. As I will show, in "Moth," lyric—which remains a commitment for DuPlessis as much as she is critical of it—isn't destroyed or, in Blake's sense, negated but is "complemented," is left in what becomes generative tatters, which in the radical Romantic tradition that broadly includes the work of Keats were called "pollen" (Novalis) or "fragments" (Friedrich Schlegel), that lead to the serial poetry of *Drafts*.

I. "Moth: Ode to Psyche"—Twentieth-Century Feminist Complement to Radical Nineteenth-Century Romanticism

The title of the poem, "Moth: Ode to Psyche," creates a confusion upon which the poem insists and builds, a traffic jam of contradiction and mixed expectations. Influence usually implies a hierarchy: either the precursor poem holds sway over any attempts to surpass it (anxiety of influence), or the new poem asserts a superiority on the basis of enlightenment, as with a feminist correction of a masculinist poem. But DuPlessis has never been content with such hierarchies and binaries, and the colon in her title provokes ambiguity. Is the "Ode to Psyche" a particular instance of "Moth," an elaboration of it, or the reverse, a revelation of it—the real thing? Or is it a visionary definition? Or is there an equivalence on each side of the colon—two wildly unrelated phenomena, one a member of billions of an undistinguished biological species and the other a unique poem of great "value," central to the canon—and both are somehow occupying the same horizontal plane or are in some way reciprocating or even anticipating a third thing? Are they, to invoke a fundamental DuPlessian coordinate, side by side, in a nonhierarchical relationship, in the manner of Keats's Amor and Psyche, whom the poet finds "couched side by side" (*Poems* 364)?

The opening strophe—of ten lumpy sections—frames the poem's bewilderingly condensed content and drama, and its method:

> Percussive throws of the moth-
> gambler moth-die
> moth-face soft face
> hurtling
> from one edge of the pegged down screen to the other.
> Twang of wire, wing
> rag(e)s bug "burning" with desire for some bright torch
> : dark clustered tree-eyes beyond
> and moonless scattered fanes of night
> thin stars without a name beyond unreachable light
> THROWS
> the ovoid winged egg at the emplacement
> one dry page casement.
> (*TR* 35)

A moth bangs against a screen and throws out an egg, interleaved with scattered phrases and words from the final stanza of "Ode to Psyche" ("soft," "bright torch," "fanes," "stars without a name," "casement"). Violent movement of the biological event blurs with violent "deformation" of the poem—"running the lines backward" and erasing many of them ("Darkest Gush" 6).[5] The poem seems to have infected the moth's battering of the screen, and two mythic sources converge: first, the moth's predisposition for "burning" light that means certain death, as Shelley poeticizes it by blurring candle and the cosmos, "the desire of the moth for the star" (475).[6] Second is Apuleius's second-century Roman tale of Cupid and Psyche, an archetypal journey narrative featuring a female hero, one whom twentieth-century feminist readers have noted for the success of her agency supported by growing consciousness. The wish to keep the moth away from the light (the heat), as occurs later in "Moth," is at once an act of empathy and a design to preserve the possibility of women's fulfillment and creativity. "Desire," and therefore some diffuse sense of consciousness, motivates all the furious movement in the strophe that ends with an anticipation that twines the site of moth birth with the site of writing, the page.

Embedded in the imagery of uncontrolled movement lies a poetic principle that DuPlessis calls upon to enforce the risky possibilities of feminist success, the Mallarméan "throw of the dice" that will not abolish chance. The reference frames the poem's intention to abolish mastery and to proclaim risk as the condition of its making. Biologically, chance will refer in the poem to the unpredictability, uncontrollability, and low-percentage possibility that a moth egg will find a source of nourishment for its growth. If the ostensible principle animating *Tabula Rosa* is the "overthrow" of masculinist poetics, replacing one "master" with another, the invocation of *Un Coup de Dés* looks beyond to a nonhierarchical poetic practice[7] registered in the chaotic, desiring violence of this opening section.

Amid the screen of this opening section, and indicating the double impulse animating her poesis, phrases from "Ode to Psyche" are introduced, first as an occasion for critique and second as generative compliment/complement. Critique begins with the beautiful: just as Psyche is known for her beauty, so does beauty characterize Keats's "Ode." It is replete with figures that saturate our sense of the beautiful, in particular a "verbal plenitude" (*BS* 7) of images and the overflowing of sound and rhythm. It foregrounds the waking dream as a lyric state of mind beneath and above the quotidian; framed by apostrophe ("O goddess!" [Keats, *Poems* 364]), the poem travels unhindered from the personal to the mythic, and the mind of the poet unfolds a utopian vision. The addressed Psyche remains silent, the muse for the male poet, whose interior vision swells passionately to an Enlightenment fulfillment ("a bright torch and a casement ope at night" [366]) that has led Anahid Nersessian to call the poem an ode to joy. By contrast, "Moth: Ode to Psyche" is a radically ugly poem. It eschews the sonorities of apostrophe, the sensuousness of Keatsian vision and sound. It contracts the distance between today and the ancient space of myth. Instead of the comic marriage plot of the Cupid and Psyche story, DuPlessis's poem scrupulously follows the life cycle of the moth. Consciousness is diffused through a moth and a shadowy poet figure without ever becoming congruent with its lyric structure.

The poem narrates the life cycle of the moth, which consists of four stages: the egg, fertilized by the sexual union of male and female moth and then nurtured in moist growth; the larva or caterpillar that grows spectacularly over a period of time from eating away at a leaf; the pupa, in which the cocoon shell protective of the larva is made out of silken threads and then stunningly dissolves the larva into an "accumulation of goop," which leads to the realized winged moth, called an "imago" (*TR* 36) In the poem, the moth is filled with a stubborn energy that insists upon the laying of eggs regardless of adverse circumstances, its beating against a "blank" window pane. It makes sounds, "ultrasonic sexual communication," that get transcribed in the poem as "moise noise," "wehing wehing," and "ple ple." As it metamorphoses into a moth, the pupa releases a waste product called "meconium" through its anus. The last three sections attend to the pupa's active life mired in dirt and slime, but instead of presenting the newly formed moth, the sections layer pupa imagery with references to book, leaf (in both senses), and "writing lines." The barely audible sounds of moth mating and warning explode and magnify at poem's close: "bareness blaring unarranged."

The poem's interest in this biological cycle is not neutral or disinterested but "burns" with what might be called human empathy and the actualities of human life. The layering of moth life and the poet's life—a queering of the latter—begins through projection of human responses—"desire," "thrill," "rage," "embittered," "sobs"—and intimations of phallic sex. By the middle of the poem, human concerns, though always mediated by the moth's life cycle, take over, coalescing, in contrast to the ahistorical nature of myth as well as biology, in a local historical and autobiographical geography. We are suddenly in Philadelphia, at sites of transition: "to this day where Broad / crosses Columbia," where the Temple University campus begins, and where Rachel Blau DuPlessis emerges from the subway to go to work and later to leave for her home in Swarthmore; and at the Thirtieth Street "station" where a train could take her north to Boston and south to Washington, DC (*TR* 35–37).[8] At these crossroads, a person pauses, a "vision" that seems to extend back to the opening strophe and forward to the end of the poem wells up in her. At these crossroads, she tells us, writing takes place (in notebooks, on sketch pads), but the character of these references, between professional public life and intimate life, and therefore defined by neither, indicates something comparable in the human being, where she crosses into a poet, recalling to me Marina Tsvetaeva's remark that a poet dwells not at home but at the crossroads.

> Writing in the station notebook all the codes
> broken, a vision
> white and brown moth feathering against
> the hard square of "its" desire.
> Resisting normal linkages
> barnacled thoughts of the psyche
> forsaken, . . .
>
> And bitter, hitting words onto the sketch pad
> cool rooted resistance shredded
> Pen-sylvia station sheets banded together. . . .
>
> Wrath of the layered silence to avenge.
> Bundled a human packet
> exists to this day where Broad
> crosses Columbia trussed
> a messages band(i)ed bonded in leaves of rags and ropes
> for she alone Alone
> inedible rage,
> her thready fascicle.
> (*TR* 37)

These dense middle sections of the poem (five and six) coalesce a sense of the "lyric subject" but with no indication of a lyric "I" as a principle of conscious organization. Less interested in presenting an "I" of the woman poet, DuPlessis seeks an "I" as an "Other," her "queering" of gender that is central to her reimagining wide-ranging poetic possibilities available to a woman poet ("Singing Schools" 63). The projective

"I" of the traditional "Ode" vanishes before a kind of flat anonymous witnessing of events. At the crossroads, a negative capability of self rises up in these passages blurring human and moth action and location; it allows for "all the codes / broken, a vision / white and brown moth feathering against / the hard square of 'its' desire" (*TR* 37). Indeed, a visionary apprehension seems to spread back from the beginning of the poem to this point, when an identification with the moth occurs, and her writing nearly becomes indistinguishable from the moth's eating and beating. A moth eats "leaves" the way a poet writes on them—green nourishment (devouring a leaf) equates to poetic creation. Moreover, it is here, as confused, conflicted writing erupts, that gender enters the poem: "for she alone Alone / inedible rage." Bitterness and rage produce the "percussive" hits and drum-like beats, against the resistances of the window for the moth and the equally square space of what was a "blank" page.

Sections five and six begin to sketch a blueprint for DuPlessis's revisionary poetry that rejects the self-enclosed, well-situated, song-full character of lyric. Notes taken at a station, words hitting a pad at the crossroads, suggest the fragment, even the "draft," which, however, are not singular but "multitudinous." Dispersive (political) emotions of "wrath" and "rage" and paranoia, not the affective conditions one associates with lyric, lead to a bundling and gathering of written stuffs—secretive, song-less, but endless (*TR* 37–38). Although from the beginning, shards of the "Ode to Psyche" have appeared, in these sections they are shown to be fundamental to poetry now fully tabula rosa:

> She strings herself through fond believing lyre,
> she stuns herself against the form of the window—
> the screen resounds in flat no tune no chord.
> The utter wings dark scorch
> yet still demand, compel, another's bright(er) torch.
> (*TR* 37)

Here the fusion of Philadelphia poet at the crossroads, predecessor poem, and moth proposes the character of the poetry coming into being. Throughout these sections there are notebooks and sketch pads and sheets and packets and leaves and even a Dickinsonian fascicle; all these signs of fragment and incompletion point away from lyric to seriality, from singular to alternative readings, with its principle of poetic aperture and its possibility for endless iterations.

At the same time she is abandoning traditional expectations of lyric poetry, DuPlessis is constantly reminding us of their presence. For example, rhyme that brings "tune"-fulness to verse, and is often associated with lyric as consolation, even visionary consolation, the nostos, an anchor for poetic certitude and a principle of closure, persists in "Moth" with metronomic regularity, almost every strophe ending with a rhymed couplet; yet it is hard to hold onto, its discovery as one passes from section to section only a faint memory, a roseate blush amid the chaotic free verse.

From here to the end of the poem, the self, maker of poems, as ephemeral as it was in sections five and six, gets further absorbed into the phases of moth emergence. It appears faintly in a radical Romantic gesture of poetic facilitation of the life of the other: "how to protect them [moths] from their desire to leap / into the rigid square of light" (*TR* 38). But mostly it is revealed as "matting" of biological references into poetic and Keatsian ones, an absorption or coloring of one domain in the other. The fascicle holding together the gathering of poems is composed of the silk threads of the pupa's cocoon. In the phrase "thready fascicle," a string focuses not on the revelation of the "imago" but on the slime produced by the pupa that dissolves the caterpillar in order to *transform* it into a moth (37). The slimy waste product, the *meconium*, ejected through the anus of the pupa, becomes the poet's abject triumph of female poetic production resistant to establishment poetic principles—slime instead of words, dark, earthy, organic life instead of air and light:

> writing lines of eager slime
> black and rotten warmth, cell-meaty mass
> rooted in the muddy and blank
> tunnels the multitudinous tuneless numbers,
> bareness blaring unarranged.
> (*TR* 40)

The poem, monumental in its weight and feel and in the sense of achievement against the odds (the throw of the dice), ends with a vision of multiple beginnings, without a structure "arranged" from above ("Singing Schools" 63); the turbulence of closure here anticipates its near abandonment in her serial poetry.

From a distance, the earlier poem torqued in "Moth: Ode to Psyche" would seem to be a stable target or object of critique, but DuPlessis responds to Keats's own vital experimentalism with "compliment and complement" ("Darkest Gush" 6). After looking at that vitality in "Ode to Psyche" as guided by the principle of what I am calling active Romanticism, I will turn to her later work that, I believe, incorporates that principle in order to extend and transform it into a vital poetry of the present.

II. The Function of "Ode to Psyche" in "Moth"

In the course of "running Keats' 'Ode to Psyche' backwards" ("Darkest Gush") in "Moth," DuPlessis scatters a monumental odal lyric in the slime (the semantic returned to the semiotic) that is her new poem. She reduces the poem with its expansive personal voice to a collection of shards of the original; each one of which is repositioned and thus radically defamiliarized. Climactic words at the end of the "Ode" work as opening frame devices—the "bright torch" that concludes the vision of Cupid's well-lit future visits to Psyche now become an initial focus of the moth's desire that needs to be eliminated for moth writing to occur.⁹ And conversely, the "tuneless numbers" characterizing Keats's speech at the beginning of the "Ode" appear at the end of "Moth" in a phrase that not only describes the poetry of "Moth" but characterizes the serial poetry of *Drafts* to come: "multitudinous tuneless numbers" (*TR* 40). As an instance of back-to-front deformance, "Moth" becomes palimpsestic; similarly while the "plot" of "Ode to Psyche" occurs at the end of the Cupid and Psyche story after the two have been reunited in heaven, "Moth" runs that plot backward into the troubling middle of Apuleius's account with a Psyche embattled with Cupid, his mother Venus, her jealous sisters, and the rigid patriarchy of both her family and the gods.

The binarism that seems to define the principle behind *Tabula Rosa* is challenged, where one side of the binary contains the other side within it. For example, Keats's "Ode" begins with a highly prayerful, projective, and sonorous voice, a rich texture of decorum in its address to the mythological figure ("pardon that thy secrets should be sung / Even into thine own soft-conched ear" [*Poems* 364])¹⁰ and its mid-poem wondering ("Surely I dreamt to-day, or did I see / The winged Psyche with awaken'd eyes?" [364]); in contrast, "Moth" assumes a flat, disinterested voice of reportage and witness, and yet it actually is a "vision" of moth/poet realization and thus not all that far from that of Keats's speaker.

"Moth," in its challenge to traditional lyric poetics, from the beginning signals a rejection of "mastery" as a poetic outlook, but in fact Keats's poem does as well. It rejects "Olympus' faded hierarchy," and at the end creates a "rosy sanctuary" in which the independent life of Cupid and Psyche, a kind of otherness, can take place in the future at their will and as often as they wish (365). This vision of "Ode to Psyche" reflects a careerlong concern of Keats: how to fashion, or facilitate, poems without the intrusion of mastery. He says, "We hate poetry that has a palpable design upon us" (*Letters* 61).¹¹ To use DuPlessis's word, Keats strives for a vision of "unpossessibility" ("Marble Paper" 113). To this end, the stanza form in the "Ode to Psyche" and the subsequent "Odes" is the culmination of a series of sonnet experiments theorized in the sonnet on the sonnet: "If by dull rhymes our English must be chained," with the intention, "if we may not let the muse be free, / She will be bound with garlands of her own" (*Poems* 368). (The "sonnet" in this regard is Keats's tabula rosa occasion.) Observing at one point that the sonnet discourages free, fanciful, spontaneous mental movement, Keats builds an ode stanza that lightens the sonnet by hollowing out one quatrain. Thematically, the "Odes" conclude with images of a life or object acting or being independent of the poet's ego,¹² and his contemporary sonnets to fame urge the poet to resist the appeal of immediate fame, to be free of ego (fame) anxiety¹³: "Make your best bow to her [Fame] and bid adieu; / Then, if she likes it, she will follow you" (367). Finally, for DuPlessis, the rejection of mastery concurs centrally with her queering of gender for the poet; but, as Anahid Nersessian reveals, Keats also queers or blurs the gender distinctions of Cupid and Psyche in his "Ode" (101–2). Keats, in other words, challenges an assumed adherence to a masculinist poetics.

III. Radical Romanticism in the Creative and Critical Writing of Rachel Blau DuPlessis

Just as "Moth: Ode to Psyche" "complements" Keats's "Ode," so does DuPlessis's later poetry and prose complement "Romanticism." What follows is a synthesis of her critical and creative updates, in her own historical present, of Romanticism in work after *Tabula Rosa*; while I do not claim that "Romanticism" is *the* source of her later work, I find that *radical* Romantic poetics can account for some of its basic principles. DuPlessis's feminist Romantic poetics begins and ends with the requirement of "unpossessibility," which relies on a fusion of political and spiritual expressions—what the Romantics called "imagination."

A passage in the brilliant "Preface" to *Surge* (2013), where "escape" is her word for "unpossessibility" (15), is a good starting place for the rest of this essay, moving away from *Tabula Rosa* to her critical writing in *Blue Studios* (2006) and *Active Romanticism* (2015) and then to *Drafts*, as a principle of her feminist postmodern poetics that fights against predetermined outcomes: "No poem is totally the poem you meant to write, but every poem you've written is the one you did or could write, brought to the poise or level of interest to which you could then bring it. That is, the poem escapes the poem. Or the poem escapes the poet. Or is it, the poem escapes the poetics? With the simultaneity of making and a sense of loss, something escapes inside the work. This 'escape' authenticates the work" (*S* 15).

Writing with the form of poems in *Drafts* and of subsequent poems in mind, DuPlessis argues that every poem has a potential for such authentication, and every poet can write with the "Negative Capability" that allows materials to enter and escape the poem without severe authorial control (Keats, *Letters* 43). The radical Romantics insist upon a political dimension of escape. Her passage recalls Blake's line from *Milton*, "There is a Moment in each Day that Satan cannot find" (35–42, 194). In Keats, it is the element in a poem that can circumvent the "palpable design" required by the ego of a poet committed consciously or otherwise to a repressive "affirmative character of culture" (*Letters* 61).

DuPlessis explores this poetic "struggle to escape" in her exemplary analysis of Wordsworth's "The Solitary Reaper" ("Marble Paper"). Listening to the "thrilling" voice of the reaper from afar, the poet-speaker asks: "Will no one tell me what she sings?" but, in the course of the poem, seems content with asking and not finding out, even precisely gratified by a beautiful song not understood arising from an attractive female figure whose historically specific artistic autonomy goes unacknowledged. Readers, particularly feminist readers, have challenged Wordsworth's poem on its seeming celebration of the reaper as traditional muse figure. DuPlessis agrees with their position but radically complicates it, granting Wordsworth at the very least an important intuition of "escape," the route to which, in her argument here briefly summarized, begins with the need to recover the historical specificity in the "other" in lyric and, indeed, to imagine a poetry in which the other speaks, a poetry of dialogue.

She establishes (as does Jeremy Prynne in greater detail in *Field Notes: 'The Solitary Reaper'*) the verifiable actuality of the language and song of the reaper in order to show that Wordsworth's idea of lyric does not accommodate that otherness but then proposes a reading of his question about her song in which he intuits a poetry of dialogue. As she puts it: "The tension around female work and autonomy is clear in this poem of yearning within romantic modernity" ("Marble Paper" 120). "In Wordsworth the sense that something has escaped him over which he had almost assumed he would have an overview makes for a quick anguish of failed possession that breaks through the tone of the poem" (120). Furthermore, he enacts a Romanticism that looks forward to modern poetic experiments, including her own; indeed, the Romantic vision is fundamentally generative of unexplored iterations of itself: with "The Solitary Reaper" "a new formation is emerging. An artwork—even a poem—can express contradictions about social relations, can negotiate its own inquiries, and can leave traces of those contradictions and queries for those willing to engage them" (121).

Wordsworth doesn't write but intuits a poetry comprised of what DuPlessis calls a "dialogue" between the speaker and the female other singing in Erse, a form that she explores in her later essay, "Singing Schools and 'Mental Equality,'" about the dialogic poetry between Mary Robinson (1758–1800) and Samuel Taylor Coleridge. How does this eighteenth-century woman poet achieve mental equality (Robinson's phrase)? First she offers two poetic exchanges between Coleridge and herself,[14] with two poems on a snowdrop, and second she provides her détournement of "Kubla Khan." "To the Poet Coleridge," DuPlessis shows, acknowledges the visionary ecstasies of "Kubla Khan," the whirling, centrifugal, and often contradictory poetry and the final rapturous dancer with "His flashing eyes, his floating hair!" which it then incorporates—often "running" Coleridge's words through her own lines—into its own, somewhat domesticated, vision. Coleridge's silent "damsel with a dulcimer" sings in Robinson with her own ecstatic agency: "Thy nymph, her dulcimer swift-smiting, / Shall wake me in ecstatic measures / Far, far removed from mortal pleasures" (Robinson 330–32). As DuPlessis states, "This poem, complementary and complimentary both, offers an example of a female poet proposing and producing and claiming 'mental equality' in the cultural realm" ("Singing Schools" 63).

We can contextualize DuPlessis's analysis of Robinson's "dialogues" with Coleridge as most immediately an instance of radical Romanticism with its link to experimental modernism and finally her own signature practice. The spirit of the French Revolution inspired Romantic poets toward writing some dialogues highlighting "mental equality." Her reading here applies easily to "Moth: Ode to Psyche," which in turn extends to her vision and method in *Drafts*.[15] (This extension describes accurately the transmutation of "The History of Poetry" in *Tabula Rosa* into that book's second part, particularly the long serial poem "Writing.") The final part of "Singing Schools" tracks DuPlessis's own practice of "torquing" poems often from the canon in poetic realizations of gendered mental equality achieved in her case in part by "queering" gender so that the woman poet, working out of her own historical specificity, achieves, just as male poets have been able to do, a multiplicity of subject positions. She shows that Mary Robinson's rough quotations from "Kubla Khan," a linguistic "dialogue" with that poem, anticipate the various forms of "overwriting" and "twisting and untwisting" that torquing includes. The palimpsest of tabula rosa becomes the dialogue of "To the Poet Coleridge" that in turn becomes the torquing of earlier texts, what DuPlessis calls "posthumous dialogues," that characterizes *Drafts* ("Singing Schools" 64–65).[16]

Of the 114 poems that comprise *Drafts*, "90," "91," "92," and "93," poems that end the major section of *Pitch: Drafts 77–95* (2010),[17] comprise a clutch of poetry driven by explicit radical Romantic sources that DuPlessis recasts for her contemporary feminist purposes. Here I can only gesture at the richness of what is in these poems a verse essay on DuPlessis's postmodern Romanticism, with references to Blake, Coleridge, and the theory of the German Romantic fragment. Together, they concentrate the major Romantic legacy in her work, the insistence upon performing "unpossessibility" as a vision of democratic ethics.

"Draft 90" and "91" channel Blake's "Proverbs of Hell" (*Poems* 71) in an exploration of the "excess" or overflow of energy required to overcome engines of social control (possibility) over human identity, social expression, and freedom of mind. Excess in Blake is about realization of any object, human or otherwise, on its own terms, which is to say, excess is a democratic principle (following the goals of the French Revolution) of inclusivity, the "numerous," the "multitudinous." "Draft 90," called "Excess," while alluding to contemporary poets, anticipates "Draft 91: Proverbs" as a massive riff on Blake's "Proverbs of Hell": "The road of excess leads to the palace of wisdom"; or "You never know what is enough unless you know what is more than enough" (*Poems* 71). DuPlessis arrives at excess as an imaginative and intellectual uncovering of its "fallen" counterpart, material excess in runaway capitalism. The poem dramatizes a movement of deep awareness of the latter, as blocking agent, toward the revelation of the former.

> Words? why even
> say them, as they fall aslant
> of it, of glut,
> buffeted and baffled
> by things without provenance,
> all sleek and shiny bright,
> their Shadows
> photo-shopped out.
> (*PI* 128–29)

Words are expressed "aslant" (Dickinson) of consumption capitalism's framing of reality. Seemingly one with capitalism's "waste," words find in their waste a freedom to observe shadows as the nearly erased truth of human life:

> This poem almost became its own erasure.
> Almost blanked itself out.
> But it's to see those shadows
> that this is. . . .
>
> My excess gathers shadows in.[18]
> (*PI* 129)

In the latter part of "Draft 90," a vision of poetry that breaks past the possessable emerges under the sign of excess: "Excess: the Verb / without a verb, / the Noun of all / and none, / a no and yes, / a rapture / and a doom" (131). Excess, pushing past consistencies, allows for a poetry of contradictions and oppositions. To write the multiple "shadows" accurately is to invest them with unpossessibility; in the case of *Drafts*, this often means writing with a sense of oppositional dialogue (as in Blake, "Opposition is true friendship" [*Poems* 78]).

In "Draft 91," DuPlessis builds upon Blake's *The Marriage of Heaven and Hell* and the "Proverbs of Hell" within it (catching startlingly Blake's "imperial" tone as well as his crisp formulaic sentences and phrases) that formulate an ethics for poetry based upon the acknowledgment, through "energy" and "excess," of multiple others in their unique individualities. "The bird a nest, the spider a web, man friendship" (Blake, *Poems* 135). "Let the mite live. Let the girl become literate" (DuPlessis, *PI* 35). Her proverb reveals the politics left implicit in Blake; "let" requires a conscious act in the service of gender equality and agency. Both poets believe that the acceptance of the uniqueness of the other extends to mind—including "the fancy," fantasy and so-called delusion, all mental activity not immediately accessible to, as the Romantics say, "custom" or "habit" or "reason," to poetry itself and the fancy or fantasy of the mind in its freedom that can guide the making and the content of a poem. Blake: "Every thing possible to be believ'd is an image of truth." And DuPlessis: "No matter what, it cannot be called back" (*PI* 138). In both poets, bringing to light demands an act of trust in the mind and the senses, which in turn requires excess of energy, and such trust opposes the drive of consumer capitalism to pitch individuality into the shadows. DuPlessis adds the specter of surveillance repression.

DuPlessis repeatedly genders the Romantic ethics in "Proverbs of Hell." When he says, "Poetry fetter'd, fetters the human race," Blake creates a set of interanimating correspondences between language in poetry and the life of the collective beyond poetry (*Poems* plate 3, 211). "To read well, you must open the whole stained cloth" (*PI* 134). Alluding to menstruation as woman's reality, she tells us that the clean cloth (a blank slate) doesn't give us the full truth. In this context, women's writing troubles familiarity and legibility: "If legible, find the illegible in it" (135). Illegibility leads to a writing instruction, "Reduplicate the awkwardness" (137),[19] to a visionary one, "Wherever there is critique, there is a third grammar" (134), and then to the nature of unpossessable, visionary coordinates that occupy the drama of DuPlessis's verbal and collage poetry, "The beyond is in two places: here and there" 134. For her, poetry needs to make all familiar coordinates and standards tremble and blur and yield to a new coordinate, a new grammar, for the liberation of the human race, which means, as she says in "Draft 92," establishing "interest in one's own foreignness of time, place, and language" (*PI* 180).

In "Draft 92," DuPlessis wittily torques one of her favorite Romantic poems, Coleridge's "This Lime-Tree Bower My Prison" (1797), acknowledges its Romantic virtues—the sympathetic imagination, its vision of both communal and "bare" life, and its precise detailing of the "condition of things"—while rejecting or seriously glossing the (masculinist) binaries of "here" and "there," center and periphery, idealism and materialism, male and female, self and other, and monolithic sense and nonsense. The poem torques "This Lime-Tree Bower" as much as "Moth" torques "Ode to Psyche," by running lines from Coleridge into her own poem but also, comically, running them first through Google translate (French, German, and back again into a mishmash of English syntax) in order to emphasize that a "national" language is a fantasy of the truth and an act of hegemonic control (*PI* 180). Coleridge's own definition in *Biographia Literaria*, XIII, of the "Fancy" (the poetic faculty that he subordinates to the synthetic "Imagination") as "a mode of memory emancipated from time and space" (305) applies: DuPlessis emancipates his poem from its late eighteenth-century poetic coordinates and linguistic expectations into a drama of self, achieving a vision of genuine otherness. From the perspective of "Draft 92," the sympathetic imagination marked repeatedly in "This Lime-Tree Bower" may actually be a kind of narcissism based upon preference for a "center" ("Here I must remain" [Coleridge, *Poems* 138]) from which to projectively impute experience to his far-off wandering friends—that is, a deficit in the original manifestation of Romantic ethics is reworked, complemented. Much of beauty in the latter poem, its absorption in glimmering natural detail, "richly tinged," is passed by in DuPlessis's relentless quest for an otherness perceived missing in it. Coleridge was famously criticized by the poem's interlocutor Charles Lamb, who complained that the poem's epithet, "my gentle-hearted Charles," was infantilizing—"my virtues have done sucking"—and added "or at least do it in better verses" (45).

DuPlessis responds to both criticisms, beginning with a framing disruption of the opening line in the signature blank verse of the early Romantic "conversation poem," so named by mid-twentieth-century critics.[20] "Well, they are gone, and here I must remain" (Coleridge, *Poems* 138) becomes:

> "Welly, they are gone." Nyahh
> "And here I must remain." Yeahhrr.
> (*PI* 140)

The blankness of the blank verse becomes a critical rosa, contestatory, the "reconciliation" of "gone" (there) and "here" is broken, while the meaning of "here" and "there" is questioned, as is the aestheticized and purified poetic language of the tradition ("Nyahh... Yeahhrr"). And while the five-stress and often ten-syllable lines of the rest of the poem, turned from the blank verse stream into couplets, keep an eye precariously on the original blank verse line replete with enjambments, they, in sync with her poem's vision, are othered, or, as the poem's subtitle indicates, translocated.

Spinning off the trajectory of "This Lime-Tree Bower" where the speaker "remains here" (141) in one place while his friends wander away on a walk, "Draft 92" dramatizes the speaker's growing vision of translocation in which to "wander in gladness" (Coleridge) comes to mean wandering into other hierarchies of value. The binaries of "here" and "there" are dropped, allowing her and her "friends" to reject "center," "arrangement," and ultimately (poetry as) "consolation." Such torqued wandering leads to a wonderfully "pedestrian" materialism:

> Yet without centralizing Verb's or Vista's
> Clearest claims, but simply passing spaces
>
> Through along, in there or thereabouts, through time.
> Or seeing her old house, moved off to here by truck.
> (*PI* 141)

The idealism of Romantic, picturesque, dappled, natural beauty in "This Lime-Tree Bower"—"Shine in the slant beams of the sinking orb, / Ye purple heath-flowers! richlier burn, ye clouds!" (Coleridge, *Poems* 139)—is first rechanneled into the world of building construction and then (repurposing Coleridge's "shine") into a woman's bodily poesis, coming out of "Moth" and "Writing": "My period eye is filled with blood. / Like veins thickening, like railroad tracks. . . . And shining! Shining with imperfection! / Silvery clots in open spots of knotholes" (*PI* 143).

"Translocations," one slowly realizes, is finally a critique and a renewal—a compliment and complement—of the idea of the Romantic lyric, where the binaries of "lyric" and "serial," self and other blur. In this regard, DuPlessis has updated the "Moth" project, its feminist torquing of a Romantic favorite from the confident perspective of *Drafts* itself, resulting in a more "drafty," playful, and less claustrophobic poem. The "here" with which both poems begin initially points to the traditional congruence of formal perimeter and lyric subject, and that congruence assumes lyric closure as a means of highlighting by contrast the primacy of subjective experience. Toward the end of "Translocation," we feel the pressure for and resistance to closure mounting, as the speaker states:

> This history, the real true story of intricacy
> Began-begins when you-thou thought it done
>
> In foreign selves who live aside the known.
> (*PI* 142)

And later:

> ... The last ditch, the stand in the door,
> The thing declared over, finished,
>
> Was beginning something else another,
> Constellations of entanglement, ...
> (*PI* 143)

Ending, thus, is a beginning in and by foreign selves. These lines describe the end of a component of a serial poem, but they also redefine lyric as a "draft" containing a paradoxical possibility of closure-as-aperture, a threshold ("stand in the door"). We can find hints of aperture in the radical Romantic lyric too: the "Ode to Psyche"'s "casement ope at night / To let the warm Love in" (Keats, *Poems* 366) that anticipates a new beginning together for Cupid and Psyche, or the following from the last lines of John Clare's sonnet "Emmonsails in Winter": "And coy bumbarrels twenty in a drove / Flit down the hedgerows in the frozen plain / And hang on little twigs and start again" (212).

Aperture and renewal open the way in "Translocations" to a second element latent in "This Lime-Tree Bower," otherness and foreignness, "beginning something else another," often marked through spatial extensions past the familiar:

> The beyond is in two places: here and there.
> Wherever there is critique, there is a third grammar.
> What is it to go beyond recto
> Though not by turn or flip to verso page
>
> But to a sonic page called vertigo. ...
> (*PI* 134, 140)

These several indications of aperture as a facilitator of an expansive, unpredictable poetics point lead quite naturally to DuPlessis's reconfiguring of the imposing Romantic genre of the fragment realized in "Draft 93: Romantic Fragment Poem," where Jena school German Romantic theory of the fragment as the quintessential Romantic poetic genre is, consciously or not, bedrock for DuPlessis's great serial work.[21]

"Draft 93" is the shortest poem in *Pitch*, a witty burst of fanciful ideas draping the drama of a sexual climax that breaks off at the moment of orgasm ("where then abruptly thereupon ...") between two lovers as "others" ("a you absorbed, an other I") (145). The poem finishes outside the poem; its ending (as is the case with female orgasm) is incomplete. Blake's "energy is eternal delight" might be its motto; the fragment articulates a "road of excess" (70). Eroticism takes its form at once in bodies and in a poem,[22] and thus "Draft 93" defines, at least temporarily, the nature, intention, and source of the sequence generally:

> . . . and one reverberant
> titanium rod, whose
> tuning forked to pitch of A
> got embodied
> and embedded
> in the homeless
> wandering
> poem
> (*PI* 144)

IV. Coda: *Drafts* as Complement of the German Romantic Fragment

DuPlessis's poetry in *Drafts* and beyond, in its resistance to closure, embraces, we can say, the fragment as a genre. Neither the fundamental eroticism of "93" nor its development of the otherness of persons feature in the original fragment theory of German Romanticism. And yet "Draft 93: Romantic Fragment Poem"—and her work as a whole—consciously or otherwise draw on that theory of fragments and seriality. Coming toward the end of her masterwork, DuPlessis's signaling of the thought of Friedrich Schlegel and Novalis, formative for radical poetics since the post–French Revolutionary period, may reflect her characterization of all her poems in the series to that point and, less obviously, of the earlier poems in *Tabula Rosa*. Schlegel and Novalis themselves of course write fragments about fragments, their own form of "thinking through poetry" (Levinson) that DuPlessis advocates. The fragment is their formal response to what they saw as the literary requirement of a democratic revolution—reflecting inclusivity and difference, a future orientation, process and becoming (not "disinterestedness"), multiplicity, and a refusal to cordon off the aesthetic from personal and social reality.[23] Its completeness lies precisely in its incompleteness, a point emphasized repeatedly by Schlegel, and incompleteness implies DuPlessis's "unpossessibility."[24]

The formal and substantive elements of the fragment, as Schlegel formulated it and as DuPlessis seizes upon it, immediately reflect commitment to poetry of democracy that insists upon the equality of all heterogeneous elements and acknowledges the fact that a democracy is a work in progress. Closure and "perfection," in this context, signify exclusion and a satisfaction with a less-than-democratic status quo. In the most famous of Schlegel's *Athenaeum Fragments*, "116," Schlegel claims: "Other kinds of poetry are finished and are now capable of being fully analyzed. The romantic kind of poetry is still in the state of becoming; that, in fact, is its real essence: that it should forever be becoming and never be perfected" (175). A fragment is a "project," thrown forward into the future; its incompletion indicates its participation in a changing social present. Its "essential incompletion"[25] implies a future of a multiplicity of fragments: "to write a fragment is to write fragments."[26] Novalis collapses the idea of becoming and multiplicity in the image of a seed that produces something never before invented ("a book as art"): "Fragments of this kind are but literary seeds. There may be many barren grains among them: nonetheless, imagine—if only a single one sprouts!"[27] (39).

DuPlessis's feminist poetry draws on Schlegel's conviction that the form of the fragment should accommodate the heterogeneity of objects: "Many works that are praised for the beauty of their coherence have less unity than a motley heap of ideas simply animated by the ghost of a spirit and aiming at a single purpose. What really holds the latter together is that free and equal fellowship in which ... the citizens of the perfect state will live at some future date" (154–55). *Haufen* (heap) can refer to the social "masses" that artists of a democracy are drawn to include, and *Einfällen* (ideas) connotes a flash of insight, wit, and the fancy: the mind in its freedom. Put simply, Schlegel's "coherence" gives prominence to parts of an artwork just as democracy gives prominence to its citizens. The democratic impulse behind Romantic form also molds language and syntax. As he writes, "Poetry is republican speech: a speech which is its own law and end unto itself, and in which all the parts are free citizens and have the right to vote" (150).

DuPlessis develops the vision of democracy inherent in the citizenship of poetics parts in her analysis of "negative [or critical] poetics" (*BS*), which she characterizes as "segmentivity, the practice of writing in lines and gaps, and in hypersaturations of verbal plenitude, signaled by Keats's curious "'load every rift' of your subject with ore" (*BS* 7).[28] This practice in conscious detailing rejects a structural totalization for a continuous, word-by-word, line-by-line, attention, as if at every moment a "citizen" were responding creatively to a new situation, and the form of the whole would emerge from this almost as an epiphenomenon.[29] Her phrase "hypersaturations of verbal plenitude" envisions an overwhelming of the conditions from which it comes at any point but equally envisions a whole flexible enough to accommodate it. Similarly, in "Draft 91: Proverbs," excess often produces a challenge to meaning, to "perfection" of expression, and to the familiar, as in: "Reduplicate the awkwardness" (*PI* 137) and "Whenever there is critique, there is a third grammar" (134).

Her focus on a fragment as composed of citizens with independent subjectivity and agency making up the whole precludes the idea of the controlling authorial subject and opens the possibility of the queering of the subject. But there is room in a fragment if not for singular authorial control then for dialogue—a crucial word for DuPlessis both in her Mary Robinson discussion and in her synonym for torquing one text with another as a "posthumous dialogue" (DuPlessis, "Singing Schools" 64). Schlegel observes, "A dialogue is a chain or garland of fragments. An exchange of letters is a dialogue on a larger scale, and memoirs constitute a system of fragments. But as yet no genre exists that is fragmentary both in form and content, simultaneously completely subjective and individual, and completely objective and like a necessary part in a system of all the sciences" (170).[30]

The preceding sketch of German Romantic fragment theory sums up a starting point for much of Rachel Blau DuPlessis's poetry and criticism as described in this essay; how does she complement it? As I noted earlier, that the Romantic, post-revolutionary period took seriously the claims of disenfranchised persons, including women, and that Romantic poetry attempted to enact those claims is important for DuPlessis finding herself in "this difficult historical period for writing. I have begun to understand that my feelings are socially saturated.... The political world infuses everything we are. I express it continuously; I do not have to 'decide' to write a 'political' poem" (*S* 17). She continues, weaving the a priori presence of politics into the formal politics of the German Romantic theory of the coherence of the fragment as the principle of expressing inclusivity and its heterogeneity: "I write politically simply by trying to represent all the dimensions of my and our lives.... The question is how to face them, not to exclude their force by means of the purificatory or aestheticizing rituals of art" (17).

Unity ("*Einheit*" for Schlegel) imposed upon a poem, the closed form of lyric and its satisfaction with a poem's uniqueness and singularity, for both the German Romantics and DuPlessis, is a technique and vision of "purification." The *im*purity of DuPlessis's poetry and her insistence upon multiple and blurred subjects lie at the basis of her feminist poetic accomplishment; the forming strategy of such poetry is best described as coherence binding together, perhaps awkwardly but truthfully, a "motley heap."

DuPlessis has thought of *Drafts* as a counter to Ezra Pound's *The Cantos*, considering the latter totalizing and controlling and thus not truly open to the motley multiplicity of the other. For DuPlessis, feminism can intervene in all iterations of life repressed, denied, and destroyed, all the way from the too-common experiences of women to climate disaster (*S* 9). Coherence cannot be the same as "unity" for such poetry, which may account for her response to Ezra Pound's famous admission in "Canto 116" that he cannot make his "ragbag" materials "cohere" (253). According to Alan Golding, DuPlessis argued that Pound began *The Cantos* with a similar openness to inclusivity, with assemblages of "a market mess of spilled fish," but over time insisted that he assert "mastery" over his materials; he lost touch with what she called the "feminine" nature of his materials by a need to control them. But Pound's market mess and rag-bag content is precisely the "motley heap" of the disenfranchised in Schlegel's fragment, in which coherence must never be "mastered" in order to reveal the often suppressed and unspoken truth of the world according to a democratic vision. DuPlessis, we can say, in her antipathy to the totalizing Pound, draws for her feminist vision the democratizing openness of the German Romantic fragment. The writer of "Romantic fragment poem" is in this one sense, in the condition of things, not that far from the note-taker in "Moth: Ode to Psyche" where Broad and Columbia cross with a "message band(i)ed bonded in leaves of rags and ropes," the maker of "thready fascicles," who is at once the moth producing its "multitudinous tuneless numbers / bareness blaring unarranged" (*TR* 37).

Notes

1. It is worth noting that DuPlessis's concern with otherness in the mid- to late 1980s coincides with a comparable expansion, in society at large, of second-wave to third-wave feminism with its awareness of many analogs to the suppression of women.

2. In "Singing Schools," DuPlessis makes clear that her critique of poems from the tradition is woven into respect and "empathy" for them; her response is "compliment" for their achievement and "complement": her poem attempts to realize, or complete, what the earlier poem only hints at, in her case, her visionary feminism or the agency of the other, its "unpossessibility," and also the historical reality in which she situates her poem. In describing the method and principle of "torquing" in *Drafts*, where she develops severe techniques for "achiev[ing] a critical relationship to [earlier] texts," she adds that torquing is also "an act of empathy and curiosity—what is there, in that text; what remains vital in it?" (65).

3. We should not overlook her commitment to Keats's "Negative Capability" statements—his "enormously useful idea." Her explicit Romanticism, along with "Moth: Ode to Psyche," appears in four "Drafts"—"90" and "91" (based on Blake's "Proverbs of Hell"), "92" (which works off Coleridge's "This Lime-Tree Bower, My Prison"), and "93" (titled "Romantic Fragment Poem")—and two essays, one from *BS* ("Marble Paper" with an extended reading of Wordsworth's "The Solitary Reaper"), and one from *Active Romanticism* ("Singing Schools," on the dialogic poetry of the Della Cruscan school and of Mary Robinson with Samuel Taylor Coleridge), and, along with "Moth: Ode to Psyche," in poems in *Tabula Rosa* treating Wordsworth, Keats, and Dickinson.

4. What she has called "the souped-up appropriations of the already-written"; see "Darkest Gush."

5. As Jerome McGann and Lisa Samuels say in their essay "Deformance and Interpretation," "The arbitrary imposition of a reversed order on the original layout indicates that the poem possesses its own means for evading determinateness" (119).

6. Moth against window recalls Virginia Woolf's modernist essay "The Death of the Moth," in which the moth, heading for death, in the beginning radiates life: "Watching him, it seemed as if a fiber, very thin but pure, of the enormous energy of the world had been thrust into his frail and diminutive body. As often as he crossed the pane, I could fancy that a thread of vital light became visible. He was little or nothing but life." From *The Death of the Moth and Other Essays* by Virginia Woolf, copyright © 1942 by Harcourt, Inc, renewed 1970 by Marjorie T. Parsons, Executrix, reprinted by permission of the publisher. In the trajectory of "Moth: Ode to Psyche," the life of the moth, rather, is sustained throughout.

7. "Throw": the word appearing here in caps emerges "otherhow" and elsewhere; first in "Throw of the dice"; and second, not quoted in the poem but realized in the Kristevan abject that characterizes much of the moth-creativity in the poem, thrown away, or thrown to one side.

8. I am grateful to Rachel Blau DuPlessis for an e-mail conversation on this subject.

9. From Anahid Nersessian's *Keats's Odes*. She observes that "Ode to Psyche" is a poem of light.

10. Compare Robert Duncan's "Often am I permitted to return to a meadow" (7).

11. Keats's facilitative poetics in the service of "unpossessibility" is the subject of my book-in-progress, *John Keats Without Compass*.

12. The nightingale fading away from the speaker, the urn teasing the viewer out of thought, the swallows of autumn gathering on their own.

13. A position taken by Keats's friends John Hamilton Reynolds and William Hazlitt.

14. The snowdrop exchange follows the practice of so-called Della Cruscan poetry, in which Mary Robinson participated. It was a type of witty, urban, erotic poetic dialogue between a man and a woman popular at the end of the eighteenth-century and adapted by Robinson to which are contrasted the roughly contemporary "sincere" rural meditative poetic monologues made famous by Robert Southey, John Thelwall, Charles Lamb, and most notably Coleridge and Wordsworth.

15. The Romantics themselves, it should be noted, wrote dialogue poems—for example, some of Blake's *Songs of Innocence* and *Songs of Experience*, Wordsworth's *Lyrical Ballads*, Shelley's "Julian and Maddalo," and some playful poems by Keats, to name a few. Mary Robinson, in *Lyrical Tales* (1800), wrote a brilliant dialogue called "All Alone," in which a female speaker full of compassion for the poor converses with an orphan who refuses her invitation to help him by insisting again and again that he is "all alone"; the poem establishes within its frame two utterly different and incompatible representations of "mental equality."

16. The idea of torquing poems, just as that of deforming them (McGann and Samuels), suggests a conscious violence done to an earlier canonical work and thus a subordination, even a "cancelling," of it. The opposite is true. Reading DuPlessis reading earlier poems reveals an extraordinary knowledge, a sensitivity, and a love for them. In poetry and prose, she is a great interpreter of poetry that she clearly loves. Moreover, her oral performances (found on PennSound) of Wordsworth's "Arab Dream" sequence in *The Prelude Book 5*, Coleridge's "This Lime-Tree Bower My Prison," and Keats's "Ode to Psyche" make this very clear.

17. Before the collage poetry of "Draft 94: Mail Art."

18. This passage brings forward the language of "Ode to Psyche" ("shadowy thought" [*Poems* 366]) and recalls the blank slate against which *Tabula Rosa* addresses itself, suggesting a repression needing to be lifted, a rasa that photoshops a rosa, an unconscious that needs to be revealed.

19. What the British poet Allen Fisher calls "Imperfect Fit." In the Romantic period, Blake and John Clare each ascribe "perfect" spelling, grammar, and syntax to a "squad" of hegemonic forces controlling and limiting thought (Clare, *Poems* 24).

20. "Conversation" as applied to these poems is really monologue, most definitely not the same as "dialogue" as DuPlessis uses it to describe the poems of Mary Robinson in dialogue with those of Coleridge or the torqued poems of her own.

21. In an e-mail exchange about "Draft 93," DuPlessis quipped: "I never met a genre I didn't like" (November 30, 2022).

22. The desire to link erotic love to its poetic expression and its perceived impossibility that creates a "fragment" has its Romantic source in Shelley's *Epipsychidion*: "One hope within two wills, one will beneath / Two overshadowing minds, one life, one death, / One Heaven, one Hell, one immortality, / And one annihilation. Woe is me! / The winged words on which my soul would pierce / Into the height of Love's rare Universe, / Are chains of lead around its flight of fire— / I pant, I sink, I tremble, I expire!" (407).

23. Some of what follows derives from work on the fragment by Philippe Lacoue-Labarthe and Jean-Luc Nancy, *The Literary Absolute: The Theory of Literature in German Romanticism*, translated by Philip Barnard and Cheryl Lester, Albany: SUNY Press, 1988.

24. A poetic fragment, says Schlegel, while being incomplete, is at the same time a thing complete in itself. In "Athenaeum Fragment 206" he calls a fragment a "hedgehog" (*Igel*), an entity with whose spiny boundaries no one would want to interfere (*Lucinde* 189).

25. See note 23, *Literary Absolute*, 42.

26. See note 23, *Literary Absolute*, 43.

27. Again, the eggs thrown against the window screen in "Moth" remind one of Novalis's seeds.

28. See also Keats's directions for liberating the life in the otherwise imprisoning sonnet form: "Let us inspect the lyre, and weigh the stress / Of every chord, and see what may be gain'd / By ear industrious, and attention meet: / Misers of sound and syllable, no less / Than Midas of his coinage, let us be / Jealous of dead leaves in the bay wreath crown" (*Poems* 368).

29. "... in diction and sense of the line, as well as a general orientation to the serial and struggles with the socio-political, I had some things in common with Oppen's work.

    Yet no masters.
    Only practices can be adequate.
        Only Citizenship
        In languages.

(*S* 14)

30. "Athenaeum Fragment 77," in *Lucinde*, 170. DuPlessis's essay "Singing Schools" also looks forward to a similar utopian genre.

Works Cited

Blake, William. *Blake's Poetry and Designs*. Edited by Mary Lynn Johnson and John E. Grant. New York: W. W. Norton and Company, 2008.
Clare, John. *Oxford Authors: John Clare*. Edited by Eric Robinson and David Powell. Oxford: Oxford University Press, 1984.
———. *Selected Poems and Prose*. Edited by Eric Robinson and Geoffrey Summerfield. Oxford: Oxford University Press, 1966.
Coleridge, Samuel Taylor. *The Complete Poems*. Edited by William Keach. London: Penguin Books, 1997.
———. *Biographia Literaria*. Edited by James Engell and W. Jackson Bate. Princeton: Princeton University Press, 1983.
Duncan, Robert. *The Opening of the Field*. New York: Grove Press, 1960.
DuPlessis, Rachel Blau. "Singing Schools and 'Mental Equality': An Essay in Three Parts." *Active Romanticism: The Radical Impulse in Nineteenth-Century and Contemporary Poetic Practice*, edited by Julie Carr and Jeffrey C. Robinson. Tuscaloosa: University of Alabama Press, 2015, 47–69.
———. *Surge: Drafts 96–114*. Cromer Norfolk, UK: Salt Publishing, 2013.
———. *Pitch: Drafts 77–95*. London: Salt Publishing, 2010.
———. *Blue Studios*. Tuscaloosa: University of Alabama Press, 2006.
———. "Marble Paper: Toward a Feminist 'History of Poetry.'" *Blue Studios*. Tuscaloosa: University of Alabama Press, 2006, 96–121.
———. "The Darkest Gush: Emily Dickinson and the Textual Mark." *Titanic Operas: A Poets' Corner of Responses to Dickinson's Legacy*, edited by Martha Nell Smith and Laura Elyn Lauth, 1999, http://archive.emilydickinson.org/titanic/duplessis6.html.
———. *Tabula Rosa*. Elmwood, CT: Potes & Poets Press, 1987.
Golding, Alan. "Drafts and Fragments: Rachel Blau DuPlessis's (counter-) Poundian Project." *Jacket2*, 14 Dec. 2011, https://jacket2.org/article/drafts-and-fragments.
Keats, John. *Letters of John Keats*. Edited by Robert Gittings. Oxford: Oxford University Press, 1992.
———. *The Poems of John Keats*. Edited by Jack Stillinger. Cambridge, MA.: Harvard University Press, 1978.
Lacoue-Labarthe, Phillip, and Jean-Luc Nancy. *The Literary Absolute: The Theory of Literature in German Romanticism*. Translated by Philip Barnard and Cheryl Lester. Albany: SUNY Press, 1988.

Lamb, Charles. *The Works of Charles Lamb*. London: Edward Moxon, 1859.
Levinson, Marjorie. *Thinking through Poetry: Field Reports on Romantic Lyric*. Oxford: Oxford University Press, 2018.
McGann, Jerome, and Lisa Samuels. "Deformance and Interpretation." *Radiant Textuality: Literature after the World Wide Web*. New York: Palgrave, 2001, 105–31.
Nersessian, Anahid. *Keats's Odes: A Lover's Discourse*. Chicago: University of Chicago Press, 2021.
Novalis. *Pollen and Fragments*. Translated by Arthur Versluis. Grand Rapids, MI: Phanes Press, 1989.
Olson, Charles. "Equal, that is, to the real itself." *Selected Writings*, edited by Robert Creeley. New York: New Directions, 1966.
Pound, Ezra. *Ezra Pound: New Selected Poems and Translations*. New York: New Directions, 2010.
Robinson, Mary. *Selected Poems*. Edited by Judith Pascoe. Toronto: Broadview Press, 2000.
Schlegel, Friedrich. *Lucinde and the Fragments*. Translated by Peter Firchow. Minneapolis: University of Minnesota Press, 1971.
Shelley, P. B. *Shelley's Poetry and Prose*. 2nd ed. Edited by Donald H. Reiman and Neil Freistat. New York: W. W. Norton and Company, 2002.
"Why We Should Worry about Moths." GroundWork Gallery, 2023, https://www.groundworkgallery.com/why-we-should-worry-about-moths/.
Woolf, Virginia. "The Death of the Moth." *The Death of the Moth and Other Essays*. New York: Harcourt Brace, Inc., 1942.

CONTRIBUTORS

Suzanne W. Churchill is a professor of English at Davidson College. She is the author of *The Little Magazine* Others *and the Renovation of Modern American Poetry* (Ashgate, 2006); a coeditor, with Adam McKible, of *Little Magazines & Modernism: New Approaches* (Ashgate, 2007); and the author and illustrator of the children's book *Dinosaurs Drive Firetrucks* (Britt Stadig Studio, 2018). She has published on modernism and the Harlem Renaissance, and on periodicals, poetry, and pedagogy in various journals and collections. The founder and editor of the website Index of Modernist Magazines (modernistmagazines.org), she is also the cocreator of the award-winning, open-access online scholarly book *Mina Loy: Navigating the Avant-Garde* (mina-loy.com).

Maria Damon teaches at the School of Art at the Pratt Institute. She is the author of several books and many articles and essays on poetry scholarship. She is the coauthor (with Alan Sondheim, Adeena Karasick, mIEKAL aND, and Jukka-Pekka Kervinen) of several books of poetry, and the author of two chapbooks of cross-stitch visual poetry.

Joseph Donahue's most recent volumes of poetry are *Wind Maps I–VII* (Talisman, 2018) and *The Disappearance of Fate* (Spuyten Duyvil, 2019). He is the cotranslator of *First Mountain* by Zhang Er. With Edward Foster, he edited *The World in Time and Space: Towards a History of Innovative American Poetry, 1970–2000* (Talisman, 2002). Two volumes of his ongoing poetic sequence, *Terra Lucida*, are forthcoming from Verge Books. In 2022 Black Square brought out *Infinite Criteria*, a collection of haiku-inspired poetic suites. He has published critical essays on George Oppen, William Bronk, Susan Howe, Nathaniel Mackey, and Ed Roberson, among others.

Jeanne Heuving is most recently the editor of *Nathaniel Mackey, Destination Out: Essays on His Work* (University of Iowa Press, 2021). She is the author of *The Transmutation of Love and Avant-Garde Poetics* (Modern and Contemporary Poetics series, University of Alabama Press, 2016) and coedited with Tyrone Williams the collection of essays *Inciting Poetics: Thinking and Writing Poetry* (Recencies Series, University of New Mexico Press, 2019). Heuving is the 2022 Judith E. Wilson Fellow in Poetry at Cambridge University, UK. She has recently published two volumes of poet's prose, *Mood Indigo* (Selva Oscura Press, 2019) and *Brilliant Corners* (Chax Press, 2022). Heuving is a professor in the Interdisciplinary Arts and Science Program at the University of Washington (UW) Bothell and is on the graduate faculty in the English Department at UW Seattle.

Megan Jewell is English faculty and a core teaching and research faculty member in the Women's and Gender Studies Program at Case Western Reserve University. She has a PhD in nineteenth-century American literature and twentieth-century American poetics from Duquesne University. Dr. Jewell researches and teaches twentieth- and twenty-first-century American and British poetry. Combining her scholarship on poetics with a longstanding interest in writing studies, Dr. Jewell's current work focuses on women poets of the Language Poetry school and their innovative engagement with the writing process. In articles and book chapters, she has explored poet Susan Howe's revisions of the practice of bibliography and the history behind Kathleen Fraser's development of her poetic voice and subsequent establishment of *HOW(ever)*, the first journal dedicated solely to publishing women's post-1950s experimental poetry. She has presented her work at national and international conferences, with the most recently accepted paper focusing on women's poetry and social media (#Instapoetics) at the University of Glasgow.

Adeena Karasick is a New York–based poet, performer, cultural theorist, and media artist, and the author of twelve books of poetry and poetics. Her most recent is *Massaging the Medium: Seven Pechakuchas* (Institute of General Semantics Press: Language in Action, 2022). Other publications include *Salomé: Woman of Valor* (University of Padova Press, 2017); the libretto for her spoken word opera, *Salomé: Woman of Valor* (NuJu Records, 2020); and *Salomé Birangona*, translation into Bengali (Boibhashik Prokashoni Press, 2020). Karasick teaches Literature and Critical Theory for the Humanities and Media Studies Department at the Pratt Institute; she is the poetry editor for *Explorations in Media Ecology*, an associate international editor of *New Explorations: Studies in Culture and Communication*, a 2021 Andrew W. Mellon Foundation Award recipient, and winner of the Voce Donna Italia award for her contributions to feminist thinking. The Adeena Karasick Archive has been established as part of the Special Collections at Simon Fraser University.

Linda A. Kinnahan is a professor of English at Duquesne University in Pittsburgh. She is the editor of *A History of Twentieth-Century American Women's Poetry* (Cambridge University Press, 2016) and the author of *Mina Loy, Twentieth-Century Photography, and Contemporary Women Poets* (Routledge, 2017). She has published books on modernist and contemporary poetry, including *Poetics of the Feminine: Authority and Literary Tradition in William Carlos Williams, Mina Loy, Denise Levertov, and Kathleen Fraser* (Cambridge University Press, 1994) and *Lyric Interventions: Feminism, Experimental Poetry, and Contemporary Discourse* (University of Iowa Press, 2004). She is the coauthor of the digital humanities project *Mina Loy: Navigating the Avant-Garde* and the digital book *Mina Loy Baedeker: Scholarly Book for Digital Travelers*. Her forthcoming monograph is *Feminist Modernism, Poetics, and the New Economy: Mina Loy, Lola Ridge, and Marianne Moore*.

Eric Keenaghan is an associate professor and chair of the Department of English at the University at Albany, SUNY. He is the author of *Queering Cold War Poetry*

(Clemson University Press, 2009), and his essays on modernist poetry, Cold War poetry, and queer literature have appeared in such journals as *Modernism/modernity*, *Feminist Modernist Studies*, *Contemporary Literature*, and *Journal of Narrative Theory*. He is also a contributing author to many published volumes, most recently *The Beats, Black Mountain, and New Modes in American Poetry* (Clemson University Press, 2021), *The Beats: A Teaching Companion* (Clemson University Press, 2021), *War and American Literature* (Cambridge University Press, 2021), and *The Palgrave Handbook on Cold War Literature* (Palgrave Macmillan, 2020). Current projects include two monographs, one on American anarchist and antifascist poetry ("Life, Love, and War") and a second on Cold War poetry and New Left–era politics ("The Impersonal Is Political"). He also is the coeditor, with Rowena Kennedy-Epstein, of *The Muriel Rukeyser Era: Lectures, Essays, Scripts* (Cornell University Press, 2023).

Amber Manning is a fourth-year doctoral candidate in English at Duke University. She teaches and works on twentieth-century and contemporary US literature and culture, with an emphasis on biological and textual reproduction in contemporary media; intersections of the literary, spiritual, and legal; and forms of writing that elide traditional methods of textual closure. She is currently working on a dissertation that considers how novels with ambiguous endings, the serial poem, comic strips, and text sets work through social tensions that emerged after World War II.

Peter Middleton is a professor of English at the University of Southampton. His research interests include science and literature, modern and contemporary poetry, poetry performance, ecology and climate change, codes in new media, and creative nonfiction. He has published books on science and poetry, gender, memory, and poetics, and edited with Nicky Marsh a book on the teaching of modernist poetry. Other writings include essays on modern and contemporary poetry, and a book of poems. Currently he is collecting published and unpublished essays on poetry in public culture, and writing a new book on the legacy of wartime code breaking on current models of communication. He is on the editorial boards of *Textual Practice*, *English*, *New Formations*, and the *Journal of British and Irish Innovative Poetry*.

Andrew R. Mossin is the author of ten books of poetry, including most recently *Black Trees* (Spuyten Duyvil, 2023); a memoir, *A Son from the Mountains* (Spuyten Duyvil, 2020); and a collection of critical essays, *Male Subjectivity and Poetic Form in "New American" Poetry* (Palgrave, 2010). He has just completed a new manuscript of poetry, *A Common World*, and is at work on a critical study of the photographer, sculptor, and installation artist William Christenberry. He is an associate professor in the Intellectual Heritage Program at Temple University in Philadelphia.

Ariel Resnikoff, a poet, scholar, translator, editor, and educator, completed his PhD in comparative literature and literary theory at the University of Pennsylvania in 2019.

His research and teaching focuses on Hebrew, Yiddish, and English multilingual Jewish literatures, translingual (language-crossing) poetries and poetics, global modernisms, diaspora studies, genocide studies, and translation studies. His most recent works include *Ten Four: Poems, Translations, Variations* (Operating System, 2015), with Jerome Rothenberg, and *Between Shades* (Materialist Press, 2014). *Unnatural Bird Migrator*, which the poet-critic Jake Marmer has described as "Deep Ashkenazi Voodoo," is forthcoming. Ariel's writing has been translated into Russian, French, Spanish, and German, and has appeared or is forthcoming in *Jacket2*, *Golden Handcuffs Review*, *Full Stop Quarterly*, *Tinge Magazine*, and the *Wolf Magazine for Poetry*. A long excerpt of his dissertation, *Home Tongue Earthquake: The Radical Afterlives of Yiddishland*, recently came out in German translation in *Schreibheft, Zeitschrift für Literatur*, and another excerpt was published in Hebrew translation in spring 2020. With Stephen Ross, he is at work on the first critical bilingual edition of Mikhl Likht's modernist Yiddish long poem, *Processions*; and with Lilach Lachman and Gabriel Levin, he is translating into English the collected writings of the translingual Hebrew poet Avot Yeshurun.

Jeffrey C. Robinson is an honorary senior research fellow at the University of Glasgow, now living in the United States. Recent publications of his include *Unfettering Poetry: The Fancy in British Romanticism* (Palgrave Macmillan, 2006); *Poems for the Millennium, Volume Three: The University of California Book of Romantic and Postromantic Poetry* (coedited with Jerome Rothenberg, University of California Press, 2009; 2010 winner of the Before Columbus Foundation American Book Award); *Untam'd Wing: Riffs on Romantic Poetry* (Station Hill Press, 2010); *Active Romanticism: The Radical Impulse in Nineteenth-Century and Contemporary Poetic Practice* (coedited with Julie Carr, University of Alabama Press, 2015); and *Poetic Innovation in Wordsworth 1825–1833: Fibres of These Thoughts* (Anthem Press, 2019). He is presently completing a book on Keats as a Romantic avant-garde poet.

Susan Rosenbaum is associate professor of English at the University of Georgia, where she teaches courses in twentieth-century American literature, modernism, and poetry/poetics, and codirects the Interdisciplinary Modernisms Workshop. She is the author of *Professing Sincerity: Modern Lyric Poetry, Commercial Culture, and the Crisis in Reading* (University of Virginia Press, 2007); and with Linda A. Kinnahan and Suzanne W. Churchill, coauthor of the website and digital scholarly book *Mina Loy: Navigating the Avant-Garde* (University of Georgia Press, 2019), supported by a 2017–2019 NEH Digital Humanities Advancement Grant. She is currently working on a book about Elizabeth Bishop (provisionally titled *Experimental Bishop*), and she has recently completed a monograph titled *Imaginary Museums: Surrealism, American Poetry, and the Visual Arts, 1920–1970* (under review). Her essays have appeared in *Dada/Surrealism*, *Genre*, *Journal of Modern Literature*, and *Studies in Romanticism*.

INDEX

abjection/abject, 163, 173, 178, 180, 189, 207, 212, 224n7. *See also* forlorn/forlornness
absence, 157–58, 185, 190
Abulafia, Avraham, 199
abyss, 31, 176. *See also* void
accumulation/accumulating, 64–72, 74, 75n3
activism, 41–42, 44, 46–47, 55, 100–102, 112, 117n1
Adorno, Theodor, 5, 61, 70–71, 148
agency, 74, 101–2, 104, 163, 208, 215, 217, 222, 224n2
Ahmed, Sara, 100–101, 113
Aji, Hélène, 3
Akedah, 193–94
Alley Cat Books (San Francisco), 147
alphabet, Hebrew, 197–200
ambiguity, 69–70, 74
ambivalence, 180, 182
"among the actives," 175–78
amor fati, 178, 182
Anderson, Laurie, 34
Andrews, Bruce, 1
Angel Deixis, 186–93
aperture, 211, 220
aporias, 19, 157, 159
Apuleius, 208
arche-écriture, 31
Arendt, Hannah, 26, 35, 71
artisanal cosmologies, 82–83, 92–94, 96
art practice, as embodied feminist philosophy, 81–96
atoms, analogy of, 23–24
atrocities, 64–67
Auerbach, Erich, 48
authenticity, 28, 155–56, 184, 188
autobiography, 44–48
avant-garde, 28, 122, 124–25, 141, 157, 188
awe, 181–83, 185, 187–89

Bahir, 202n6, 202n10
"ball of yarn" image, 94–96
Barnard College, 112. *See also* Columbia University
Barthes, Roland, 21, 31
Baucom, Ian, 75n3
Beckett, Samuel, 27
Bee, Susan, 140
Belamy, Dodie, 147
Benjamin, Walter, 5, 33–34
Berlant, Lauren, 124
Bernstein, Charles, 37n16
binaries, 158–59, 189, 218–19
binarism, 213
Binding of Isaac, 181, 193–94
black bar/square, use of, 69–70, 191
Blake, William, 206, 214, 217, 220
blank verse, 218–19
Blaser, Robin, 70, 191–93
bleeding, 66, 158
Bloch, Ernest, 70–71
body, human, 66, 68, 76n8, 84; and eternal forces, 62–64; female, 84, 122, 199–200 (*See also* menstruation; motherhood); and fold, 86; and surge, 62–64
Bookchin, Murray, 100
book publishing, 139–50
Bourriaud, Nicolas, 108–9
Brain, Josephine, 47
breakage, 115–16
breastfeeding, 125
bricolage, 88, 90–94, 112, 121
Bronk, William, 175
Browne, Laynie, 140
Butler, Judith, 61–62
butterfly image, 59–60. *See also* moth image

Caesura (online journal), 193
Camboni, Marina, 3

INDEX

"cannibalization," 85
Carbery, Matthew, 7, 20
caring, 104–5, 110, 118n5
censorship, 69–70
chance, 208–9
choosing/chosen, 178–86. *See also* Judaism/Jewish
citizenship, 101, 222
Cixous, Hélène, 28, 37n11
Clare, John, 220, 225n19
climate change, 62
close reading, 34, 126, 131
closure, resistance to, 81, 220–21
coherence, 222–23
Coleridge, Samuel Taylor, 206, 215–16, 218–19
collaboration, 121–36
collaborative gesture, 24
collage/collaging, 82, 88, 90–94, 110–17, 129, 140–42
collage/homage, 121–36
collagist lyricism, politics of, 106–17
collective/collectivity, 41, 43–44, 46–47, 49–51, 55–57, 101, 103
Columbia University, 41, 45–46, 112, 175–77. *See also* Women's Liberation
commonality, 101–2
comparative religion, 191
comradeship, 102, 117n1
consonants, 199–200
consumer capitalism, 116, 216–17
Conte, Joseph, 7
conversation poem, 218, 226n20
counter-archive, 41–57
COVID-19 pandemic, 62
Crane, Hart, 177
creation, 197–203, 202n9
creation hymns, 188
Creeley, Robert, 85, 157, 189
critical returning, 56
crossroads, 74, 210–11
Cudd, Ann, 54
Cullen, Countee, 131
Culler, Jonathan, 36n4, 102, 117n2

cultural formalism, 126
Cupid and Psyche, 208, 213
curation, of inner speech, 27

Dada/Dadaists, 113–14, 118n8, 122
Dahlen, Beverly, 147, 157, 161
dailiness, of writing, 103
daily politics, 99–106
Dante Alighieri, *Divine Comedy*, 83
Dean, Jodi, 102, 117n1
debris, 94, 143; ethics of, 26
deconstruction, 32, 113, 162
deixis, 186–93
Deleuze, Gilles, 72, 89, 101
democracy, 221–22
depth, 175, 192–94
Derrida, Jacques, 20, 31–32
desert, wandering in, 143–46
destruction, 63–64
dialogue, 215–16, 222, 225n15, 226n20; posthumous, 216, 222; silent, 32, 35
Dickinson, Emily, 24, 181
DiFeo, Jay, 86
différance, 20
difference-with-a-repetition, 85
digital flash mob, 122
digital post(card)s, DuPlessis's, 122; "Crisis in Consciousness," 122–25; "Domesticity is BACK," 125–26; "Mona Lisa Corrected," 127–29; "Time's Up," 135–36; "What the Actual," 134–35; "WOW Are You Ever," 129–31; "Wrenches," 132–34
distance, 175, 177, 179, 184–85
Dobbs v. Jackson Women's Health Organization (US Supreme Court, 2022), 47
Donahue, Joseph, 74
donor drafts, 83–87
Douglas, Mary, 95–96
"draft," 87, 90, 211, 220
drafting from the fold, 87, 90
Drafts (DuPlessis), 2, 19–36, 82–83, 153–54, 156–57, 166–67, 176–77, 181, 205–26;

234

"Draft 1: It," 87–88, 181, 205; "Draft 2," 205; "Draft 5: Gap," 191; "Draft 6: Midrush," 192; "Draft 20: Incipit," 86–88; "Draft 23: Findings," 182; "Draft 29: Intellectual Autobiography," 184–85; "Draft 33: Deixis," 187–89; "Draft 34: Recto," 194; "Draft 48: Being Astonished," 29; "Draft 49," 41–57; "Draft 51: Clay Songs," 89; "Draft 52: Midrash," 89; "Draft 87: The Trace," 20; "Draft 90," 216–17; "Draft 91: Proverbs," 216–17, 222; "Draft 92," 216, 218–20; "Draft 93: Romantic Fragment Poem," 216, 220–21; "Draft 99: Intransitive," 20, 70; "Draft 102: One-on-One," 63; "Draft 103: Punctum," 74–75; "Draft 104: The Book," 89; "Draft 106: Words," 21–26, 63, 70–71; "Draft 107: Meant to Say," 34; "Draft 111: Arte Povera," 67–69; "Draft 112: Verge," 64–67; "Draft 113: Index," 69; "Draft 114: Exergue and Volta," 63, 71–75

drowning, 174–75, 177–78, 183, 192

Ducasse, Isodore, 125

Duncan, Robert, 24, 69, 73, 82, 86, 108, 110–11, 113, 176, 191–93

DuPlessis, Rachel Blau, works: *Active Romanticism,* 214; "Adventures of the Book," 31; "Angelus Novus," 33–34; *Around the Day in 80 Worlds* (ATW), 4, 195; *Blue Studios* (BS), 5, 25, 29, 41, 44–46, 51, 214; *Churning the Ocean of Milk,* 112, 115–16; *The Collage Poems of Drafts,* 111, 139; "Cosmos, a Nocturne," 30; "Crowbar," 160–61; "Darkest Gush," 208, 212; "Dark Matter," 94; "Desiring Visual Texts: A Collage and Embroidery Dialogue" (Damon and DuPlessis), 92; *Drafts,* 2, 19–36, 82–83, 153–54, 156–57, 166–67, 176–77, 181, 205–26 (*See also* separate entry); *Drafts 1–38, Toll* (T), 173–95; *Drafts 1–38: Toll* (T), 6; *Drafts 15–XXX, The Fold* (TF), 86–89; "Eurydice," 159–60; "For the Etruscans" (DuPlessis), 19–20, 90, 129–31, 133, 136, 157; "from *The 'History of Poetry',*" 155, 159, 160–61, 205; "*f*-Words: An Essay on the Essay," 49–50, 156; "The Gendered Marvelous," 34; *Genders, Races and Religious Cultures in Modern American Poetry* (GRRC), 44, 126; *Graphic Novella,* 112–13, 116; *H.D.: The Career of That Struggle,* 61, 155; "*Late Work* (LW), 4; "A Letter on Loy," 135; *Life in Handkerchiefs,* 92, 143, 148–50; *Long Essay on the Long Poem,* 12–13; "Mackle, Shard, and Trace," 109, 116; "Marble Paper," 214; "Midrashic Sensibilities: Secular Judaism and Radical Poetics," 179–80; "Moth: Ode to Psyche," 205–26; "No Moore of the Same," 127; *Numbers* (N), 82, 90–94, 112, 140–48; "Of Being Numerous," 175–76, 179; "On *Drafts*: A Memorandum of Understanding," 49, 55; "Otherhow," 124, 154, 162; "Pater-Daughter: Male Modernists and Female Readers," 133–34; *Pink Guitar* (PG), 19, 44, 50, 121, 123, 129, 132–36, 153–58, 162, 168; *Pitch: Drafts 77–95* (PI), 20–21; "A Poem of Myself," 159; "Preface" to *Surge,* 214; "Psalm 151," 193, 197–203; *Rage* (collage), 112; "Reader, I Married Me," 44–46, 51, 54, 117n3, 129, 132–33; "Seismic Orgasm: Sexual Intercourse and Narrative Meaning in Mina Loy," 128; "Singing Schools and 'Mental Equality,'" 206, 210, 212, 215, 224n2; "Summer Poem," 99–106; *Surge: Drafts 96–114* (S), 4, 59–75, 89; *Tabula Rosa* (TR), 153, 155, 159, 205–7, 225n18; *Traces, with Days,* 82, 110; "Translocations," 219–20; "Uncannily," 167; "Undertow," 174; *Wells* (W), 155, 159–60, 174–75; "'While These Letters Were A-Reading': An Essay on Beverly Dahlen's *A Reading,*" 154;

DuPlessis (*continued*)
    Wood-Machine (collage), 112; "The Work of Susan Howe," 128–29; "Writing," 153, 156–57, 161–68, 205; *Writing Beyond the Ending: Narrative Strategies of Twentieth-Century Women Writers,* 51, 129, 155; "Yod—Its Little Eye," 145. *See also* digital post(card)s, DuPlessis's
Duras, Marguerite, 163
durational performance, 94–96

echolalia, 26
écriture féminine, 28–29, 31, 108, 154, 162
ecstasy, 182–83, 187, 191
Ein Sof, 202n13
elective affinities, 179–80
Eliade, Mircea, 191
Elijah's cup, 194–95
Eliot, T. S., 31, 191
elision, 53, 189, 194, 202n9
embodied feminist philosophy, art practice as, 81–96
embodiment. *See* body, human
Emerson, Ralph Waldo, 180
empathy, 179, 208–9, 224n2
emptiness, 189–90
encyclopedism, 55
"en dehors garde," 121–36
Enlightenment, 144, 179–80, 209
enumerating/enumeration(s), 64–72. *See also* numbers/numbering
eroticism/erotic, 88, 93, 108, 220–21, 225n14, 226n22
escape, 4, 31, 214–15. *See also* unpossessibility
essayer, 129
essay genre, 49–50
essaying, 104
Ethical Culture movement, 179–80
Eurydice, 175
excess/overflow, 216, 220–21
excitability/excitement, 103, 105, 133

experimentation/experimentalism, 104, 112, 128–29, 133, 142, 206, 212–13, 215
expressionism, 101, 155

failure, 31, 81, 94, 105–6, 143
fascism, 176, 191
fate/fatedness, 178–86
fear and trembling, 181, 194
fearlessness, 94
Felski, Rita, 169n7
felting, 90–94
feminism/feminist, 5, 7–8, 100, 106, 117n3, 132, 153–70, 184; and activism, 41–44, 102; analytic, 42, 54–55; and/as art practice, 81–96; and autobiography, 44–48; and disruption of masculinist tradition, 205–26; first wave, 41–57; poetics, 121–22, 214–21; postmodern, 206, 214, 223; second-wave, 41–43, 46–47, 81, 224n1; third-wave, 224n1; weak resistance, 99–117. *See also* Women's Liberation
Feminist Studies (journal), 47
Ferneyhough, Charles, 37n21
f-essays, 156–57
Fest, Bradley J., 3, 13, 26, 33–34, 75n4
Finch, Annie, 133
finger, pointing, 76n8. *See also* pointing moment
Fisher, Allen, 225n19
"flattened dialectics," 186
fold/folding, 72–75, 83, 93–94, 167. *See also* unfolding
footnotes, DuPlessis's use of, 85, 103, 189, 192
force moving, 157–58, 168
forlorn/forlornness, 173–74, 178, 181, 185, 189–90, 194
fort/da, 189
Foster, Ed, 177
foundational cluster, 154
found objects, 132
fracturing, 115–16

fragment, the, 131, 159, 206, 211, 220–23, 226n24
"Frank O'Hara's Last Lover" (reading series), 140
Fraser, Kathleen, 122, 126, 163
Fraser, Nancy, 100
free indirect discourse, 31
French Revolution, 215–16
Friedan, Betty, 52–53
Friedman, Susan Stanford, 47
Frost, Elisabeth, 3
Fuhrman, Joanna, 91
fundraising, 147

gap, 55, 155, 158
gender dynamics, 153–70
gender equality, 217
Genesis (biblical book), 188–89
German Romantics, 220–23
Ginsberg, Allen, 42
Glatshteyn, Jacob, 144–45
global violence, 62
Goethe, Johann Wolfgang von, 179
Golding, Alan, 3, 106, 223
Google Translate, 218
Gorra, Michael, 31
grief, 61–62, 116, 190. *See also* forlorn/forlornness
Grosz, Elizabeth, 74
Guattari, Félix, 101
Guest, Barbara, 34

handmade, the, 81
handwriting, 162
hashtag, 113
Hasidism, 202n4
Hatlen, Burton, 36n1
H.D., 52, 61, 69, 140, 150, 169n6, 186
Hebrew language, 197–99
Heidegger, Martin, 188
Heist, Ursula K., 62
Hemmings, Clare, 47

heterogeneity, 11, 55, 222–23
"heuristics of suspicion," 169n7
Heuving, Jeanne, 6
Higgins, Scarlett, 111
hirik, 144–45
Höch, Hannah, 114–15, 118n8
Holocaust, 181, 191, 194
hooks, bell, 56
Horkheimer, Max, 61
Howe, Susan, 29, 37n14, 180
HOW(ever) (feminist journal), 121–24, 127–33, 135
Husserl, Edmund, 32
hybrid works, 2, 9, 140–42, 144, 149–50

"I," dispersed, 50
illegibility, 217
illusion of distinction, 190
imagination, Romantic, 214
"immerginated rapture," 177–78, 185–86
improvisation, 25, 87
inclusiveness, 25–26, 48, 55, 216–17, 223
incompleteness, 211. *See also* fragment, the
index/indexing, 64–72, 74
infant, 163–65
infinite, the, 59–75, 202n13
Ingold, Tim, 85
inkwell, 192
in medias res, 158
inner speech, 19–36
interrelationships of traditions, 10–11
interruption, 21, 25–26, 31, 81, 159
intersectionality, 55–56; DuPlessis and, 44–45
intertextuality, 81–96; and collage, 28, 92; intratextual, 86–89
interviews, with DuPlessis, 3, 43, 92
"in the desert," 143–46
Iraq War, 62
Irigaray, Luce, 88
irony, 181–83
Isaac (biblical figure), 181, 193–94

Jabès, Edmond, 199
James, Henry, 31–32
James, William, 32
Jaussen, Paul, 3, 5–7, 83, 106
Jewell, Megan, 24, 36n5
Jewish Enlightenment, 144
Jewish identity, 178–80
Job (biblical book), 181
joy, 68, 72, 74, 86, 95, 101, 180, 185–86, 209
Judaism/Jewish, 30, 83, 93–94, 115, 142–46, 178–86, 194–95, 197–203. *See also* alphabet, Hebrew; Hebrew language; Kabbalah; midrash

Kabbalah, 92, 94, 193, 197–203, 202n5, 202n9–202n13; "one-woman collage Kabbalah," 92, 94
Kafka, Franz, 178
Kalaidjian, Walter, 3
Kaplan, Carla, 123
Keats, John, 214, 224n3; "Ode to Psyche," 205–26
Keenaghan, Eric, 68
Keller, Lynn, 7, 126, 159
Kelly Writers House, 139
Kennedy-Epstein, Rowena, 108
Khullar, Dhruv, 62
Killian, Kevin, 146–47
Kinnahan, Linda, 7, 126
"kintsugi ethos," 197
Klee, Paul, 33–34
Kristeva, Julia, 38n23, 132
Künstlerroman, 51
Kushner, Lawrence, 202n10

Lamb, Charles, 218
language, and light, 197–99
language poets, 169n5
Laporte, Dominique, 107
Lautréamont, Comte de, 125
layers/layering, 88–89
Left, the, 175–76. *See also* politics

Levertov, Denise, 108
Levitsky, Rachel, 140
light, and language, 197–99
Lilley, Kate, 72
linguistics, 185, 190
lists/listing, 64–72, 74. *See also* enumerating; numbers/numbering
literary/cultural theory, 20–21
little words, 188, 191–93. *See also* punctuation
Lorde, Audre, 84
loss, 173–74
lost/found, 149
Loy, Mina, 128, 135
Lucretius, 23
Lynn, Greg, 88
lyric subject, 205, 210–11

Machoan (Greek warrior), 60
Mackey, Nathaniel, 73, 75n2, 82
Maggid of Mezritch (Rabbi Dov Ber), 198
magic/magical, 183–86, 189, 193
Majewska, Ewa, 101–3
marginalizing/marginalized, 9, 108–9, 116, 121–22, 130, 163
marking devices, 162. *See also* punctuation
Martin, C. J., 48
masculinist tradition, feminist disruption of, 205–26
mastery, rejection of, 208–9, 213
material culture, 90–91
Materialist Press, 92–93, 139–50
materialist studies, 90–91
materiality, of poetic production, 8–10, 106–17, 149, 201
McGann, Jerome, 224n5
meconium, 209, 212
mending, 201
menstruation, 217
metonymy, 158–59
micropoems, 116
micropolitics, 101–2, 104–6. *See also* politics; weak resistance

"middle voice," 31
midrash, 30, 37n17, 83, 93–94, 146–47
Miller, Livingston, 141
Mina Loy: Navigating the Avant-Garde (website), 131
minimalism, 189
minoritized Americans, 99–100
minor literatures, 101
Mitchell, Jason, 140
modernism/modernists, 123, 125–26, 129, 134, 157, 191–92; Yiddish, 142
Moi, Toril, 43
monologue, 25, 32, 225n14, 226n20
Moore, Marianne, 127
Morrison, Toni, 100
Mossin, Andrew R., 112
moth, life cycle of, 209–12
motherhood, 163–65
moth image, 205, 207
MSA Conference, Penn State University, Seminar on Modern and Contemporary Women Poets, 126, 132
multizonal thinking, 10–11
muse, figure of, 214
mythic transformation narrative, 177
myth/mythological, 51–52, 175, 191. *See also* Cupid and Psyche; Orpheus

Nahmanides, 200
negation, 182–86
negative capability, 214, 224n3
negative theology, 183, 190
Nersessian, Anahid, 209, 213
New American Poetry, 185
New Left, 102
New Narrative, 147
newspaper clippings, 110
Newsweek (issue of March 23, 1970), "Women in Revolt," 42
New Woman, 114
Nicosia, Cyprus, 66
nonbeing, 175

Notley, Alice, 51
Novalis, 221–22
Numbers (biblical book), 143, 145
numbers/numbering, 145–46, 198. *See also* alphabet, Hebrew

Obenzinger, Hilton, 177
objectivism/objectivist, 29, 37n14, 48, 174, 192–93
objectivist poetics, 153–70, 169n5–169n6, 181
Objectivist Press, 141–42
objectivist sublime, 177, 181–82, 189, 193
O'Hara, Frank, 24
Oliver, Mary, 37n10
Olson, Charles, 156–57, 169n6, 207
open-field poetry, 29
open form poetics, 108
openness, 19, 143, 223. *See also* closure, resistance to
Oppen, George, 29, 37n16, 51, 139, 142–44, 147, 154–55, 166–67, 174–78, 180–86, 188; "Psalm," 187–88
Oppen, Linda, 147
Oppen, Mary, 115
oral performances, by DuPlessis, 225n16
organ/body donation, 84–86
Orpheus/Orphic, 175, 177
Orwell, George, 169n5
otherness, 163, 166, 190, 205, 214–15, 217–18, 221, 224n1
Others (little magazine), 124–25

page, the, 186, 193–94, 208; as ocean, 192; turning of, 192, 194
palimpsest, 87, 167, 213, 216
Papadakis, Yiannis, 66, 75n5
participation, and perception, 175–77
Passover, 194–95
perception, and participation, 175–77
Perloff, Marjorie, 169n6
Philadelphia, 139–40, 210
piecework, 90–94

pleasure, 1–2, 72, 94, 96, 159. *See also* joy
poesis, 13, 81, 207, 209, 219
poetics: objectivist, 153–70, 169n5–169n6, 181; projectivist, 153–70, 169n5–169n6; radical Romantic, 214–21
pointing moment, 187–90
politicization, 44–46, 48, 117n2
politics, 104, 223; antipolitical, 101; daily, 99–106; encrypted, 109; poetic politics/political poetics, 111, 113
Pope, Alexander, 144
portal poem, 153, 157, 167, 168n1
positional (located) writing, 156
postcards, 121–36. *See also* digital post(card)s, DuPlessis's
postmodernism, 2, 5, 8, 10–11, 13, 20, 191, 205–6, 214, 216
post-objectivism, 106
post-structuralism, 31–32
Pound, Ezra, 110–11, 128, 166, 169n5–169n6, 191, 223
prepositions, 167. *See also* little words
presence, 3, 10, 69–70, 102, 162, 183, 185, 188–90. *See also* "vibrant void"
Pritchett, Patrick, 3, 72
projective prose, 154, 156, 161
projectivist poetics, 153–70, 169n5–169n6
Prynne, J., 38n24, 215
Psalms (biblical book), 189
Psyche (goddess), 205, 208, 213
Puig de la Bellacasa, María, 118n5
punctuation, 64, 106–7, 113, 165, 167, 182, 202n9, 207–8
purification, 182, 223

queering of gender, 205, 209, 213, 215, 222
queerness, and waste, 108
quilting, 90–94

Rachel (name), 178–80
radical Romanticism, 214–21

Ramban (Moses ben Nachman), 203n14
rapture, 177–78, 180, 182, 185–86, 193. *See also* "Immerginated rapture"
reading practices, of DuPlessis, 5
readings (public events), 1–2
recording, 28, 157
recycling, 81, 85, 94, 114. *See also* donor drafts
redaction, 69–70
Redstockings of the Women's Liberation Movement, 53
referentiality, 70, 81, 89
reflexivity, 19, 33, 48, 54, 202n9
refolding, 94–96
refuse/refusal, 2, 9, 71, 106–10, 112, 143. *See also* debris; recycling; waste
register, shifts of, 19–20
Resnikoff, Ariel, 93
return, 47–48, 51–57, 108, 186, 200–201
reuse, 90, 92, 95. *See also* recycling
Reznikoff, Charles, 141–44, 147, 176
Rich, Adrienne, 52, 108, 174
Riding, Laura, 155
Rig Veda, 188
Riley, Denise, 26–28, 32, 35, 36n8
Rilke, Rainer Maria, 175
risk, 208–9
Robertson, Lisa, 19
Robinson, Mary, 206, 215, 225n14–225n15
Romanticism/Romantic, 179, 205–26
Rothenberg, Jerome, 149
Rowan, Lou, 177
Rukeyser, Muriel, 107–8
Ryle, Gilbert, 32

sacrificial violence, 193–95
St. Mark's Poetry Project, 124
salvage/salvaging, 8, 26, 94–96, 111–12, 184
sampling, 91–92, 110
Samuels, Lisa, 224n5
scale, 12, 19, 193
Scappettone, Jennifer, 140

scattering of light, 197–203
Schlegel, Friedrich, 206, 221–22, 226n24
Schneeman, George, 142–43
Schor, Mira, 197
Schwitters, Kurt, 112–14
Sefer ha-Bahir, 198
segmentivity, 222
Seidman, Hugh, 177
self-: actualization, 50; confidence, 177; consciousness, 102, 113, 117n2, 183; correction, 26; expression, 101; identification, 117n3; interrogation, 27; irony, 95; portrait, 194; presencing, 162; referentiality, 89; reflexivity, 48; reproduction, 67; sacrifice, 43
Semina (art magazine), 111
semiocapitalism, 116
seriality/serial, 4–5, 11, 48, 56–57, 72, 161, 166, 211, 221
Shapiro, David, 177
shattering of the vessels, 197–203
Shekinah, 202n5
Shelley, Percy Bysshe, 208, 226n22
Sheshet, Rabbi Jacob Ben, 200
Shevirat ha Kelim, 197, 201
"shit," as word, 106–7
Showalter, Elaine, 90
silence, 7, 32, 35
Silliman, Ron, 71, 168n1
"singing smudge," 109–12
sit-in, at offices of *Ladies' Home Journal* (spring 1970), 46, 54
skepticism, 83–85, 95, 184
Snitow, Ann, 47
solidarity, 101–2, 112, 176
sonnet, 213
source texts, 85. *See also* donor drafts
Spicer, Jack, 193
Stacey, Jackie, 45
Stein, Gertrude, 86, 108
Stevens, Wallace, 123, 133, 178

The Strawberry Statement (film), 175
subjectification, 88
sublimity/sublime, 180–86, 193; objectivist sublime, 177, 181–82, 189, 193
Supplement (coedited by Resnikoff, Tierney, and Warner), 139, 147
Surge, as title, 60–64
surge(s), 59–75
surrealism, 125
surveillance repression, 217
suspicion, heuristics of, 169n7
Swados, Elizabeth, 54
swallowtail image, 59–60
"sweaty concepts," 101, 116
sympathetic imagination, 218

Talmud, 86, 93–94
talush, 148–49
talushkeyt, 144
Tarlo, Harriet, 21
tearing, 115–16
Tel Quel group, 28
temporality, 24, 62
Ten Commandments, 203n16
terrorist attacks of September 11, 2001, 61–62, 125
terza rima, 83
textiles, 87, 148–50
textile studies, 81, 90–91
textual reproduction, 71–72
"Theory of Everything," 82
thinginess, of language, 106
thinking, 35–36, 36n7, 38n23, 221
"throw of the dice" (Mallarmé), 208–9
Tierney, Orchid, 139
tikkun olam, 95, 201
tokenism, DuPlessis and, 45–46
toll, 190–91
Torah, 181
Torah scroll, 200
torquing, 215–16, 218–19, 222, 224n2, 225n16

touch/touching, 71–72, 118n5
trace, 20, 36n3, 110
translocation, 219–20
transplantation, 85
triumphalism, rejection of, 105, 174
truth, inscribed in/through language, 200–201
Tsvetaeva, Marina, 210
Twitter (X)/tweets, 113, 116
typographies, 161–63

ugly poem, 209
Ullstein Verlag, 114
unending, 64–67, 70, 72–75, 75n2
unfinished, 68
unfolding, 84, 94–96
unity, 223
University of Pennsylvania, Creative Writing Program and Center for Programs in Contemporary Writing, 139
unpossessibility, 213–14, 216, 221, 224n2
unwriting, 36n4
upcycling, 90, 92, 95

Valéry, Paul, 35
Vaneigem, Raoul, 100
vector, 74
verbal prism, image of, 82–83
verse essay, 24–25, 28
"vibrant void," 183, 185, 189–90, 192
voice, poetics of, and inner speech, 19–36. *See also* inner speech
void, the, 182–83, 194. *See also* "vibrant void"
Volosinov, V. N., 26

volta, 64, 72–75
vowels, as female, 199–200
vulval voyages, 199–200

Wachter, Robert, 62
Wagner-Martin, Linda, 126
Waldman, Anne, 55
wandering, 143–46
Warner, Julia, 139, 141–42, 149
waste, 99–117
weak resistance, 99–106, 116
weaving, 90–94, 201
"weird shit," 104–17
wells, 159–60, 174–75, 177, 183, 192, 194. *See also* drowning
Williams, William Carlos, 24, 85, 130, 157, 164
wine, 194–95
Winterson, Jeanette, 66
Wittgenstein, Ludwig, 27
womb, 178
Women's Liberation, 41, 45–46
wonderment, sense of, 92–93
Woolf, Virginia, 100, 123–25, 224n6
Wordsworth, William, 206, 214–15

Yeats, William Butler, 23, 31, 191
Yiddish language, 148–49
yod (Hebrew letter/number), 144–45. *See also* alphabet, Hebrew

Zohar, 198
Zukofsky, Louis, 48, 54, 106, 144, 192